Fly Fishing Boston

Fly Fishing Boston

A Complete Saltwater Guide from Rhode Island to Maine

Terry C. Tessein

BACK COUNTRY

Backcountry Guides
Woodstock, Vermont

Library of Congress Cataloging-in-Publication Data
Tessein, Terry C.
Fly fishing Boston : a complete saltwater guide from Rhode Island to Maine /
Terry C. Tessein.—1st ed.
p. cm.
ISBN 0-88150-517-X
1. Saltwater fly fishing—Massachusetts—Boston region. I. Title.
SH507 .T47 2003
799.1'066145—dc21
2002028138

Cover and interior design by Faith Hague
Cover photograph copyright © Eric Kulin
Color photographs by Larry Largay
Black and white photographs by the author unless otherwise noted
Illustrations on pages 96–98 by Barbara Smullen,
copyright © 2002 The Countryman Press
Tide chart on page 37 copyright © 2002 Tidelines; reproduced by permission
Maps by Mapping Specialists Ltd., Madison, WI,
copyright © 2002 The Countryman Press

Published by Backcountry Guides
A division of The Countryman Press, P.O. Box 748, Woodstock, Vermont 05091
Distributed by W. W. Norton & Company, Inc.,
500 Fifth Avenue, New York, NY 10110

Printed in the United States of America
10 9 8 7 6 5 4 3 2 1

Contents

CONTENTS

Acknowledgments

You might be able to imagine what it took to research and record the information in this book. I like to think of it as good news and sort-of-bad news. The good part of the effort to produce this book was that I got to meet a lot of great people as I visited the different areas. Though I may have fished in an area, there is nothing like local, firsthand knowledge. Part of being a successful angler is getting to know the people who run the tackle shop in your fishing area. They are in business to help you with your fishing.

I cannot tell you how appreciative I am of the help, interest, and support given by the people I met while gathering information for this book. If there was any bad news about this effort, however, it was choosing which fishing locales to include in the book. I can honestly say that the wealth of information I received relative to the numerous good fishing spots for any given section covered in this book could comprise a book all by itself. Everywhere I went, people with local fishing knowledge gave me tips about a number of fishing spots. The difficulty was that each person would tell me I couldn't write this book without including his or her suggested fishing locations.

This made for difficult decisions on my part. As I stated earlier, I could have written a single book on just one state or major location. So for all those who helped with providing information, when you read this book and don't see a particular spot that you told me about, please forgive me. It was simply a question of space. This was one of the most difficult aspects of putting this book together—what would or would not be included. My objective was to tell the reader of some well-known fishing destinations as well as others that may not have received much press.

I also owe thanks to some specific people who gave of their time and willingly offered advice. In particular, I wish to express my appreciation to Captains Jeffrey and Lynn Heyer of Cross Rip Outfitters, Nantucket, Massachusetts; Chris Grill of Kennebec Angler in Bath, Maine; Dana Eastman, The Tackle Shop in Portland, Maine; Jim Bernstein, Eldredge Bros. Fly Shop, Cape Neddick, Maine; Peter Jenkins of The Saltwater Edge, Newport, Rhode Island; Captain Doug Jowett, for his Spey rod information; Captain Tom Koerber of Roccus Charters for his flies and knowledge of Boston Harbor; Karen Hill, Sports Port, Hyannis, Massachusetts, for her generosity in lending equipment for photos; Eric Kulin, for the wonderful cover picture; Kent Jackson, for his advice and computer wizardry; and Captain Jim White of White Ghost Guide Service, Coventry, Rhode Island. Jim's a friend whom I admire and whose fishing company I enjoy; I want to also thank him for the photographs he contributed to this book.

There is my special appreciation for Nick Curcione for his friendship, advice, and, in particular, willingness to share his knowledge of Spey rods. Nick, I want you to know the stripers are waiting, so come on up.

I want to offer a special thanks to Jack Gartside, a talented fly tier and author, who gave me a fishing lesson on a hot summer's afternoon that I will long remember. Jack, you made me a believer and a member of that eclectic fan club of yours.

While I was writing this book, I learned of the passing of a very dear friend. Phil Genova, over the years, had been my long-distance fishing buddy. Though we didn't fish together that much, we sure spent a great deal of time on the phone discussing fishing, which was the next best thing. Some of Phil's pictures appear in this book. He gave them to me a number of years ago when I was doing a magazine article on getting youngsters into fly fishing. That was his great passion. Phil, you will be greatly missed.

Additionally, my special thanks go to two very good friends who gave of their time and shared their saltwater fly-fishing expertise. Bob Mitchell, an outdoor writer, guide, and fly tier, has a contagious love of the outdoors. I am so grateful for his willingness to help with fishing information on the Massachusetts North Shore and New Hampshire coastline.

I first met Chip Bergeron in 1995 when I was paired with him to fish the Martha's Vineyard Rod & Gun Club's one-night Fly Rod Striped Bass Catch & Release Tournament. His experience and understanding of fly fishing the waters of Martha's Vineyard are second to none. Every time I have fished with him I've learned something new about the Vineyard and techniques for catching fish there. Thanks, Chip, for what you taught me, and the many enjoyable hours on Martha's Vineyard.

Finally, this book would never have been completed without the support and assistance of my wife, Paula. Since the very beginning of our marriage she has fished with me whenever time has permitted. She, as much as anyone, instilled the love of fishing in our son David. Before he ever attended school, he had spent many hours standing in front of his mother, helping her hold her surf rod as she fished. She has been, from the start, my cheerleader, adviser, and proofreader. But most of all, she is my best friend.

Introduction

While I was growing up in New Jersey, my father often took me fishing and passed on to me his love of the sport. I loved the surf and beaches of my youth, but when I began to read about the striped bass of New England in the late 1950s, I knew I had to go there. In 1963 a job offer from Honeywell, located just outside Boston, gave me that chance. As soon as I moved there I began to fish the beaches of Cape Cod. It has been an ongoing love affair with New England's saltwater fishing ever since.

When I arrived in Massachusetts, I was what was fondly known as a surf rat. I fished the surf with conventional and spinning gear, using plugs and metal to catch striped bass and bluefish. I became a member of the now defunct Intrepid Striper Club, a group of about 30 anglers, which gave me the unique opportunity to learn from some of the best saltwater anglers around. Besides getting a first-class education in fishing New England, I also formed some valued friendships. It was during this time that I bought a 14-foot aluminum boat with an 18-horsepower motor and joined some of the club members who launched their boats through the surf at the tip of Cape Cod. The striped bass fishing of the 1960s was legendary, and I am lucky to have experienced it.

Sometimes it's hard to break from the familiar and try new things. I didn't begin to fish regularly with a fly rod until about 1991. Still, there was an incident years earlier that laid the groundwork for my immersion into the sport. Since the early 1970s I have gone to the Outer Banks of North Carolina every year in late November or early December to extend my fishing season. Though all my fishing is usually with large surf sticks, from the beginning I carried a fiberglass fly rod that I'd had since my college days; I used it occasionally when freshwater fishing. Back in the 1970s there were some big bluefish blitzing the Outer Banks surf, and I hoped that I might find the right conditions to catch one of those powerful fish on my fly rod.

About my third year there I did get the opportunity, and was able to catch and release six or eight bluefish, all in the 15-pound-plus range. After the action had died down, an angler nearby, who had been watching, informed me that I had released several potential saltwater fly-rod records for bluefish. I was having so much fun that afternoon that I never considered keeping those fish. They were part of a wonderful experience. To this day I have no regrets, because I have a grand memory of catching those bluefish on a fly rod.

There is another little wrinkle to this fishing tale. The big blues were chasing bait around a shallow flats area, inside a bar. The water there was only about 4 or 5 feet deep. I wanted to catch at least one of these fish on the fly rod, but back then I didn't own any saltwater flies. I did the only logical thing that a largemouth bass fisherman could do: I tied on and caught large bluefish with Gaines freshwater bass poppers. One popper lasted only a fish or two. That memory is what fishing is all about!

I started seriously saltwater fly rodding about 10 years ago. While at a Coastal Conservation Association banquet in Maine, I bought a fly-rod outfit donated by L.L. Bean. That year Brad Burns, whom I met through the CCA, invited me on a fly-fishing trip on the Kennebec River, where my interest and love of the sport was rekindled and grew. Since then I have been able to fly fish from Maine to Florida and have been fortunate enough to experience many more memorable saltwater fly fishing days.

But no matter where I fish, New England remains at the top of my list. People from all over the world come here to fish. I have heard anglers who have been fished the globe describe New England's fishing as world class. I live here and may be biased, but I have to agree with them.

The shoreline of New England is more irregular and varied than some of its more southerly neighbors. Formed by glaciers many centuries ago, it features every fishing environment that an angler could possibly want. Maybe that, coupled with the quality of fishing, is what draws so many to fish here. There are long sandy beaches, rocky shorelines, marshes, flats, rips, large rivers, and small estuaries. The last thing you can say about the shoreline of New England is that it's boring. One of the major prerequisites for catching fish is structure, any irregularity in the monotony of open water—whether that is bottom shape, obstructions, or whatever. And you would be hard pressed to find many spots along the New England shoreline without structure. Additionally, an angler has the opportunity to fish in some of the most picturesque surroundings on the Atlantic coast. As I worked to put this book together, I was pleasantly surprised to find so many good fishing sites for each locale.

This leads me to what I think is a key to angling success. Take the time to learn an area that you fish regularly; it will pay off. But expand your angling opportunities by occasionally scouting new locations. There are no doubt spots that you often pass by without realizing the fishing potential that may exist there. Let me give you an example.

I have lived on Cape Cod for 25 years and fished here for nearly 32 years, and I thought I knew most of the places to fish. An excuse to get out on an early-spring day taught me that I knew many of the most-frequented spots on the Cape, but not nearly all of them. A fishing buddy and I decided to explore the towns of Chatham and Orleans to find new fishing sites. We used detailed town maps to go down every road that was marked as a town landing or public access to water. Now, these two towns aren't that big, but it took us a whole day to do this, and we didn't fish. We just visited each spot and marked the map with some general notes of description and access. That day we discovered more than a dozen potentially good fishing spots.

You'll find many such saltwater fly-fishing locations in this book, beginning with Boston Harbor, which is a gem of a location for the fly caster. We will also look at fishing destinations to the north of there, all the way to the Kennebec River of Maine. South from Boston but still within easy driving distance are Cape Cod, Nantucket, Martha's Vineyard, and Rhode Island. The variety of fishing situations and locations in this section of New England can make for a lifetime of fishing trips.

Throughout the book I'll give you directions for getting to the locations I describe, tell you how and when to fish them, and give you any other pertinent information that might help you if you're fishing the locale for the first time. In addition, I've tried to include some background and history for the different areas presented in this book. I believe that when fishing a new destination it adds much to the experience if you're aware of its history. This is especially true in New England, whose past is so much a part of our country's heritage. For me, it is a richer fishing experience when I know something of the people, the place, and its history.

The shoreline from Maine to Rhode Island is as varied as anywhere along the East Coast. One section of the book highlights the types of shoreline conditions you can experience. Basic information on how to fish these watery environments will put you on the road to becoming a better angler. There will also be information on basic tackle selection and suggestions on how to make your fly fishing easier and safer. Additionally, this book looks at the fish you will encounter along the New England coast, as well as what they eat—which is important to your fly selection.

Lastly, I hope you take from this book a principle that comes from my days as a surf rat: You will never be successful unless you put in your time. That means taking the time to study and learn the area you fish. Learn what tides are best for what time of the day, and at what part of the season. Beyond that, and most of all, have fun with your fly fishing. When you learn that the enjoyment of fishing is more than just catching fish, you will be getting the most from the sport.

Passing on to future generations of anglers our love and enjoyment of the sport is the greatest gift we can give. It is priceless, and unlike many gifts, it lasts a lifetime to be passed on again.

PART I

The Shorelines of New England

It wasn't too many years ago that Boston Harbor was known as one of the most polluted bodies of water along the East Coast. Today, however, Boston Harbor has taken its place as one of the best fishing destinations in New England. Boston has seen huge improvements in not only the water quality of its harbor but also the fishing there, and along its adjacent shorelines. Boston Harbor now sits in the middle of some of the best fishing along the Atlantic coast. Within a couple of hours' driving time either up the coast to Maine or south to Rhode Island, you'll find numerous outstanding fly-fishing locations that are head and shoulders above coastlines of similar size. From early spring to late fall the shoreline waters of this region hold the number one target of New England fly anglers, the striped bass, along with a variety of other game fish. From the Kennebec River of Maine to Boston Harbor and south to Napatree Point in Rhode Island, the diversity of shoreline structure and angling opportunities are second to none.

To someone fishing an area for the first time, determining when and where to fish can seem a daunting task. Learning what location is best at what tide will take time. Initially, all anglers operate on a hit-or-miss basis; then they begin to see the patterns that produce the most success. For unlike the bait fisherman who casts out his baited rig and waits for a passing fish, the fly angler must find his quarry.

Any type of shoreline can be intimidating to the first-time fly fisher. This is particularly true when trying to learn to fish a long, sandy beach. It seems to be without the structure to hold fish, and with only endless waves sweeping up the sand. Those who have fished this type of shoreline, however, will tell you it has a good deal of structure. They know that this point on a dropping tide or that cut in the bar just offshore on a rising tide will produce fish. How do they know? That knowledge is gained through time and experience.

Let me state up front that gaining experience in reading the water and the associated shoreline takes time. There is no shortcut to this education. There are, however, ways to help gain that experience. One is fishing with someone who has the knowledge and is willing to pass it along. Reading as much as possible about the sport will also help. If you want to learn more about reading coastline waters and how to fish them, I highly recommend Ed Mitchell's *Fly Rodding the Coast*. This book contains the most complete information I've seen on the various types of shoreline you'll encounter, and how to fish them. Whether you're a novice or seasoned fly rodder, you will benefit from Ed's many years of experience fishing the shorelines of New England.

Every angler, when starting out, has experienced hit-or-miss fishing. One day your favorite spot will be hot and you'll hook a number of fish; the next time you'll come home skunked. The conversation after the latter trip usually refers to not having any luck. But luck has nothing to do with it. Certain elements were different from the time when you were successful. This book will assist you in your journey to become a better fly fisherman by giving you a fundamental understanding of the shoreline you'll encounter, the game fish of the area, and basic tackle and gear. I'll also give you some suggestions for making your fishing safer, easier, and more fun, plus tell you about some really fine fishing locations.

CHAPTER 1

Shorelines

From Rhode Island to Maine, there are all types of shorelines with outstanding fishing opportunities. There are sandy beaches and rocky beaches, and combination of both. There are fishing locations described in this book that are made up of long sweeping beaches bounded at each end by steep, rocky shorelines. Some beaches are comprised of sand and cobblestone, while others are all cobblestone. New England also has its fishing flats, some with sand bottoms and others with soft, muddy footing. Throw in numerous estuaries large and small, salt ponds, and marshes, and you have fly-fishing variety at its best. This is what makes this part of the Atlantic coastline such a delight to fish and why the fishing is considered to be so good.

The key to all shorelines, or locations fished, is structure. Structure is any change or irregularity in the bottom where bait can hold or hide from predators, and where predators themselves can ambush a meal. If you add to that structure current or moving water, then you've got potentially good fishing. Any small baitfish that becomes caught in the current, tumbling along with it, will be dinner. The surf is a prime example of such a situation.

There are any number of other combinations of structure and tidal movement that provide likely spots where bass, weakfish, or bluefish can lie in wait for a meal to be swept by—around a boulder, past a point or jetty, over a drop-off, or through a rip. These are all prime examples of structure and moving water that can hold fish, both prey and predator. One of my favorite

One of my favorite types of beaches to fish is one with sand plus rocks or boulders, especially when they are within casting distance of the shore. Add moving water and you have a near perfect combination for success.

types of beach to fish is one with sand plus large rocks or boulders, particularly when they are situated within casting distance of shore.

If you've never fished a particular location before, regardless of the type of shoreline, check it out at low water during daylight hours. This is especially important if you plan to fish it at night. It will prevent accidents like stepping into a deep hole or off a steep drop-off. Beyond the safety issue, you will get a good look at and understanding of the structure that exists there. This can mean the difference between maybe being lucky and spending your time fishing the right area, the right way.

Let's say you decide to fish a new beach because you heard from fellow anglers that they've been catching striped bass there for the last two nights. You head out, arriving after dark, and slowly proceed to the water's edge armed with your favorite fly. You are using an intermediate line since that's what you recently used on a similar beach. You spend several hours without even a hint of a fish. Yes, you went to the location indicated by your friends, but with no results. What you didn't know was that the spot was a deep hole where the bass were lying in wait for baitfish to be swept in by the tide. With your intermediate line, your fly was passing right by the bass, well over their heads. If you had gotten there before sunset, on the other hand, and had seen that a very deep hole was there, would you have used a sinking line instead? That one adjustment would have changed the results of your fishing trip.

There is an old trick that anglers have been using for years. When you scout the beach during the day, at low water, leave a marker at the exact spot you think will be the best to fish. When you come back at night to fish, then, just look for that same spot. You want to use a marker that you can find at night, but not so obvious that others can readily see it. If they do, they will either be in your spot when you get there or they will remove it, and you'll never be able to determine precisely where to fish. If the marker is too subtle, of course, you may totally miss it in the dark.

Modern technology has given us another way to mark good fishing locales—and the best part is, there's no visible marker for the passerby to see. We now have handheld GPS units that can help you mark and find prime fishing locations. The current accuracy of these units is good enough to put you within several yards of your favorite point, even on the darkest of nights.

The information provided in this book, or others, is a beginning, but nothing beats experience. I can't say this enough: If you want to become a good fisherman, you have to put in the time. Each fishing trip should not only bring enjoyment but also more knowledge, thereby making you a better angler. Over time you'll learn that one beach location may fish better at low water while another point a mile away will have feeding fish near high water. You'll then be able to fish different locations in an evening as conditions change, and improve your chances for success.

Sand, Gravel, and Cobblestone Beaches

The first time anyone walks onto a long, sandy beach, he may feel a bit unsure of how to fish it. A beach with a light surf and what seems like endless sand will often give the first-time angler the feeling that there is little structure or current.

If you explore the beach at low water, however, you will discover that it looks different. What appeared to be a beach without structure usually isn't. You'll see that that much is hidden under the water at high tide. If the beach had a steep slope from the crown, above the high-water line down to the water's edge, then normally you'll still find deep water right up to the beach, even at low tide. This is a general rule to remember: The steeper the beach, the deeper the water just off the beach. Also, darker-colored water along a beach usually signifies deeper water. Conversely, long, gradually sloping beaches usually indicate that the water is shallower there.

Some of the types of structure found on beaches are points, bowls, off-shore bars, and sloughs. Points are spots where the beach extends out from the regular contour of the beach. Some are so small that they're only apparent at low water, while others are quite visible even at high tide. I like to zero in on this type of structure since it breaks the beach line and will usually have fish holding somewhere nearby. Points will often form a rip off their tip at a certain stage of the tide. It's hard to forecast where fish might be feeding in this situation. They could be above the rip, downtide close to the rip, or even farther downtide. Again, the tide and its strength will normally dictate where they are. This is where time spent fishing a spot like this will fill in the blanks of how, where, and when to fish a particular point.

Bowls are the areas where the beach has a large inward curve. The water here will be darker in color and deeper. This type of structure can be fished at all stages of the tide. However, fish may only be there during low water when the surrounding areas become shallow, just before and after low tide. Other bowls can be most productive just before and after high tide because that's when access to that water is easiest. Bait may hold in these bowls for safety through all stages of the tide.

Offshore sandbars, and the deeper water between them and shore, are known as sloughs; they are the main highways for prey and predator. Beaches with long sandbars and deepwater sloughs are great spots to fish. Don't worry if the bar is so far out that you can't reach it on a cast. Quite often the section from the center of the slough into the beach can be the most productive to fish, particularly at night.

Because there are tidal changes, there is movement of water along every beach. Also contributing to current or movement is wave action. The current along a beach can be parallel to the beach, running to either the right or the left; the direction depends upon location and the stage of the tide. If the location is near an opening to an inlet or estuary, the flow can be fairly strong. Water also moves out from the beach as the waves wash up on the sand and recede. This current will be along the bottom and out, off the beach. Such flow can be very pronounced if you're standing in front of a break in an offshore bar. The water brought over the bars by the waves on each side of the opening will be flowing out through this one point.

Along the New England coastline you will encounter not just sandy beaches, but also gravel beaches, small rock or cobblestone beaches, rocks and sand, all rocks, and any combination of these. One big difference is that sandy beaches have a tendency to change. Sandy beaches can be transformed, re-formed, reshaped, and changed by the strong winds and tides of a storm. Therefore, after any major storm it's a good idea to rescout the beach for changes in structure. Do so in spring, as well, for the winter's weather can modify a beach greatly.

Even over periods of quiet weather, such as through a summer with fairly consistent conditions, sandy beaches can slowly modify. Sand will build up here and widen the beach, while taking sand from another spot. Sandbars can form, disappear, and then re-form. Your favorite bowl will fill and a new one will develop a few hundred yards down the beach. Points that formed rips on a dropping tide will flatten out, while new ones might develop a short distance away.

Gravel and cobblestone beaches are fished much like sand beaches; most of the same types of structure exist on both types. Their biggest difference from sandy beaches is that they will not change contour during a storm as quickly. Still, they will change some if the storm is strong and lasts for any extended period. Gravel and cobblestone beaches generally have a shallow slope and therefore shallower water adjacent to the shoreline. The good news is that these beaches, especially cobblestone ones, attract crabs, shrimp, and other marine life that can hide within the small crevices on the bottom. You will also find more mussel beds in the waters off these types of beaches, which feature an irregular bottom that the mussel can cling to. This means that all types of fish, from small baitfish to large predators, will be there to dine.

Regardless of what type of shoreline you're fishing, the biggest challenge is finding the fish. Often this means working your way along the shoreline until you hook up. One way to search for fish is to use a fan-pattern approach from the shoreline. Start at about 10 o'clock and make several casts; make enough casts in that one direction to allow you to also vary the speed of your retrieves. The right retrieve can mean the difference between fish and getting skunked. If there is no action, move your casting to about 11 o'clock and repeat the process. Keep this pattern up until you are casting to your right at about 2 o'clock. If you've covered the area in a fan and haven't raised a fish, move about 50 feet or so and begin casting again at 10 o'clock.

Here's another suggestion for fly fishing from shore. When you get to the spot you want to fish, don't wade right in, particularly at night. So many anglers just can't wait to get waist deep in the water and begin casting. Before you do that, however, first cast in a fan pattern from the shore. Often you'll find the fish very close to shore—just beyond the first breaker, where the wave hits the beach. The reason for this is that many beaches have a ledge or drop-off just beyond where the last wave breaks onto the beach at low tide. Fish will cruise and feed along this drop-off, especially at night. This brings up a caution about fishing the surf: Be careful if such a ledge or drop-off is present. If you're not, you can step off into some deep water.

Tony Stetzko, a guide in Orleans, Massachusetts, who knows as much about fishing the surf of Cape Cod as anyone around, gave me a great tip. One of the biggest problems when fly rodding in the surf is maintaining contact with your fly. The wave action makes it difficult to keep slack out of the line and feel the take of a fish. As Tony explained it to me, after making his cast and as he begins to retrieve the fly, he slowly backs up the beach, helping to keep slack line to a minimum. By the time he has completed his retrieve, he will be up the beach a ways from the surf. This slow retreat during his retrieve allows the fly to cover the water all the way to the last wave. Not only does this give him greater control of the line and fly, but the fly will be in the water up to that last drop-off zone, where bass are often feeding.

The surf is one of those spots where less is better, at times, when it comes to fly movement. I know of a very successful fly rodder who uses a Spey rod in the surf to catch some nice striped bass. The longer rod gives him the added distance he needs to get his fly out over the breakers. He then lets the fly drift in the current, as is done when salmon fishing. He calls this greased-line fishing, as described in the book *Greased Line Fishing for Salmon [and Steelhead]* by Jock Scott.

Spey rods are getting some attention from saltwater fly fishermen. There are many situations where these rods, which run from 12 to 15 feet in length, can be useful. I'll discuss Spey rods later on in the book.

If you're fishing the salt for the first time, be aware that this environment can be tough on your gear. First, sand can cause as much damage as salt water. If you drop a reel in the sand, get it to a place where you can rinse it with fresh water. Remove the spool and rinse the sand from the internal workings. When you replace the spool, if you hear any grinding sound or the reel seems to not move as freely as it should, do not use the reel. Fishing with a sandy reel will allow the sand to work its way into the gears and drag, causing serious harm.

Anytime you're fishing around salt water, corrosion is a fact. At the end of every trip, use fresh water to rinse off your reel and rod. Also, rinse all the flies you have used. When fishing the surf, it's not only the salt water but also the sand suspended in the water from the surf's action that creates a problems. Besides corrosion, salt water can carry fine sand into your reel. Again, if you hear gritty, grinding sounds in the reel, stop and clean it. Given the price of fly reels these days, it's important to take care of your gear. And if you do have a problem with a reel, a backup can save a trip.

Rocky Beaches

Rocky shorelines do not change their characteristics over time. They seem to remain the same from one year to the next. Their shorelines are often irregular and are the epitome of structure. Due to their unchanging nature, many rocky shoreline spots have become famous within the angling community for their ability to consistently produce good fishing; the names given these various fishing destinations have become a part of local angling vocabulary. These names are passed from generation to generation of fishermen.

If you're planning to fish a rocky shoreline for the first time, a scouting trip at low tide is a must. Stay through high water to see how things change. What may have looked good at low water could be unfishable at high tide. Look for where you might fish at different stages of the tide. Are spots reach-

Scouting an area at low water will reveal structure like these boulders that are hidden at high tide. Stripers will set up around these boulders to ambush an unsuspecting meal swept by the current.

able from the shore, or will you need to venture out into the water to cast from a rock? When looking for a stable platform to cast from, look for the flattest rock possible. But don't be disappointed if you arrive at the beach and find someone else on that rock. In many locales there is strong competition for the better spots.

The prime time to fish rocky beaches is two to three hours before and after high tide. This provides enough water for larger fish to move in and feed on bait that hides in the shallow pockets of water at lower tides. But when selecting a spot to fish, make sure you won't be cut off and be in a dangerous situation at high tide. That rock may look great at low tide—but will the waves make it impossible to maintain your footing when the water rises? If you can, look for places that have deep water within casting distance. Watch to see how the water moves around the rocks and where fish might hang, waiting for a meal to come by.

Having noted that the best tide to fish rocky shores is around high tide, don't pass up fishing a spot if there's sufficient water within casting distance even during the lower stages of the tide. In fishing, you soon learn never to say "never." Also, if you plan to fish a new location at night—which often is the best time—fish it at least once during daylight hours, if possible, to get the feel of the area.

In *Fly Rodding the Coast,* Ed Mitchell makes a very good recommendation about what types of flies to use around a rocky shoreline. Flies that ride with their hooks up, like the Clouser Minnow, help to reduce the hang-ups that often occur around rocky structure. Otherwise it's almost impossible to avoid this problem unless you're using a floating line and poppers. This is just a single example of the useful information in Ed's book.

A Clouser Minnow is a versatile fly that will get down deeper in the water column than an unweighted fly will, when fished on an intermediate line. Clousers with different-sized eyes can also help you adjust to fishing different depths without changing lines.

If you're fishing a location where the water is being pushed around the rocks by the tide and waves, try an unweighted fly and let it drift in the swirling water. This can be a very productive method, but if this approach causes too many hang-ups, switch tactics.

The downside of this type of fishing is that it can very dangerous. Do not attempt to fish the rocks without the use of some kind of footwear with cleats. A number of different types of metal cleats are made to fit over your boots. The ice creepers sold in catalogs also work well. Felt-soled shoes will do okay on bare rocks but not so well in other situations.

You'll often find weeds on rocks that are covered at all but low water, or remain just under the surface even at low water. Such rocks are extremely slippery. You'll also find rocks that have no weeds but are covered with a slippery slime; these appear darker in color than the other rocks or boulders. Rocks that receive spray or are covered by water during the higher stages of tide will be slippery, as well.

Always be on the lookout for darker water near the shoreline. If it's within casting distance, all the better. It could be deep water, a submerged rock, grass beds, or a mussel bed. Check it out at low water. Each has the potential to attract and hold fish.

A good bit of your fishing will be done during low light or darkness. At these times a slower retrieve is better than a fast one. It gives the fish a greater chance to find the fly, and there is less chance of rejection since the fish are primarily seeing the fly's silhouette.

While we're on the subject of retrieval speed, be aware that if you're fishing in a mix of striped bass and bluefish, the general rule is that a fast retrieve will attract bluefish while a slower retrieve will take bass. I have experimented with this on a number of occasions, and the rule seems to hold true.

I've had people tell me that bluefish only feed during the day. Bluefish will eat anything they can, at any time. My experience is that if I'm fishing at night and there are bluefish around, they will hit a fly. There are some instances when they will ignore your fly, but these are special situations and will be covered in the section about bluefish.

Saltwater Ponds

Saltwater ponds offer some of the most enjoyable fly fishing you can find. They are, in some respects, much like fishing freshwater ponds. They can also be a great way for the beginning angler to get into saltwater fishing. Many anglers start their seasons here in spring when small striped bass enter these ponds to feed after a long winter. Later, the first bluefish arrivals often follow the same pattern. This is because the waters of these ponds are warmer than the open ocean and there is a good food supply.

Early-spring fishing in ponds will usually be during the day. The one exception is when worm hatches occur during the early-evening hours and into the night. As the summer progresses, the water in the ponds warms and the better fishing is at night. In fall you will again find action during the day as fish enter the ponds to feed and fuel up for their migration south.

Saltwater ponds are great spots to get used to fly fishing at night. One thing to remember is that stealth is very important. Vibrations from walking or wading in small, confined waters will spook the fish. Any fish that enters here to feed at night will be wary of being in shallow water. You may want to initially fish from shore so as to not disturb any fish that might be feeding close to shore. If you don't encounter fish, then slowly work your way into deeper water, fishing as you go.

In spring you'll find small stripers and blues feeding in saltwater ponds. As the season progresses, however, the bigger bass will come in to feed during the higher tides at night. But again, this is a general rule. There will be times when there is so much bait in the pond that the fish won't wait until dark but push in during the day on a high tide to feed.

If there are deep holes or channels, do not pass up fishing these spots during the day. When these spots are deep enough, the fish will feel safe and hold there during low water. Like all the different shoreline situations, struc-

Saltwater fly anglers begin their season in the spring when schoolies enter the coastal ponds and estuaries to feed after a long winter.

ture is important. Look for deep water, drop-offs, channels, and rips that form on a dropping tide. Also, on a dropping tide, work the ocean side of the opening to a pond. Fish often position themselves here to waylay a meal being brought their way by the current. Remember, most fish are opportunistic feeders; if they can conserve energy yet still get a shot at dinner, they will.

I had a memorable experience a number of years ago while night fishing on Martha's Vineyard. I was wading across the opening of a pond when I encountered a large bass that either was exiting the pond as the tide was dropping or was feeding on bait being washed out the opening. That dark night I learned a valuable lesson about striped bass behavior. Bass will swim through water so shallow they scrape their bellies, if a good meal is to be had.

The second lesson from the night was about taking more care when moving around, particularly at night. This particular bass was spooked when I none-too-quietly waded across the opening. He bolted for deeper water. The problem was that I was between him and his objective, the open water. He hit my leg and threw spray all over. It reminded me of one of those pictures of salmon wiggling up a shallow stream to spawn, only at higher speed. I'm not sure who was more frightened that evening.

You can read about things like this but when it happens to you, you'll definitely remember it. I learned to move through water with more care and stealth, and I am no longer surprised to find fish in the most unlikely places. I also know that striped bass, under the cover of darkness, feel comfortable navigating shallow water, especially if there is a meal involved.

That same night on Martha's Vineyard, my friend and I heard popping sounds back in the pond as bass fed on the surface. I now realize that it could have been a worm hatch. At the time I was not aware of such an event. Most saltwater fly rodders know all about the worm hatches in saltwater ponds and watch for this event each year.

What's called the worm hatch in New England is when sandworms— also known as cinder worms, sea worms, and clam worms—spawn. It takes place in saltwater ponds and small estuaries from spring into early summer, normally in the evening or at night, and around the times of the new and full moons. The worms drift on the current, an easy meal for stripers. When striped bass find a worm hatch under way, they will gorge themselves on these small tidbits. Like trout, they swim along sucking in the worms as they go.

This event can provide great fishing or sheer frustration. There are times when the bass will ignore whatever fly you're using—there's just too much to eat, and your fly is lost among all the food. At these times, try switching from a fly that resembles a worm to something else, but keep it small. Though there are several patterns of flies that resemble the cinder worm, I have had success with small bunny flies, with a short rabbit strip tail.

Some saltwater ponds are better than others because from year to year they have more resident bait. If any marsh area is associated with the pond, this is a good sign that you've found an environment where young baitfish are born and live during their early years. These nurseries are an important part of the marine food chain and why these marshes need protection. For regardless of how good a management plan we might have for striped bass, bluefish, and the like, our game fish will not survive without the food they need—much of which begins life in the marshes, bays, and ponds along our coast.

Lastly, saltwater ponds not only provide fine fly fishing but are also good spots to learn about the prey you're trying to imitate with your fly. I know of a number of top anglers who have spent hours just standing or crouching along a shoreline, watching baitfish and observing how they move in the water. It's important to understand something about the fish you're trying to catch, of course—but you should also know about what they eat and how that prey looks to them. It will make you a better angler.

Flats

Many shorelines with little wave action and a very flat slope will turn into large flats at low water. Other flats areas are never dry but can be waded at the lower stages of thc tide. The bottom of a flat is normally either sand or mud; it can be small or cover many square miles. But regardless of size and bottom type, flats can provide some of the best fly fishing you'll experience.

Many large flats areas are devoid of water during low tide. However, there will be channels and pockets of deeper water that hold fish. When you're on this kind of flat, be very mindful of the tides. You can end up in trouble if you're not careful. The water can move in quickly with the tide, filling the holes and cuts that you waded through on your way out. With a tide differential of just 6 feet, the water in those spots can be over your head. In some locales a tide of 8 feet is standard. The channel you easily waded at low tide may be impassable if you wait too long to return.

You'll want to fish the channels and deep pockets of water on this type of flat. Fish will hold in these spots, waiting for the tide to flood the flats. You may also want to wade out to a reasonable depth to explore the deeper edges. But again, keep an eye on the time and the tide. The farther you are from shore, the longer it will take for you to get back.

You will be able to sight cast to fish during the daylight hours on flats that are covered throughout all the stages of the tide. You'll need polarized glasses to spot the fish when doing this type of angling. The fish will usually be moving from location to location in search of food. However, do not ignore places where they might wait for prey; look for them hanging over darker bottom spots, waiting to ambush an unsuspecting meal. I've seen bluefish holding over dark grass patches in just 4 feet of water. Casting to these grass patches brought a strike on almost every cast.

One fly pattern that has worked well on striped bass patrolling sandy flats is a light-colored crab fly. This is another instance where very little fly movement is needed to get a take. When sand eels are present, patterns that imitate this baitfish will also produce.

A good flats area is one where there is deep water close enough that the fish can retreat to it as the tide drops, or if threatened. Good flats or shallows will have fish feeding at different times of tide. Usually the incoming tide brings the fish in to feed, so your fishing time may be confined to just a couple of hours. Again, look for those drop-offs where the fish may be hanging during the lower stages of the tide.

One additional piece of equipment that I recommend is a compass. This is a must for night fishing but also a lifesaver when the fog rolls in. Trying to find your way to shore in the dark or heavy fog with a tide rolling in is not a good situation.

A friend once told me about such an incident, which occurred when he was fishing the Brewster Flats on Cape Cod. It was a foggy night, and he was making his way back to shore using his compass. He was about halfway back when he saw a light to his left and coming his way. He stopped and waited. He soon saw another angler approaching at right angles to him. When the man got close, my friend shouted to him and asked where he was going. "I'm heading in to my car," was the answer. My friend then assured the man that he wasn't, adding that he had a compass and the fisherman should follow him. The angler, if he'd continued on his course, was headed for gradually increasing water depth and sure trouble. A small compass should always be part of your gear when fishing locations like flats. Be mindful that in New England the fog can settle in even during the day and leave you with no points of reference.

Estuaries

Whenever I drive along a New England coastal road, I'm impressed with the number of small streams, creeks, and rivers I see—and this is after living here for nearly 40 years. The majority of them feature shallow bays and marshes. These are prime nursery areas for baitfish, shrimp, and crabs, all of which are like hors d'oeuvres for bluefish, striped bass, and weakfish. They are key links in the marine food chain.

As a general rule, feeding fish move into an estuary on an incoming or rising tide and then slowly drop back out as tide falls. Besides the buffet resident in the estuary, additional baitfish often move in and out with the tide, as well. All these fish use the channel as their main highway. As the tide floods the bays and marshes, predators large and small move in to feed.

Just as if you were on a beach, look for structure—points, rips, holes, and such—where fish will have a tendency to set up and feed. If there are deep holes or channels even at low water, get a fly to the bottom of these hiding places. Striped bass and weakfish will hang in these holes until the tide comes back in. They're waiting for a meal to come through these deeper hideaways, carried along by the current.

In many New England estuaries, you may only be able to reach these

Wading and fishing the shallow areas of an estuary on an evening tide can be some of the most enjoyable and successful angling you can experience.

deeper sections during the last few hours of low tide. At that time you can wade to these spots with ease and reach the deepwater channels and holes. Also, if there are turns and bends in the waterway, pay attention to these at low water. Fish the water on the outside section of the bend. This is where the current will cut deeper channels, often right against the bank. If you can reach the far side of the bend, cast to the bank and use a slow retrieve. If there's current, drift the fly through these sections.

Trout anglers already understand an important principle of fly fishing that also holds true in salt water: A fly moving in an unnatural manner, such as at right angles to the current or upstream against a dropping tide, is not exhibiting the normal movements of a baitfish or shrimp. That same fly drifting in the current has a more natural appearance and appeal. However, when drifting a fly with the current, pay attention to when it reaches the end of the drift and starts to swing across the current. You will find that fish that were following your fly will often attack it then.

Estuaries are unique relative to the tides. There is a delay in the times of high and low tide in estuaries. The farther a point is from open water, the longer the delay at that point. A river will continue to flow seaward for a

Knowing how much of a time difference or delay in tide there is for a particular location on an estuary is part of learning to fish that water. It is as important as knowing where key structure is located.

while after the time of low tide, and conversely will continue to flow in after high tide has been reached at its opening. As an example, let's say you're at a point on a beach that is adjacent to a river. Your tide chart indicates that at your location high water will occur at 12:13 PM, and shortly after that time you see the water beginning to recede. Up the river, however, the water will still be rising; it won't begin dropping until sometime later. Knowing how much of a time difference there is for a particular location on an estuary is part of learning to fish that estuary. Once you're sure of the delay or differences for high and low water, make a record of it.

In the example above, you were probably at that spot near the mouth of the river because fishing the outflow on a dropping tide can be very productive. Predators set up to feed, waiting for baitfish to be carried downstream by the current. Fish any rips that form as the dropping tide sweeps out into open water. As the tide drops, fish this situation until the current slackens. In fall migrating bass and blues will often use the openings to creeks and rivers as feeding stations, fueling up for their journey south. If there is sufficient prey available, when the tide rises, they will pursue it up into the estuary.

One very important point about fishing the openings to estuaries needs to be stressed. They can be very dangerous places to fish, particularly during the dropping tide. And if you aren't familiar with the area or are fishing at night, they can be doubly dangerous. The tide will cut channels and create drop-offs that change location and characteristics over time. In the excitement and anticipation of fishing, you can step off an edge and be swept out into deeper water. This has happened several times on Cape Cod, with fatal results. You should always use a flotation device like the inflatable suspenders or belt units that are now available in tackle shops and fishing catalogs. They can save your life.

Jetties

When I was growing up in New Jersey, my favorite fishing places were the jetties along the shore. The ones I liked to fish were broad, long, and fairly flat on top. They were there as structures to stabilize beach erosion. These jetties were such a popular place to fish that a new breed of fishing rod was developed just for jetty jockeys—the nickname for those who fished these rock piles on a regular basis. Though I didn't feel I qualified as a jetty jockey, I did like to fish the jetties, especially at night. While in high school, a trip to the shore for me usually meant some time casting plugs from a jetty, into the dark night.

New England has single jetties scattered along its coastline that were built to control erosion. You will often hear them called groins, but to me they will always be jetties. Now, in some places in New England, you'll hear of breachways. These are jetties that protect the two sides of an opening to a saltwater bay, pond, or estuary. The opening or inlet is what's called a breachway. The jetties on either side are man-made structures built to stabilize the opening. These breachways usually feature swift-moving water between the jetties and around the ends, as the tide flows in and out of the opening.

Certain jetties can be difficult to fish and turn dangerous in heavy seas, especially at night. Still, they can also provide some very productive fishing. It's like fishing a pier; it takes you out to deeper water where the fishing can often be better than that on shore. However, like any location, you will need to fish a jetty at different tides, various times of day, and through the season to really learn how to make the most of what it offers. Learn its fishing characteristics, for every jetty or breachway is different.

I like to have a partner with me when fishing a jetty. Not only is this wise from a safety point of view, but a second person can also be a big help in landing a fish. Even the most experienced jetty jockey will tell you this can be a difficult task when alone, especially if you plan to release the fish. A long-handled net can help you, but it's just one more thing to carry out onto the jetty, as well as something that can get lost in the rocks or kicked into the water.

Another hazard of fishing jetties is nicked leaders and hang-ups. But be aware that many anglers simply put up with these to catch the quality fish taken from some of the better-known breachways and jetties. The best advice is to check your leader and fly often. The rocks around the jetties will take their toll on your flies, so carry a good supply in your bag. The eyes of Clouser Minnows seem to disappear from one cast to the next. Jetties quite often have mussels on their rocks that can be severe on both flies and leaders. Check both between every few casts, because there is nothing more disappointing than losing a fish to a nicked leader or dulled hook point.

Some jetties are covered with water at high tide, especially at ends. On others, high tide and the right wind direction cause waves to wash over the end, and even other sections of the jetty. At a minimum the spray will cause slippery conditions that are potentially dangerous. Sometimes these conditions can make the fishing downright miserable. If you have even a minor fall or slip, you can sustain some nasty injuries. This is why metal cleats, ice creepers, or similar devices that fit over your boots are a must on jetties and rocky structures. But given all of that, experienced jetty jockeys tend to be a safe lot, and few accidents occur.

As I've noted, the end of a jetty is a prime fishing location. This is where the water is the deepest and where the current of the open water sweeps by. On a dropping tide, water from the inlet will also form a rip in this area. The end of the jetty, if not crowded, offers an additional advantage. You can avoid casting into the wind because you have more options as to the directions you can cast. Still, there will be times when you have to cast into the wind, since that's where the fish are feeding.

Because the tip of the jetty offers such good fishing, it can be crowded. Many jetties may have limited space at the end to fish, accommodating just a couple of anglers. If there are fishermen drifting eels on the dropping tide, this also limits where you can cast. This is a good time to explore other sections of the jetty, especially near the shore.

Fishing the breachway is much like fishing an estuary. Cast across the

Fishing a breachway is similar to fishing an estuary with fast-moving water. Cast up-current or across, keep in contact with the fly as it is swept along in the current, and pay close attention when the fly begins to make the swing in the current. Also, work the quiet water.

current, give the fly just enough movement to stay in contact with it, and pay careful attention to the fly as it begins to make that swing in current. Besides fishing the current with a drift, also work the outside. If fish are on feeding on top, an intermediate line will work well. If they're feeding below the surface, try a sinking line. And if you know the fish are there but aren't getting any strikes, you may have to go even deeper to get the fly down to them. A weighted fly and a fast-sinking line will do the trick.

When you hook a fish on a dropping tide, it will usually swim away from the jetty, with the current. So it's a sound idea to have sufficient backing on your reel. This is where a large-capacity reel can mean the difference between landing a fish and getting spooled. Try to work your fish along the outside of the jetty and land it from the beach. This can be done if the jetty is easy to negotiate and the fish is willing to cooperate. On an incoming tide, the fish will take advantage of the current and run up into the inlet. However, do not depend upon the fish always behaving in this manner and going with the current. They don't read the rulebooks.

The jetties of inlets or breachways are some of the better places where a shorebound fly rodder can catch bonito and false albacore. Standard practice for these fish is to attack baitfish being carried out by a dropping tide. There will also be times when the bonito and false albacore chase the bait into the breachway. The best time for this to happen is on an incoming tide.

Striped bass regularly enter inlets to feed upstream or in the back pond; this usually happens at night when the bass feel the safest. But when the fall migration starts, look for bass and bluefish to regularly stop and feed at the open-water end of breachways, on an outgoing tide.

Lastly, like estuaries, there will be a delay in tide times in breachways, often by an hour or so. The tide in the open water can be on the rise for some time and yet the water of the inlet will still be flowing out. This is something to make note of, for the delay is different in each inlet.

CHAPTER 2

Tides

Throughout this book I've made reference to the tide and the important role it plays in fishing. It's one of the elements, along with weather, that influence just about everything in the coastal marine environment. Tide changes the water level, and produces current and the movement of water. Tide quite often dictates when and where the fish will be feeding, for it's the tide that allows them to get to a food source or have the food carried to them.

So if tides, and when they occur, are so important, what causes them? Simply put, it is the gravitational pull between the earth and the moon, plus some influence from the sun. Our oceans, as well as the earth's surface, are pulled out toward the moon. And when the sun is aligned with the moon, the pull is stronger. The times of the tide change from one day to the next because the moon rotates around the earth at a frequency greater than 24 hours.

Along our Atlantic coast, we have two high tides and two low tides each day; however, there are places on our earth where only one high and one low tide occur per day. The difference in the time of tides from one high tide to the next one is approximately 12 hours and 25 minutes. The same holds true for the time between low tides. A full day's tide cycle will repeat about every 24 hours and 50 minutes. So the high tide today during the daylight hours will occur tomorrow, during the day, some 50 minutes later. This is why the tide affects the fishing at a particular location over a moving period of time. If the fishing was good last night at sunset and high tide, it may not be good a week from then at sunset because the tide will be different, and closer to low water.

If you would like more information on tides, waves, and currents, plus many other aspects of the marine environment and how to fish it, get yourself a copy of the book *The Fisherman's Ocean*. A good friend, David A. Ross, who is a scientist emeritus at Woods Hole Oceanographic Institution, wrote this book. He is not only a well-known oceanographer but also a first-class fly fisherman.

The moon influences not only the time of high and low tides but also the height of the tide or amount of change between high and low tide. Some high tides are higher than others, just as some low tides are lower. Fishermen call the higher tides moon tides; the more proper name for them is spring tides, though they have nothing to do with the season. These higher tides, and accompanying low tides that are lower than normal, occur during the full- and new-moon phases. The wide variance in tide differential will produce the strongest currents, which is a key for anglers.

The high and low tides with the least amount of difference between them are called neap tides and occur about every two weeks during the first- and third-quarter phases of the moon. Currents caused by tidal movement are weakest at this time. If all of this seems a lot to keep track of, a later chapter will introduce you to the fishing log and how it can help.

The most important piece of gear that you can carry is a tide chart for the area you are fishing. Not only will it become your guide to good fishing, but it will also keep you from placing yourself in a dangerous situation, cut off by a rising tide. Learn how to read a tide chart and use it. A tide chart lists the tide times for a major location in a particular region. It also gives time adjustments for high- and low-tide times for a number of different locales in that area. For example, I use a tide chart that lists the tide times and heights for Boston Harbor. If I'm fishing Race Point, at the tip of Cape Cod, the chart tells me that I should subtract one minute from the high-tide time indicated for any given day and two minutes from the low-tide time to determine the tides at Race Point. The tide chart should also list the tide-height difference for each spot that should be applied to the primary location's tidal differences.

Tackle shops stock tide charts for the areas they service, usually free of charge. You can also get tide information on the Internet. Most saltwater fishing web sites provide tide information or link to tide information elsewhere. Just make sure the web site is giving the tides for the area you want to fish. One that I use is www.tidelines.com; it gives tide information for the Atlantic and Pacific coast plus Alaska, Hawaii, and Mexico.

Here is a bit of information that might be of help to you. During the full- and new-moon phases for a given area in New England, the times of the high tide, and low, will always occur at about the same time of day or night. For example, on Cape Cod, if there is a full moon or new moon, the high tide for that night will occur sometime near midnight—always. It may be 11 PM or some minutes after midnight, but always in that time frame. The same holds true for the associated low tides. This can be useful in the long-range planning of fishing trips.

Remember that with tide there is always moving water. Even along a straight stretch of beach there will be a current. If they are not swimming along with it and searching for food, the fish will take a position facing into the current. They will be waiting for baitfish, crustaceans, worms, and shrimp to be swept by in the current, providing them with an easy meal.

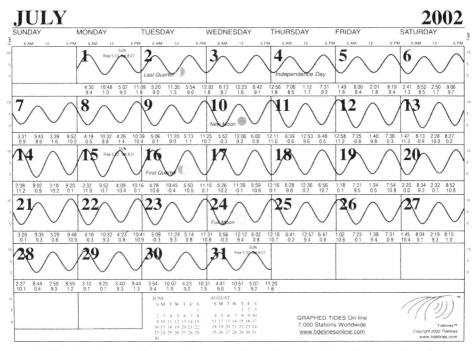

A tide chart is one of the most important items for an angler to have and use. I like this one from the Tidelines website (www.tidelines.com). They also sell a tide calendar and handy pocket chart with the same information, which I use. (Reproduced by permission.)

Keep in mind that some locations may not have their best fishing at high tide. You may only be able to effectively fish a flats area from the last hours of the dropping tide into the first few hours of the incoming. Remember that the good flats or shallow areas are usually located close to deeper water, where the fish can retreat on a dropping tide; this is important if there are no holes or deep cuts in the flats.

The key to becoming a better fly fisherman is learning what are the best times of the tide for a particular location. In his book *Fly Rodding the Coast*, Ed Mitchell notes that for most locations the opportunity for fish comes at only one stage of the tide, either the ebb or the flood. He adds that hooking a fish in that spot may be restricted to very small segment of that stage of the tide. It may just be a one- or two-hour window of opportunity.

There are countless locations along the coastline of New England where you can park your car and walk to good fishing. Pick any given area in any state and you'll find it has a number of places to fish, and sometimes the choice as to which one is best may be difficult. My advice is to select one or two locations with different structure, and maybe different tide times, and concentrate on learning how to fish them. Study them at low tide and on through a complete tidal cycle to learn where rips form, where drop-offs are, or where boulders sit, hidden at high tide. The more you know about a location, the greater your chances of success.

PART II

The Fishes
of New England

CHAPTER 3

The Fishes
of New England

The ocean is filled with a variety of marine life, all having one thing in common. Both day and night there is a continual struggle for survival. That survival is dependent upon two primary actions, which are to find food to eat and to avoid being eaten. If a fish cannot escape its enemies, it will die. Conversely, if it's unable to capture and eat enough food, it won't survive. Nature's balance over millions of years has sustained life in our oceans; only humankind has been able to upset that balance.

All fish are opportunistic feeders. If there's a chance for a meal, they will not pass it up, for in the wild you never know when the next opportunity will occur. So as fly rodders, when we cast a fly to a rip or other likely spot, we hope that it will look natural and foodlike enough in appearance and movement to entice a fish to eat it.

This is why it's important to develop a basic understanding of the habits of the fish you're pursuing and what's on their menu. You will find that many fish, particularly the larger and stronger predators, have a wide and varied bill of fare. Within this chapter is information on the game fish that we, as fly fishermen, pursue along the coastline from Rhode Island to Maine, as well as what marine life these game fish prey upon. In several instances the prey itself also makes for fine sport on a fly rod.

Some 20 years ago before their numbers dwindled, weakfish (or squeteague) like this 14-pound fish were caught along the Atlantic coastline. Their numbers are now increasing and anglers are once again experiencing good squeteague fishing.

A good way to learn about some of the baitfish and other sources of food sought by game fish is to observe them in their natural habitat. Competent saltwater anglers often take time to do this. If you can, study how certain prey moves and behaves. Estuaries, flats, bays, and other areas of quiet water are ideal spots. If you have access to a boat to travel the shoreline, this can afford a great opportunity to watch certain baitfish. And don't forget the polarized sunglasses; they are a must if you want to see down into the water column.

One good example of baitfish that can be easily observed are the large schools of sand eels found in the bays and along the shorelines of many New England areas in spring and summer. Another food source that is easy to find and watch are crabs. An angling friend once told me of how he stood on the bank of deep channel that cut through a marsh and watched striped bass rooting crabs out of the mud bank. Those that tried to swim away were an easy meal. You can bet that one of his choices when he fishes that location is a dark-colored crab fly.

Let me state at this point that if you're one of those who cast out a fly and then use the same monotonous strip, strip, strip, never varying the rhythm of your retrieve, you're in for a number of fishless trips. Understand that a variation in your retrieve, particularly matching the movement of the bait present, is as important as what fly you use and where you cast it.

This point was brought home to me several springs ago while fishing on the south side of Cape Cod. The water was loaded with sand eels and feeding striped bass, but I was having a hard time getting any hits. My fly was the right type and size; I just wasn't getting any takes. However, a friend nearby was getting hook-ups regularly. Finally I walked over to him and asked what he was doing different. I learned that he would cast the fly out, let it sit, give a short twitch of a retrieve, and then let it sit again. For whatever reason, the bass were passing up the faster-moving sand eels in favor of those hanging suspended in the water.

There will be times when, if you aren't getting any interest from the fish, you'll need to vary your fly's movement. Keep changing the speed and cadence of your retrieve until you find what works. Often a fly moving differently from the rest of the bait around it will get the interest of your quarry and work the best. As pointed up by the sand eel experience, less can often be better. And remember, the situation can change from day to day, so keep experimenting until you find the combination of the right fly, speed, and depth.

Another trick, well known by surf rats, is being on the lookout for bait that has washed up on the shore. I should qualify that by saying *bait that was probably chased up onto the shore,* rather than just washing up. How far up the beach the bait is from the waterline can often tell you when and at what stage of the tide the attack occurred. You'll also learn what type and size of bait the game fish were feeding upon.

Fish find their prey through the senses of sight, sound, and smell. Later in this chapter there will be an introduction to these senses. However, since for the most part smell is not a major factor in fly fishing unless you contaminated your fly with an odor that would be offensive to the fish, sight and sound are most important.

Striped Bass

When striped bass began to appear in better numbers after their collapse in the 1970s, they once again took their place as the number one inshore game fish in the Northeast. At about that same time saltwater fly fishing was beginning its rise in popularity; no longer is this type of striped bass fishing

The striped bass is a perfect game fish for the fly-rodder. They can be caught on a variety of flies that imitate the marine life they prey upon.

done by just a handful of anglers. This was not just a coincidence; there is a correlation. The striped bass is a perfect fit as a game fish for the fly angler.

The striped bass lives and feeds at all levels of the water column, from the surface to the bottom. Bass are found in the rolling surf, cruising the quiet waters of bays, tidal estuaries, and coastal flats. Stripers come in all sizes, from small schoolies to females of 50 pounds or more. And most importantly to the fly fisherman, they can be caught with artificial imitations of the marine life they prey upon.

Their other appeal is that they can be caught on fly rods of varying weights and lines. A light outfit with a floating line and a cinder worm imitation, being drifted on a quiet stretch of water, will catch bass just as well as the 10-weight outfit utilizing a 500-grain sinking line and casting a large, weighted Grocery Fly into the fast, deep waters of the Kennebec River. A fly rodder can catch bass from the shore of an estuary, while wading the flats, or in the surf. It's as if the striper had been specifically designed for all aspects of saltwater fly fishing.

The striped bass, also known as rockfish in southern states, has been a prominent saltwater fish since the time the Pilgrims set foot on our country's shore. Stripers were apparently so numerous back then that they made quite an impact on the settlers of Plymouth. In his book *Striper,* John Cole gives an account of the vast quantities of striped bass described in 1614 by Captain John Smith, who spoke of, ". . . such multitudes that I have seene stopped in the river close adjoining to my house with a sands at one tyde so many as will loade a ship of 100 tonnes. I myselfe at the turning of the tyde have seene such a multitude passe out of a pounde that it seemed to me that one mighte go over their backs dreshod."

Cole also relates the well-known story of how the striper became the foundation of public education. In 1664 the leaders of the Plymouth Colony ordered that the money from the sales of striped bass, which had become valuable commercially, be used to build the first public school in our country. They also prohibited the use of striped bass for fertilizer. The bass were more valuable to the colonists as a source of revenue and food. This had to be the first marine conservation measure in the yet-to-be-established United States. It was also the first of what was to be many legislative actions seeking to protect and maintain striped bass stocks.

If you love to fish for striped bass and would like to read a well-written book on this beautiful fish, get yourself a copy of *Striper*. I am sure you'll enjoy this fine book. However, I must admit that I am biased because John Cole is my favorite writer.

The major portion of the striped bass population along the New England coast is resident here only from spring until fall. They migrate north in spring from their winter grounds in southern waters, to which they return in late fall. However, given the numbers of small bass showing up in late April in the estuaries and bays of Cape Cod's south shore, it's believed that some may be wintering offshore in deeper water, where temperatures are warmer. A number of bass will also winter over in numerous estuaries all along the Atlantic coast. This is no doubt due in large part to these estuaries being cleaned up in recent years.

In *Fishes of the Gulf of Maine,* authors Henry B. Bigelow and William C. Schroeder make note of this. They state that there is some thought that "a good portion of these bass that come from the south when they are 3–4 years old may remain in the north for the rest of their lives." This is backed up by accounts from years ago when the bass populations were high and the rivers along the Atlantic seaboard were not heavily polluted. Wintering stripers in these estuaries were so thick they could be foul-hooked as they lay on the bottom, waiting out the winter.

The majority of migrating stripers winter off the coast of Virginia and North Carolina, then enter the Chesapeake Bay in early spring to spawn before again moving up the coast. However, this is not the only spawning ground for the bass. Though the Chesapeake is the primary spawning ground, there are other bass populations in the Hudson River and the Roanoke River of North Carolina, which was once a major bass producer and is again starting to produce significant numbers of fish. On a smaller scale, Maine's Kennebec River has spawning bass, as well.

An interesting note in *Fishes of the Gulf of Maine* is that the younger stripers stay near their spawning area for the first couple of years of their lives. The book claims that they do not migrate until at least two years old.

Because the Chesapeake Bay has classically been the spawning grounds of the largest portion of the overall striped bass population, the Maryland Department of Natural Resources (DNR) a number of years ago began measuring the success of the spawning as an indicator of the health of the bass stocks. Every year the DNR issues an assessment of the striped bass population. This forecast is a result of measurements of how well the striped bass have reproduced in the Chesapeake Bay and certain tributaries. It's called the young-of-the-year index and is considered a prime indicator of striped bass status along the Atlantic coast.

Since 1954, the determination of the young-of-the-year index has been carried out by the DNR in the Upper Chesapeake Bay as well as the Choptank, Nanticoke, and Potomac Rivers. This index is determined by catches made with haul seine nets at 22 set locations. The sampling is done at all sites three times per year, during the months of July, August, and September.

Using a seine net that is 100 feet long, biologists make two hauls at each site; there is about a 30-minute wait between the first and second samplings. The total number of young striped bass netted at all locations is then divided by 132, which is the number of samplings done (22 sites x 2 samplings per site x 3 times per year = 132). The resulting figure is the young-of-the-year index for the year.

This may sound very controlled and monitored, but in 1989 there was an instance when it wasn't. That year, for whatever reason, DNR biologists decided to sample a different site. Rumor has it that they didn't find any fish at the original site. Nevertheless, the new location produced an enormous number of fish—so many that it drove the index up to 25.2 that year. Though there were protests of foul play from many sources, the Maryland DNR stood firm and that index was then responsible for reopening bass fishing in the Chesapeake Bay. It kicked off the "bass have recovered" era and changes in striped bass management practices along the Atlantic seaboard.

Striped bass spawn in brackish to fresh water and can tolerate different degrees of salinity. Stripers can even do well and survive in fresh water. They have been cut off by dams and have also been transplanted into many fresh-water locations, and have become a very popular freshwater game fish. They are an extremely adaptable and hearty fish. Stripers even survived a rail trip across our country to become the foundation of the West Coast striped bass population

They can survive in a wide range of water temperatures. Their optimum temperature range is from 60 to 70 degrees, but they can tolerate water temperatures to the lower 40s or upper 30s. During these times they become very lethargic. Their upper water temperature tolerance is about 78 degrees.

Striped bass can grow to great size, if permitted to do so. Current management policies have produced a lot of smaller bass, but the larger fish seen in the 1960s and earlier are absent. As an example of how big they can grow, several bass weighing 125 pounds were caught at Edenton, North Carolina, in April 1891. A striper estimated to be 112 pounds was taken in Orleans, Massachusetts, many, many years ago. And for those who think big bass never made it to Maine, one was taken in Casco Bay that weighed just over 100 pounds. All of these fish were taken commercially and are documented in *Fishes of the Gulf of Maine*.

Every one of these striped bass was a female. The females are larger than the males; those who fished for them during the 1960s, when these bigger bass were around in much larger numbers, rightly referred to them as cows.

The first recorded, record striped bass was C. B. Church's fish of 73 pounds. It was caught in August 1913 in Vineyard Sound, somewhere along the Elizabeth Islands. This record was thrown out a number of years ago, however, when it was contested.

I once had the pleasure of being a member of the Intrepid Striper Club along with a fellow named Charles Cinto. Charlie is a great fisherman and proved so in June 1967 by catching a striper of 73 pounds. That bass was taken on a boat in seas so rough, those onboard had trouble standing up. It was taken off the tip of Cuttyhunk Island in a nasty spot called the Pigs and Sows—a tough place to fish even on a good day. It was not recognized as an International Game Fish Association (IGFA) record because it was caught on a swimming plug, with treble hooks and wire line. At that time it was the largest bass taken on hook and line since Church's fish, and not that far from where Church caught his striper.

As striped bass get older and bigger, there are fewer members of their year-class around. The profile of the total bass population, when in a healthy state, would resemble a pyramid with the youngest year-classes and greatest numbers in population at the bottom, while the oldest year-class of larger bass, having the fewest numbers, would be at the top. Prior to the collapse of the striped bass population in the 1960s, we saw a classical pyramid profile of the bass. Today, though many claim that the bass population has recovered, there are also many who say the profile is a pyramid with the top cut off and flattened because the larger-sized bass are not around in the numbers they enjoyed in the 1960s.

Large bass are normally solitary feeders. They do not expend their energy in feeding as they did when they were smaller and traveled in large schools. A fly being stripped quickly through the water in their vicinity may not get a strike, but a fly drifting by slowly like an unwary sand eel or silversides looks like an easy meal that can be captured with minimum effort. This is not to say that 40-pound bass won't chase and grab a fly moving at a moderate speed, but the general rule is that the big fish are lazy and want an easy meal.

How larger bass feed was taught to me when I was fishing in my 14-foot boat off the beaches of Provincetown in the 1960s. My buddy Charlie Cinto saw me throwing away dead mackerel after a day of striper fishing and told me to fish those dead ones, as well. Up until that point I had thought only a live mackerel would work. After his advice I learned to anchor on the edge of drop-offs with a live mackerel swimming in the deeper water and a dead one drifting back on the flats, the latter rod in free-spool. I did this since I had often seen the bigger bass cruising the flats, looking for an easy meal. Though I didn't get as many bass on the dead mackerel as I did on the live ones, they were always bigger. I never took a striper of less than 40 pounds on the rod with a dead mackerel.

Larger striped bass usually don't feed in big schools. But in the 1960s when there are a lot of them around, we did see schools of 30- and sometimes 40-pound fish, feeding together with smaller ones. Overall, though, they are solitary feeders that will use the least amount of energy to get a meal. When they do mix in with smaller bass, you won't find them chasing bait on top with the younger, more energetic fish. Rather, they will be feeding underneath on the stunned, wounded, or dead that drop down from above. It's also known that these larger bass will do the same thing with bluefish: As the blues slash through bait on the surface, the bass will be underneath dining on the pieces that drift down to them.

In this scenario, the problem is getting the fly through the upper layer of smaller bass or blues and down to the big bass underneath. And here is a general rule of thumb for you when bass and blues are mixed together: A fast retrieve will take bluefish, while a slower retrieve will take bass.

During their early years, striped bass live and feed in schools. The larger fish, as they approach and grow past 30 pounds, are usually found as singles or just a few together. The bigger fish, however, will school up during their migration. This is when you can run into a school of larger bass fueling up as they travel, most often during their fall migration south.

While on the subject of migrating bass, there is something to point out to the newcomer to striped bass angling. If you catch a bass with small brown "bugs" on it, the fish is okay. These are sea lice, which means the fish has just come in from deeper water where it picked them up; this is usually seen during the spring migration. The bass seem to lose these sea lice after spending some time in shallower water.

Striped bass are very strong fish. They love the tumble of the surf, the current of a rip, or the dropping tide of an estuary. They like to feed in these situations where every other living creature fights to maintain equilibrium. This is where stripers have the advantage. And they will feed upon almost anything.

Their menu is long and includes such entrées as alewives, eels, herring, bay anchovies, menhaden, mullet, sand eels, shad, silversides, shrimp, crabs, lobsters, worms, clams, and squid. For fly fishermen, that's a lot of food to imitate. However, knowing when and where to use what fly is the first step toward being a good angler.

Bluefish

There is no doubt that the striped bass is the premier game fish for the fly fisherman in New England, and I thoroughly enjoy catching them, but my other favorite fly-rod fish is the bluefish. I love fishing for blues, and contrary to popular belief, there are times when they will frustrate you and seem to have a total disregard for whatever you throw at them. But once you do hook up, look out. A 10- or 12-pound blue will introduce you to your backing in a hurry.

I may be a bit partial to the bluefish because it was the first saltwater game fish I caught on a fly rod. As I noted in the introduction, the memory of that event is still fresh in my mind. I can almost feel the sore knuckles I had from the handle spinning wildly as each fish made rapid runs up and

The bluefish is built for speed. They overtake their prey by attacking from the rear or striking at the middle, disabling or killing their quarry.

down the beach. I must admit that I knew little about taking fish of such size on my freshwater outfit. It was one of those times when everything just worked out well, despite my lack of experience with saltwater fly fishing; but that's how we learn and become better.

This happened about the same time that large bluefish showed up off Cape Cod. Suddenly the mackerel that we had been using to fish for bass were missing. In their place were marauding schools of 15- to 18-pound bluefish. Many of the regulars fishing the outer beaches of the Cape had not, in their fishing experience, seen bluefish in such numbers and that large. Within a year even Maine was enjoying these big blues. But after a number of years their numbers dwindled in the Pine Tree State.

Those who know bluefish will tell you that they're very cyclical. Records show that over the times when fish populations have been recorded, the bluefish has enjoyed cycles of abundance followed by times when numbers were down. In *Fishes of the Gulf of Maine*, the authors recognize these bluefish cycles but offer little by way of explaining why this happens. It just seems to be the nature of the species.

Most books state that the bluefish appear to spawn offshore, in deep water. Once hatched, the young move inshore. There is some evidence, however, that the bluefish spawn closer into shore while in New England waters.

For example, Jim White of White Ghost Guide Services told me that in the last few years he has seen big blues come into Narragansett Bay in spring; then, some weeks later, the bay is loaded with very small bluefish. Jim feels that the blues may be spawning in the bay.

He may be right. Over the last few years Narragansett Bay has had incredible bluefish action. I fished there with Jim last August and could not believe the numbers of bluefish. Everywhere I looked there were large schools of blues just beating the water to froth. Jim said he had measured a number of schools that were several square miles in size. If I closed my eyes it sounded like applause.

The best times to find bluefish are in the early morning and the evening, when they will move into shallower water. Though they can be taken in the surf, the best spots are flats, openings to inlets and bays, and rips within casting range of shore.

The best approach to finding bluefish is with poppers. They can hear the commotion and will be drawn to the sound. A floating line on an 8-weight rod will handle most bluefish situations. Where there is faster-moving water around inlets and rips, switch to an intermediate line and a fly like a Clouser Minnow, Lefty's Deceiver, or similar pattern that imitates the bait in the area. Whether you're using a popper or another fly, however, always use a short wire leader.

Bluefish travel in schools and feed in schools. Even when they aren't feeding on the surface, you can locate blues: Look for the telltale slick on the water's surface, which is visible even when the surface is rough. The oil from the baitfish that the blues have been eating creates that slick.

Bluefish have a narrower temperature tolerance range than striped bass. The ideal water temperature for bluefish is around 68 degrees, but they will vacate any water that reaches their upper range of mid-80s in temperature. When the water temperatures in fall start getting down toward the lower end of their range—about 50 degrees—the bluefish will begin their migration to warmer waters to the south.

Bluefish move north up the Atlantic coast in spring, arriving about mid-May in Rhode Island, Martha's Vineyard, and Nantucket, and then into Nantucket Sound on the southern side of Cape. They will eventually reach Maine by late June. Their migration south in the fall begins as water temperatures cool; leaving Maine first, they are last seen in the region around Nantucket, Martha's Vineyard, and Rhode Island in November.

People will tell you that a bluefish will attack any lure, anytime. I am here to tell you that there are times when this isn't so. And when this hap-

Scenes like this of bluefish feeding on bunker occur every August and September in Rhode Island's Narragansett Bay. Sometimes these schools of marauding blue-fish will be a square mile or more in size.

pens, it can be the most frustrating time you'll experience. Here is what has been described as the most "the most ferocious and bloodthirsty fish" there is—and it just looks at your fly or popper, then swims away with disdain. This usually happens in spring and early summer, soon after they arrive. I have asked marine biologists about this, and they all agree—they don't know why blues do this.

I've experienced this behavior both in Cape Cod Bay and on the south side of Cape Cod in spring. The big sign that you may be in for a frustrating day of fishing is seeing the blues cruising on the surface, often with their fins showing. If you throw your fly at or near them at these times, they will just move out of the way as it comes through the school. Luckily, this odd behavior is very short in duration and they soon become aggressive again.

I have a fishing buddy who calls bluefish "swimming buzz saws." Of all the game fish that you'll encounter along the New England coast, none has a set of dentures like the bluefish. Their teeth are very sharp and triangular shaped; they interlock when the fish close their jaws, leaving no space between them. They are totally different from striped bass, which have more abrasive, holding-type teeth and try to swallow their prey whole, headfirst. When they can, bass seem to home in on the eye of their quarry. That is why I like eyes on the flies I use for bass.

Conversely, bluefish will attack from rear or hit at the middle, disabling or killing their prey. In *Fishes of the Gulf of Maine,* there is a line that aptly describes these fish; it reads, ". . . it is perhaps the most ferocious and blood-thirsty fish in the seas, leaving in its wake a trail of dead and mangled mackerel, menhaden, herring, alewives, and other species on which it preys."

I can't say enough to the newcomer to saltwater fishing about the care needed when handling a blue. Their teeth are like razors. An incident several years ago serves as a reminder to me even today. I've caught a number of bluefish during the years I've been fishing and always considered myself careful when handling them. On this day, however, I guess I was too nonchalant. As I was removing the hook from a particular blue, I felt something barely brush my finger. When I looked down I had about a three-quarter-inch cut that was bleeding.

There are a number of stories about lost fingers, courtesy of bluefish. And once they bite down on something, it takes a lot of pressure to force their mouth open. When it comes to bluefish, you can't be careful enough. Even the small "snapper" blues can give you a nasty cut or serious wound.

When fishing for blues, you'll need a wire leader on your fly or popper. It doesn't have to be very long—maybe 3 inches. I like to use those wire leaders made for fly fishing that have a very small snap on them. This allows me to change flies on the wire leader quickly and easily—because when you get into a batch of blues, they'll destroy your flies in a hurry. The snap is convenient, and it doesn't bother the bluefish.

If you are fly fishing for bluefish, you cannot have too fast a retrieve. For many fly rodders this can be a problem. How do you get enough speed in your retrieve, especially when using poppers? A rapid hand-over-hand retrieve seems to produce the most speed. This is done with the rod tucked under your arm. When using a popper, I have found that bluefish seem partial to the fluorescent-colored ones, especially orange. I have been outfished by a buddy on several occasions when he used the fluorescent orange poppers that he makes.

Though bluefish can be taken anytime during the day, early morning and evening seem to be the best times. This is when they move onshore to feed, particularly near and around inlets and openings to bays. You will also hear that bluefish can't be caught at night. Don't believe it. Though their eyesight might not be as good then, they can still home in on your fly by picking up the vibrations it makes in the water.

Lastly, if you want to read a good book about bluefish, let me recommend John Hersey's *Blues,* on fishing for bluefish in the waters around Martha's Vineyard. It is well-written book that is very entertaining on a cold winter's evening, when fishing is months away.

Weakfish

In New England you'll hear anglers call weakfish by their American Indian name, squeteague. They are also referred to as gray trout and sea trout in the southern portion of their range. These last two names are quite appropriate considering the square tail, body shape, and vivid coloration of the weakfish. It looks like it is a cousin of the freshwater trout, but it's not. In fact, it's part of the scientific family of croakers and drum. With two large, close-set teeth that resemble fangs and protrude from the upper jaw, you know this fish is a true saltwater predator.

The name *weakfish* can be misleading to anyone who hasn't caught one. The name has nothing to do with its performance when hooked. To the contrary, it's a fish that gives the fly rodder a good battle. Weakfish get their name from the condition of the area around their mouths. This thin, membranelike skin is easily torn. Therefore, when working to land your weakie, don't horse it. It's the quickest way to lose the fish. Due to this fragile tissue around their mouth, you may land fewer fish than you hook until you get the feel for playing them. You can't horse them in, but conversely, taking too long to land them will also increase the odds that the hook will pull out.

The squeteague has beautiful coloration, with a blue-gray to gray-green dorsal area, silver sides, and a white belly. Adding to this are the spots on the upper body, which can be of many colors including gold, yellow, copper, and green. I've even caught weakfish that had an iridescent purple hue. On top of this, there are orange fins on the adult fish. They are truly a saltwater trout.

The average size of weakfish in New England is about 4 to 10 pounds. However, there are larger fish taken. Squeteague travel and feed in schools; they will arrive here, migrating from North and South Carolina, in May and take up residence in the waters south of Cape Cod to Rhode Island. They are rarely caught north of the Cape. Weakies will be around until early to mid-October, when they again migrate south. The best time for the large squeteague is May and June, with Narragansett Bay being one of the better locations for the bigger fish. During the summer you'll catch mostly smaller fish, with the larger ones making a brief appearance again in fall. I believe the bigger fish did not leave the area but are just harder to find. They will hang in

The coloration, shape, fins, and tail of the squeteague resemble a freshwater trout,
hence the names sea trout *or* gray trout. *But the two fang-like teeth that*
protrude from the upper jaw indicate that it is a saltwater predator.

the deeper holes or move into the open ocean along the shore. In spring you
can catch them during the day, but during the summer, night is the best time
overall for weakfish.

It's not uncommon to take squeteague alongside striped bass and bluefish. They will often be feeding in the same location, where bait is being
swept along a channel, through a rip, or into a hole where they are waiting.
Weakfish, for the most part, like moving water when they feed. When I was
a child fishing for them in New Jersey, I was told that this is why they called
the larger fish tiderunners.

Weakfish like to stay close to the shoreline, even while in the ocean.
They prefer a sandy bottom in bays, estuaries, and marshes, but will hunt
shrimp and crabs in the mud. Weakfish also feed in the surf. I have caught a
number of them in surf, especially if the water is reasonably clear. They like a
water temperature between 55 and 65 degrees, but can tolerate temperatures
into the mid-70s.

A squeteague's menu is a varied one consisting of crabs, shrimp, worms,
squid, and small baitfish, including menhaden, silversides, herring, and sand
eels. Though I have seen weakfish at the surface feeding on baitfish, they usually like to wait at or near the bottom for their meal to come to them.

Overall, a very slow retrieve works best for weakfish. Any exaggerated, long pull during the retrieve will usually make the fly move too fast for a weakfish. The standard retrieve for weakfish is slow, and on the bottom, especially during the day. It isn't that the weakfish are especially looking for slow-moving prey; this tactic simply gets the fly down to where they normally feed.

As noted, there are exceptions when the weakfish will come to the surface to feed on schools of bait. If striped bass and blues are crashing bait on top, look for weakfish to be below them, picking up the scraps.

I've had good success when fishing for squeteague by lifting the fly up off the bottom and then dropping it back down during a slow retrieve. Very often a weakie will pick up your fly on the drop or during a hesitation in the retrieve. You should also be alert when the fly is dropping to the bottom, after you've made your cast. Weakfish will rise off the bottom and eat a slowly dropping fly. There are times when they will also chase and hit a fly as it is slowly lifted from the bottom at the end of the retrieve. So don't be too quick to yank your fly out of the water at the end of the retrieve; raise it slowly to the surface.

It would be hard to pick just one fly as the best for weakfish. However, there are several that should be at the top of your list. You can't beat a Clouser Minnow, Half-and-Half, or Bob Popovics's Jiggy Fleye fished on the bottom with a sinking line. I would also include a shrimp pattern like Popovics's Ultra Shrimp on my list. Fish your shrimp pattern using an intermediate or floating line, and let the fly drift with the tide.

The fly colors that produce the best for weakfish are chartreuse and white, olive and white, yellow, and yellow and white. When fly fishing at night for weakfish, if you want to try something other than a shrimp pattern, consider using a black-and-purple or all-black fly.

Fly rods in the 7- to 9-weight range are ideal for squeteague. The 9-weight rod is handy when there is some wind to contend with or when working the surf; you may even want to move up to a 10-weight rod under certain conditions. There are also times, such as on a windless evening, when a 6-weight rod will do just fine. Since weakfish feed mostly in the lower depths of the water column, sinking lines of various weights are your best choice. You'll want to use a faster-sinking, heavier-grain line when fishing deepwater spots or dealing with a fast-moving current. When drifting a shrimp fly on the tide, use a floating line. Still, I've found that even an intermediate line works well when wading the shoreline and fishing more shallow water near deep channels.

Your leader lengths should be in the 5- to 8-foot range. The shorter leader length is best with unweighted flies to keep them near the bottom, when fishing sinking lines. The longer leaders are best with weighted flies and when drifting a fly on the surface. A good suggestion is to use a tippet section of 10- to 12-pound-test fluorocarbon leader material for decreased visibility. Also, regardless of what flies I'm fishing, I always tie them to the tippet leader using a loop knot, as opposed to a knot that cinches the leader tight to the eye of the fly. I use the nonslip mono loop because it's strong and allows for better fly movement.

When fishing estuaries, bays, and marsh areas, look for squeteague around the entrances to small creeks, on a dropping tide. Like bass, weakfish will come into flats or shallows at night but need a deeper channel or drop-off nearby to hang in during the day. In daylight hours look for locations that have some moving water and deep holes or a channel nearby; weakfish will move along these channels or hide in the holes. Early-morning and late-evening hours are the best times for this type of fishing. During the times of low light and dark, weakies will move out of the deeper water onto the flats, adjacent to the shore-line. And one strong word of caution: Always be ready for a take as your fly settles in the water, prior to your retrieve. I have been caught napping on several occasions because I wasn't ready for the hit as my fly settled.

Finally, it's funny how certain things from your childhood can stay with you. For example, every time I see lightning bugs, or what some call fireflies, I think of weakfish. This odd association goes back to when I was growing up in New Jersey. Every summer, when the first lightning bugs appeared over the fields, my father would comment that the weakfish were in Barnegat Bay and that we should go fishing. In those days there were no fishing reports readily available. People used nature's signs as a guide.

We would go out with my father's uncle Ed, who lived next to Barnegat Bay. But before an evening of fishing, we had to net grass shrimp for our bait. We would then anchor the boat across the current, occasionally chumming with a few shrimp. Our tackle was freshwater gear, which we used to drift the shrimp in the current behind the boat. This is why I believe that one great way to catch squeteague is to drift a shrimp fly in the current on a quiet summer's evening.

Bonito and False Albacore

Both bonito and false albacore are members of the mackerel family, as are all tunas. I mentioned earlier that a bluefish would introduce you to your

Bonito and false albacore provide an exciting dimension to the late summer and autumn fishing for anglers on Cape Cod, Nantucket, Martha's Vineyard, and Rhode Island.

backing; well, these fish will show you a lot more of your backing, and faster. The prime time for these fish is in summer and early fall from Rhode Island to Martha's Vineyard and Nantucket, plus Nantucket Sound and along the southern beaches of Cape Cod.

Both species like to feed around inlets, breachways, and similar tidal openings. They will also work along the shoreline that is adjacent to these openings, as well as sandy beaches. This is where they hunt their favorite baitfish like silversides, bay anchovies, and sand eels. When these fish are chasing bait, what may at first glance seem to be chaos isn't. They often feed in a pattern that they repeat as they work an area. So if you see these fish working up the beach at a frantic rate, they're probably traveling too fast to follow. The best course of action is to stay put, since they will usually repeat their feeding pattern and be back your way.

With an incoming tide, they will often move into an opening, and even back into the bay to feed. When fishing a jetty, the ends are where the action will begin—but don't be surprised when it moves up inside. On an incoming tide they will also be closer to the beach; there's more water where the bait can try to hide, and the fish will follow. Like many others, bonito and albacore seem to be most active in the early morning, from first light, and late in the evening, just before sunset. However, don't discount catching them at any time during the day.

One of the best ways to find bonito and albacore is to look for the birds. Sometimes, however, there will be no birds—just a small splash or two on the surface as they chase bait. Fly casting for albacore and bonito is like dove shooting because these fish are so fast. You need to cast to where they are heading, not where they are. If you don't do this, by the time you fly gets into the water column where they were when you started your cast, they will be gone. This is why they are a frustrating fish to many anglers. Quite often I have seen hook-ups when no fish were showing, so be on your toes.

A lot of experts will tell you that you need to match the size and general appearance of what the fish are eating. Others will tell you they've taken albacore on flies larger than the bait they were chasing. The tendency is to go with flies on size 1 or 1/0 hooks. A smaller fly seems to work better because the fish can get it into their mouths, giving you a better chance of not losing your catch.

It's also believed that a fast strip is the only way to catch a bonito or albacore. However, anglers have discovered that a fly placed to the outside of a school of bait and allowed to sink slowly works quite well. These fish are always looking to pick off wounded prey. A slow-sinking line will do the trick in this instance, and some fishermen even prefer to use an intermediate line. I believe that a sinking line gets your fly down to where there are more fish than seen on the surface.

Since most scientists hold that albacore and bonito have very good eyesight, the use of fluorocarbon leader can be an advantage. A number of fly rodders have told me that they have experimented and found fluorocarbon to be superior. Most use leaders with a 10- to 16-pound-test tippet, and will go to the lighter strength if their fly is being ignored. Additionally, a slightly longer leader—at least 8 feet—will improve your success.

The bonito that visits New England waters goes by several names, including common bonito, skipjack, horse mackerel, and Atlantic bonito. They arrive here at the end of July or first of August, and will normally be around until the end of October. Bonito prefer a water temperature of 65 degrees or warmer, and when it drops below 60 degrees, they will be gone. Though they can grow to a weight in the midteens, the average size range for bonito in this area is 5 to 8 pounds.

The bonito is a bit more striking in color than the albacore with its blue to bluish green back, and silver sides and belly. It has dark bluish bands that run forward and down over the lateral line. When young, the bonito's back is barred with 10 or 12 dark blue stripes, which are almost triangular in shape. These stripes disappear before the fish matures.

The albacore or false albacore is also known by the name of little tunny. And you'll hear anglers refer to them as Fat Alberts—a reference to their round, football shape. They appear at about the end of August and are gone by mid-October. When the albacore arrive the bonito become hard to catch, mainly because the albacore seem to be more aggressive. After the albacore leave, you can again catch bonito for the next week or so, until they leave.

The Fat Alberts of New England average between and 8 and 12 pounds, though they can reach nearly 30 pounds. These fish have a steel-blue color to their backs, along with glistening white sides and bellies. Their most notable markings are the dark wavy lines on their backs. There are no markings below the lateral line except a few dark spots below the pectoral fin. Their forward dorsal fin has more of a peak and is shorter than that of the bonito.

Spanish Mackerel

I am including the Spanish mackerel in this section because you may encounter them when fishing for bonito and albacore. Though they're great game fish on light tackle, they can also be a problem. Because of the Spanish mackerel's very sharp teeth, they will easily cut your leader. When they are around, often mixed with the bonito or albacore, you will lose some flies to these speedsters. If you land one, however, you've caught yourself a very tasty meal. If you are going to keep your fish, be sure to clean and ice it as soon as you can.

Spanish mackerel are long and slender for their size. They have bluish or blue-green backs, silvery sides, and a number of oval spots—both above and below the lateral line—that are orange or yellow in color. These fish average 3 to 4 pounds but put up a good fight.

Spanish will be around from the end of July through late September or early October, if the water remains warm. They are not found everywhere, but look for them on Nantucket, Martha's Vineyard, particularly on East Beach, and along the south beaches of Cape Cod, especially around and near the entrance to Waquoit Bay in Mashpee.

CHAPTER 4

What They Eat

A ll fish have certain items that are favored on their menu. When these foods get scarce, however, they will look to other sources, including the smaller sizes of their own species. For the fly angler it's helpful to know something not only about the habits of the fish you're pursuing, but also about what they're eating. Using the right size and type of fly is important.

There have been a number of good books written that will give you in-depth information about the varieties of baitfish, worms, and crustaceans that game fish eat. Many are geared for the fly rodder and suggest what flies imitate the food source. I recommend the following: *Lou Tabory's Guide to Saltwater Baits and Their Imitations,* by Lou Tabory; *A Fly Fisherman's Guide to Atlantic Baitfish & Other Food Sources,* by Alan Caolo; *A Fly-Fisher's Guide to Saltwater Naturals and Their Imitation,* by George V. Roberts Jr.; *Prey,* by Carl Richards; and *L.L. Bean Fly Fishing for Striped Bass Handbook,* by Brad Burns. All of these books are must reading for the serious saltwater fly fisherman.

This section will give you some basic information on each of the food sources to get you started. Your biggest teacher will be experience. Learning what food source is where, and at what time of the season, is key. Sure, I've seen times when an angler threw a large, brightly colored fly into a school of bass feeding on small sand eels and hooked up. But that is the exception rather than the rule.

What is important is understanding the habits of the fish you are pursuing and what they are feeding upon when you're there at the water's edge. Key factors include matching the size and coloration of the food with your fly, and placing the fly at the proper point in the water column, with as natural a movement—or lack thereof—as possible.

Sand Eel

The sand eel is not an eel but a fish with the proper name of sand launce. It's the prime food for all the game fish in New England. Sand eels have a range from Cape Hatteras to the Canadian Maritimes, and are found in areas with sandy bottoms. They burrow into the sand at night and then reappear in the morning. When cut off by a receding tide, sand eels also bury themselves in the sand above the low-water line until the tide comes back in. They're about 4 to 6 inches in length, as an average, with the younger ones in spring being around 2 inches.

Sand eels are found in large schools and are favored by all game fish, large and small, as well as whales. They have olive, brownish, or bluish green backs, silvery sides, and a white belly. Some have a longitudinal stripe on both sides that is an iridescent blue. They are imitated by any number of sand eel patterns sold at local tackle shops. Fly colors include white, white and olive, and white and chartreuse, all with some flash. For best results, the fly length should be close to the size of the sand eels you observe; this is especially true if fish are feeding on the smaller-sized sand eels. Good fly choices include the Clouser Minnow, Bob Popovics's Surf Candy, and Tabory's Sand Eel.

Menhaden

A member of the herring family, menhaden go by many names depending upon where you're fishing; you will hear them called bunker, pogy, mossbunker, and fat back. The smaller ones seen in the fall are called peanut bunker. They are usually about 3 to 5 inches long. Menhaden are found from Maine to Florida, and are an important food source for larger predators. They migrate north to New England in spring and return south in fall; they arrive in May and leave by October or early November, at the latest. Menhaden travel in tightly packed schools and are found along shorelines, in bays and harbors. They are taken commercially for fertilizer and for their oil, which is used in everything from paint to lipstick.

When they are in calm waters, menhaden often give themselves away by the ripplelike surface action from the school. At other times you will see small splashes and the flashes from the light reflecting off their sides. Because of these schooling tactics, game fish will frequently pack them against the shoreline and feed for periods of time. If you're in a situation where predators are feeding on a school of menhaden, cast to the edges of school, not into the middle of it. Otherwise your fly will only be lost in the mass of fish packed together.

Menhaden have dark blue or blue-green backs, silvery sides and belly, and a yellow or brassy iridescent glow. They have a large dark spot on each side, near their gills, plus a number of smaller ones farther back, along their sides, in irregular lines. The average size for menhaden is 10 to 12 inches, with young peanut bunker averaging around 4 inches.

The best fly imitation for bunker is a white Deceiver with a dark top and flash added. Tabory's Slab Fly is another excellent selection. Using poppers to simulate the way menhaden splash on the surface is also a good tactic.

Silversides

Like many fish, the silversides is known by a number of names, including spearing, sperling, green smelt, capelin, and sand smelt. They are a schooling fish but not in the large numbers of menhaden, and all the silversides in the school will be the same size. Their range is from Maine to the Chesapeake Bay, and they spend their time feeding along shorelines, and in bays and estuaries. However, they are not found in any large numbers along rocky shorelines. Silversides are around throughout the fishing season and spawn from May to July, with the young developing and growing quickly. They are on the menu of all the game fish in New England.

The silversides' average length is 2 to 5 inches; it has a light, almost transparent green back. Its sides are speckled with dark brown, and the belly is white. There is a silver band running along each side with dark thin stripe above it.

Most flies that imitate silversides include a piece of silver tinsel or similar flashy material on each side. Good flies that mimic silversides include Deceivers in a size to match the bait, Popovics's Surf Candy, Tabory's Snake Fly, and Gibbs's Striper Fly. When fishing in estuaries, you may want to try drifting your fly on the current.

Alewife

The alewife is also known as branch herring and freshwater herring; some of the old-time anglers call them buckies. They are often confused with other members of the herring family, especially the blueback herring. The alewife is an anadromous herring, which means that it spends most of its life in the open ocean but spawns in freshwater streams and ponds. They are found from Nova Scotia to North Carolina.

Alewives enter and move up estuaries in spring to spawn in fresh water. In southern areas this begins sometime in April; look for it in May or a bit later in the northern sections of New England. Alewives will return to the sea after they spawn, passing those still going up to spawn. Young alewives leave the fresh water and enter the sea throughout the summer and into early fall.

Their numbers were great during the early days of our country. *Fishes of the Gulf of Maine* quotes the journal of Captain John Smith: "Experience hath taught them at New Plymouth that in April there is a fish much like a herring that comes up into the small brooks to spawn, and when the water is not knee deep they will presse up through your hands, yea, thow you beat at them with cudgels, and in such abundance as is incredible."

The alewife is a favorite of striped bass, bluefish, weakfish, bonito, and albacore. They average 6 to 8 inches in length, with adult alewives being nearly a foot long. These herring have a grayish green back that is darkest on top and becomes a more pale or silver color on the sides and belly. There is also a dusky spot just behind the gill cover on each side of the fish. One of the best flies to imitate an alewife is a white Deceiver with a dark back.

Blueback Herring

The blueback herring and alewife are often confused for one another, and many people just refer to both as herring. The blueback herring is also called a glut herring, summer herring, and blackbelly; the latter name refers to the color of the lining of its belly cavity. Bluebacks are an anadromous fish and spawn in fresh water, like the alewife, but a bit later in spring. Indications are that young blueback herring leave a bit earlier for the ocean than alewives.

The blueback herring is about the same size as an alewife, with the adult reaching a length of about 11 inches. The blueback looks similar to the alewife, although its back is more bluish green in color; it has silver sides. The other thing that the blueback herring has in common with the alewife is that it, too, is a favorite meal of bass, blues, squeteague, albacore, and bonito. They are so similar in appearance that the same Deceiver pattern mentioned for the alewife will work when bluebacks are around.

Herring

The herring or sea herring has a range from Cape Cod north to Labrador. It is also known as the Labrador herring or sardine. They are found in open water and travel in schools. They can be anywhere from a couple of inches to a foot or more in length. This wide range in size is due to the fact that these fish spawn at sea and the young move in along coastal sections along with adult fish. Like their cousins, these herring are forage for all the game fish in their range.

The sea herring has a blue to greenish blue back. Its sides and belly are silver, often with an iridescent glow. White Deceivers with a blue back or top will imitate these fish quite well.

Hickory Shad

The hickory shad or shad herring looks like a herring but can grow to 2 feet in length. It is one of the larger members of the anadromous herring family. This fish is not only a food source for striped bass and blues but also a great fish to take on a fly rod. Use small flies to catch hickory shad in certain estuaries in spring. Flies should imitate their diet of sand eels, silversides, and similar small baitfish.

The hickory shad has a range that extends from Canada to Florida. It spawns in fresh water in spring like the alewife and blueback herring. It prefers to spawn in water that has warmed to over 50 degrees, which is usually around May or June.

It has a shape and coloring similar to its cousins, with a dark bluish or green back, silvery to white sides, and more white on the belly. Its most distinguishing marking is the faint dark, longitudinal lines on both sides, and the tip of the nose that is dark in color. A Deceiver with dark blue or green top makes a good imitation, as well as any fly with a similar profile and coloring.

Shad

The largest member of the herring family, the shad or American shad grows to a length of $2\frac{1}{2}$ feet. They are found from Newfoundland to Florida and spawn in fresh water in spring, starting as early as April and continuing through the month of June. Shad travel in large schools at sea; whether at sea or in estuaries, they are a favorite food of striped bass and bluefish.

Shad are a bit larger than the hickory shad and have a larger mouth. This is an interesting difference since they're primarily plankton feeders, whereas the hickory shad does eat small baitfish. However, the American shad can also be taken on small flies in spring.

This fish is dark blue-green on the back with silver sides and a white belly. It has a faint spot located closely behind the gill cover, with one or two longitudinal rows of faint spots behind that. As with the other herrings, a white Deceiver with a dark blue or green top is the best imitator of this fish.

Mackerel

Mackerel or Atlantic mackerel have a range from Canada to North Carolina. You will often hear the small ones called tinker mackerel. These fish migrate north in spring, arriving in Cape Cod Bay by the end of April or the first of May. They reach Maine later in spring to spend the summer there before they migrate south in fall.

The Atlantic mackerel's average size is between 8 and 14 inches; some of them will grow to be as large as 20 inches. All the major game fish will pursue and feed on mackerel. Though a bit oily, many people also enjoy them; they're a good-eating fish, especially when broiled.

Mackerel are also a great fish to catch on a lightweight fly rod. Your flies should have some flash in them to entice the mackerel. Look for mackerel along shorelines, and just inside and around the mouth of estuaries.

The mackerel, which is a speedster, has a torpedolike body with a greenish blue back; its head is a bit darker shade of the same color. The body is barred with numerous dark bands that run in irregular, wavy lines to the midsection. The mackerel's sides and belly are silvery white with an iridescent hue. Some flies that mimic the mackerel are Dan Blanton's Sar-Mul-Mac fly in a mackerel pattern and a white Deceiver with a dark green back; both should have some flash in them.

Pollock

The pollock, which is known in parts of New England as the Boston bluefish, is a cold-water fish. Its optimum temperature range is about 45 to 50 degrees. If the water gets above 60 degrees, they will depart for cooler places. This powerful fish can grow to be 25 or 30 pounds. The younger fish, ones 6 to 12 inches in length, are a favorite of striped bass.

Like the mackerel, this is a good-eating fish. From Boston to Maine, fly rodders will occasionally catch a pollock while seeking other fish. A number of years ago they were caught in late spring just off the tip of Cape Cod, but with the drop in population that is now a rare occurrence there.

The pollock has an olive or brownish green back and light gray sides that blend to a silvery gray belly. Its very distinctive lateral line is either very light gray or white. The younger fish are bit darker in color. Flies that imitate the pollock are Jim Bernstein's Grocery Pollock Fly, Deceivers with dark olive backs and more tan bodies, and the Half-and-Half fly with a dark olive or brown top.

Mullet

Mullet range from the waters south of Cape Cod to Florida, but in New England they're primarily found along the shoreline of Rhode Island in fall. They go by several other names, including common mullet, striped mullet, and jumping mullet. The mullet is prey for all the major game fish from bass to bonito. They are only 3 to 7 inches long in these northern waters, while farther south in their range they grow much larger. These larger mullet are referred to as corncob mullet or cob mullet in southern states. An oily fish, it is the primary choice for cut bait with southern anglers.

The adult mullet is blue-gray to a greenish gray above, with sides of silvery scales whose dark centers form lines running the length of the body. The body shape is round, with a head that is short and blunt. The younger fish are bright silver and lack the darker back. The ever-versatile Deceiver, in blue and white or green and white, in a length to match the mullet around, is a good imitation. If size is hard to determine, a fly of about 4 or 5 inches that's a bit bulky to imitate the roundness of the mullet will work very well. Make sure there is some flash in whatever fly you select.

Bay Anchovy

The bay anchovy or anchovy is found from Cape Cod south, and especially in coastal Rhode Island, during September and October. They spawn in shallow-water bays and ponds with an outlet to the ocean, leaving in late summer or early fall for the open water. These fish, which are only 4 or 5 inches long, seem to drive albacore, bonito, bass, and blues into a feeding frenzy.

The bay anchovy travels in large, dense schools in fall. This is where they get the nickname *rain bait*—the schools make the surface look like it's raining. When you encounter these fish under attack by any of the game fish, do not cast into the middle of the anchovy school. Your fly will only be lost in the countless numbers of anchovies. Try fishing edges of the school, with little movement or no movement to your fly. The predators are always looking for wounded or dead falling away from the school. An intermediate or sinking line is the best choice to accomplish this.

One of the major characteristics of the bay anchovy is that its eyes are larger than you'd expect for its body. It has a dark olive or brown back and a thin, silvery band on both sides that runs from the gills to the tail. The anchovy's belly is white and seems to have almost a pearl finish, often with a pink or purple hue. Flies with large eyes in the 4- or 5-inch range would be a good choice to imitate an anchovy. Clouser Minnows, Half-and-Half flies, and Bob Popovics's Jiggy Fleye, all with some pink, purple, and flash in them, would be good selections.

Eel

The American eel or eel matures in 8 to 24 years in fresh and brackish water, whereupon it will migrate in late summer or early fall to the Sargasso Sea to spawn and then die. The young eel, about 2 to 3 inches in length, is called a glass eel because of its lack of pigmentation; they're also called elvers. These elvers migrate into saltwater estuaries in spring and eventually into fresh water. Once there, they gain their color.

Eels are a particular favorite of striped bass, but are also eaten by bluefish and weakfish. They are active at night, and this is when any fly imitating an eel is a good choice. Any dark fly with a long, thin silhouette fished near the bottom will work. The best color for these flies is black or dark purple. One excellent fly that fits this category is Kenney Abrames's Eel Punt.

Squid

Squid are found in New England waters from early May through the fall, and will spend their time in the deeper water. However, game fish will often drive them toward the shoreline and onto the beach. Squid vary from 3 to 12-plus inches in length. Bass, bluefish, weakfish, albacore, and bonito all love calamari.

In May, numerous commercial boats mark the arrival of squid in Nantucket Sound. This commercial fishery is a great indicator of squid as they migrate north. And more importantly, anglers know that striped bass will not be far behind.

Fly movement to imitate a squid should be a quick spurt, followed by a slow glide. Fly colors in pink and white or brown and white match some of the various hues that a squid can produce. Bob Popovics's Shady Lady fly is an excellent choice when squid are around.

Grass Shrimp

Grass shrimp are generally nocturnal creatures, though they can be active during the day. They are found in shallow inshore areas, bays, and marshes. They prefer sandy or muddy bottoms, and if there's any type of marine grass present, that's a plus. They are a special favorite of both striped bass and squeteague.

Drifting a shrimp fly on a nighttime tide can be very effective—and extremely productive. When you put any motion to your shrimp fly, use slow and short strips. Clouser Minnows, Popovics's Ultra Shrimp pattern, Al Brewster's Reverse Shrimp fly, Dave Whitlock's Salt Shrimp, and similar patterns in browns and tan colors are all good selections.

Crabs

A variety of crabs are eaten by New England game fish. The green crab is found throughout the region. It is dark gray-green in color. The blue crab inhabits the tidal waters from Cape Cod south. This crab is bluish green and brighter in color than the green crab. The sand fiddler crab is brown and spends its time both on land and in the water.

A favorite fly for the flats, a crab fly is usually fished on the bottom and is used when sight casting to striped bass that are working the flats. However, this fly can be good in marsh areas, again when you know bass are feeding on crabs. Check your local tackle shop for the crab patterns that work best where you intend to fish. The rule of thumb is to use lighter-colored crab flies over sand and darker ones in areas with a mud bottom. Del Brown's Permit fly, which is a crab pattern often tied in browns from dark to light shades, and the McCrab fly are two good crab imitations.

Clam Worm

Clam worms or sandworms are those creatures responsible for the mysterious "worm hatch" that anglers often speak about. I have experienced this event on several occasions on the south side of Cape Cod. On one occasion there were striped bass feeding on the worms as they drifted on the dropping tide from a large bay. I was able to catch several fish; to my amazement, they were so stuffed with worms that these schoolies looked like striped silver footballs. I stood and watched as the bass fed on the worms the way a trout would sip a caddisfly from the surface.

In *Fly Rodding the Coast,* Ed Mitchell has one of the best sections I have read on the worm hatches in New England, and when they occur. He indicates that it usually happens on the first new moon after the second week in May and continues, to some extent, on each new moon through the summer. Like the shrimp fly, a worm pattern floating on the dropping tide of a quiet night can have excellent results with bass. Some flies that work very well are Al Brewster's Worm Fly, Page's Worm Fly, and the Palolo Worm fly.

All fish are opportunistic eaters. If a food type is not available, their survival instinct will direct them to other sources. Recently some fly anglers have discovered that striped bass along the shorelines north of Boston, and into New Hampshire, were dining on very young, small lobsters. Not being ones to pass up a challenge, fly tiers have come up with a lobster fly.

I am also aware that bass will eat small flounder. In answer to that, there has come out of Long Island a rubber flounder imitation, but it is rather large and not at all intended for casting with a fly rod. I wonder how long it will take before some innovative fly tier comes up with a flounder fly?

CHAPTER 5

Sight and Hearing

For the fly angler, two of a fish's senses, sight and hearing, are most important. The sense of smell is key when a fish is hunting prey and is the first sense to be used if the potential meal is at a distance. It will be detected first by smell, and then, as the distance closes, sound and finally sight take over. The focus of this section will just be on sound and sight, since they are the more important senses of a fish that affect your results when fly fishing. That is assuming you aren't soaking your fly in some fish attractant.

If you're like me and really love every aspect of fly fishing, you probably spend your nonfishing time reading about it. I believe that the many books I have read have helped me to improve my fishing skills. So several years ago I was thrilled to get a copy of a very special book that I consider to be the authoritative work on a subject very little has been written about—game fish behavior.

For a number of years I had read about a book that was often referenced by various outdoor writers; it was noted as being an excellent source for information on fish behavior. The book, *Through the Fish's Eye*, was written by Mark Sosin and John Clark nearly 30 years ago, and until recently had never been equaled in its wealth of information about just what makes fish behave the way they do. However, David A. Ross has written a book titled *The Fisherman's Ocean*, which not only covers the senses and behavior of fish but also includes a wealth of practical and useful information for the serious angler.

Before you rush out to buy *Through the Fish's Eye* at your local bookstore,

I should tell you that it has been out of print for some time. There are some used copies around, though. One great source for this book is the book dealers who frequent the various fly-fishing shows. Also check with your local library, which may be able to locate a copy for you.

Fly fishermen who understand that fish have keen hearing and unique sight are usually more successful overall. For example, a bulky fly will push more water; this causes sound, maybe not at a frequency that a human can hear, but certainly one a fish can detect. A fish will hear its prey before it zeros in on it and then can see it. At night a fish a good distance away will hear the noise from the wake of a fly moving slowly across the surface. Similarly, knowing that certain colors will be better seen in roiled water can be a big advantage.

Remember when you went fishing as a child and Dad told you to be quiet because you'd scare the fish? Depending on your age then, you may or may not have believed him. Though he might have just been seeking some peace and quiet, he was right. Fish do hear, and quite well. It is what helps them locate prey, and avoid being prey. Knowing how a fish's hearing works can be of great value to an angler.

To understand how a fish's hearing has developed, you must understand the environment in which the fish lives. Water is much denser than air. This means that any movement or vibration will create sound, and that sound travels much faster in water than it does in air. Sound moves through water at a rate of about 1 mile per second or five times faster than in the air.

Sosin and Clark make an important observation in their book about sound in water. Sound will ether attract or repel fish. In their watery world, there is either food or the threat of being food. The authors also note that fish seem to never make a mistake as to which type of sound is which. They will never swim away from a potential meal, or toward the sound of danger.

Normal talking by anglers along a shoreline is not a problem. Their conversation is reflected by the water's surface. But strike a rock that is in the water, walk heavily along a marsh bank, or slosh into a quiet backwater and you can bet it will send fish in the other direction.

Biologist James Moulton, who has studied the effects of sound on fish, discovered that fish exhibited some very obvious fright reactions when he merely flexed his knees while he stood in his boat. Though we are dealing with shore fly rodding in this book, his observations are important. Moulton said, "Just a shallow knee-bend with no foot movement spooked the fish." This is an extreme example, but it does show that anglers need to eliminate as much noise as possible as they move about, in and around the water. To this point is the observation that the shallower the water, the greater the need not to make any unusual noise; it will spook the fish.

Since water is a poor transmitter of light, fish have compensated by developing an extremely keen sense of hearing. Of all their senses, it is the most sensitive and versatile. Fish can determine sound through a wide range of frequencies. In fact, they possess a dual system, giving them short- and long-range hearing.

Fish do have ears, but not exactly like the human organs. Though positioned on the head much like a human's, a fish's ear has no opening to the outside water; nor does it have an eardrum. Sound is transmitted directly from the water through the skin, flesh, and bone of a fish's head.

Various species of fish can hear some sounds better than others do. Certain of these fish owe their keen sense of hearing to an internal connection between their ears and the swim bladder. Since the swim bladder is a gas-filled chamber formed by an elastic membrane, it acts as a microphone, resonating chamber, and amplifier. The bladder picks up vibrations in the water and transmits them to the ear. In *Through the Fish's Eye,* the authors add that it has been proven that fish with this system of hearing are very sensitive to soft sounds and can detect intensities of sounds some 30 decibels lower than fish without this physiology.

Both predators and what the book calls "peaceful grazers" belong in this group of species that have the ear-to-bladder connection. Thus highly sensitive hearing is beneficial to the hunted as well as the hunters. It is indicative of the constant struggle for survival in this watery environment.

Did you know that some fish have stones? No, not kidney stones, but rather stones that are located in their inner ear canal. I discovered this fact several years ago while fishing for red drum in North Carolina. We had caught a couple of drum and when we returned to the dock, a state biologist asked if he could cut open the heads of the fish and get the stones. He told us that these stones were made of calcium and had growth rings much like those of a tree. By examining these stones, he could determine the age of the fish. Now that I know a bit more about the physiology of fish, I wish I'd asked if these stones played a part in the red drum's hearing process.

Though a fish can detect sounds from great distances using its ears, it cannot determine the direction or location of a sound. That is the task of the second part of their hearing system called the lateral line. The lateral line originates on the fish's head as a network of tiny canals located just under the skin. Just behind the head, these canals join to form the main portion of the lateral line, which extends down each side of the fish to the tail. In some fish the lateral line is quite visible; in others you have to look closely to see it. The snook is an example of a fish with a very visible lateral line, marked by the black line running the length of the fish. Striped bass and bluefish have far less visible lateral lines.

At intervals along the lateral line there are tiny pods with sensory hairs inside. Known as neuromasts, they are especially sensitive to low-frequency sounds. Each of the pods is connected to nerve fibers that carry signals to the brain. There are continual pulses of electrical charges moving along these nerves, feeding the neuromasts. The neuromasts help to pinpoint the source of sound.

When a sound wave reaches the neuromasts' hairs, it will push them in one direction or the other. If they are moved rearward, the electrical charge increases, and if they are moved forward, the charge decreases. Authors Sosin and Clark note that scientists therefore refer to the lateral line as "the sense of distant touch." A fish can locate the source and direction of a sound within a range of about 20 to 30 feet using its lateral line system.

There is another interesting point about the lateral line. This hearing system has a special sensitivity to larger objects. This means that a larger bait-fish or predator can be located at a greater distance, and with greater accuracy, than a smaller one. A single baitfish will therefore have an advantage over a larger predator at night, or in murky water, when both are using their lateral lines. The smaller fish will hear the larger one first. But remember that a large school of the same baitfish would produce a more pronounced near-field sound and would be detected more quickly.

Using their ears and lateral line, fish possess both distant and close-range hearing; this is their unique, dual sensory system. Fish can locate the source of a sound within the lateral line's range of about 30 feet, but at distances beyond that they must use their ears to detect the sound and then locate the source by swimming a search pattern. Once within the range of the lateral line's capability, it can then pinpoint the location.

As you can see, fish depend very heavily on their hearing. *Through the Fish's Eye* tells the reader, "Nothing can trigger a response in fish faster than the vibrations set up by an injured fish. The sounds produced by a wounded fish are totally different from those created when a fish is swimming normally." Flies that imitate the vibrations of an injured meal seek to get that same response.

The sense of hearing is one of the most valuable assets that fish have. It helps them find dinner and avoid being one. If anglers understand this, they can decrease their chances of spooking fish and increase their chances of catching more fish. So when you were told as a youngster to be quiet and not scare the fish, once again your father was right.

The chapter in Sosin and Clark's book on a fish's sight was exceptionally valuable to me as an angler. After reading it I began to understand more about why fish ignored a particular fly at one time, then at another, attacked it as soon as it hit the water.

As fishermen we have to understand that the eyes of fish have some dissimilarities from ours due to the fact that they live in a different environment. Several major aspects of fish sight are important to an angler: the way fish make adjustments to the light of day and the dark of night; that they are nearsighted, with a limited range of sight; that they have a restricted field of depth perception; and what colors they are able to discern in water. Just knowing about these features of a fish's sight process can be extremely helpful.

The eye of a fish is like a camera, much like ours. However, when light enters a fish's eye, a lens in the center of the eyeball picks it up. Its eye is round as opposed to the more flattened eye of humans. The fish's eye cannot change focus by adjusting its shape, as we do. This is why fish have a tendency to be nearsighted. Additionally, we have an iris that opens or closes down depending upon the amount of light that's entering our eyes. Fish also have an iris, but it's fixed; it just allows light to enter their eyes and does not make any adjustment for brightness. The fish's reaction to light and dark occurs in a different manner.

A fish's eye has two types of receptors cells in the retina, which are used alternately, depending upon light levels; they are called cones and rods. The cones are the color receptors and are used during daylight hours. During the hours of darkness or when light levels are extremely low, the fish changes over to use the rods, which are about 30 times more sensitive to light than the cones. The rods record images only in black and white.

The change from cones to rods, and back again, does not happen instantly. Depending on the species of fish, the shift from daytime vision to night can take a couple of hours, or longer. However, many game fish can make the adjustment in less time, making them more efficient hunters during dusk and dawn hours, feeding on prey that might not make the change as quickly. I believe the striped bass would fall into this category of the efficient hunter. Other fish, however, take two to three hours after sunset to make the change of extending the rods and adjusting to the darkness. The rods remain extended for several hours, and then the process reverses for the coming dawn; the rods contract and the cones begin to extend. This is an automatic process, and somehow the fish's internal clock knows how long it is from sunset to sunrise, and vice versa.

Because of the construction of their eyes, fish are a bit myopic or near-sighted. As previously noted, their eyes are round, whereas a human's eye is slightly flattened; and unlike humans, a fish cannot adjust the shape of the eyeball and lens to change the focus. The fixed, round lens in a fish's eye causes their nearsightedness. Since the visibility in water is usually limited, however, fish don't need long-range vision. This is why their other senses, like smell and hearing, are so finely developed. They can locate prey well beyond their visual range through smell and hearing.

Though fish cannot focus their eyes as we can, some species can, to differing degrees, move the round lens closer to the retina by way of an attached muscle, providing some range of focus. The Sosin and Clark book notes that brown trout have an excellent capability to move the lenses in their eyes. They also have additional refinements in their lens and retina that permit them to focus on images both near and far, at the same time. By "reading" the individual images on separate parts of the retina, they acquire a type of bifocal vision similar to humans. The book explains that this occurs because the brown trout's lens is shaped much like an egg, with the more pointed end facing toward the retina. This may be why brown trout seem to be more aggressive feeders, and yet at times are harder to fool with a fly. I am sure the reader who has fished for brown trout will agree with this observation.

Our eyes face forward, focusing on objects in a way that is called stereoscopic or binocular vision. This provides depth perception, allowing us to gauge distance. Again, however, due to the anatomy of fish and the way their eyes are positioned, they do not see objects like a human. In *Through the Fish's Eye,* there is an excellent explanation of how this works. The authors note, "Since their eyes are placed on the sides of their heads, fish have a wider range of sight. But the right and left eyes each see a separate half of the field and they suffer a bit from split vision. Nevertheless, it is an advantage to have each eye able to scan an arc of 180 degrees or more on each side of the body. To the fish's rear there is a small blind spot where neither eye can see. Dead ahead, the arcs of the two eyes overlap to provide a narrow band—perhaps 45 degrees—where the fish has binocular, or stereoscopic, vision. It is in this band of binocular vision that a fish can be expected to have accurate depth perception. But sharpness of vision is lost in the tradeoff because the image is focused out near the periphery of the retina. The sharpest vision would occur when objects are at a right angle to the eye."

Given this information, the authors also suggest that rather than presenting a fly to a fish by pulling it in front of it—which we usually do, because we have a tendency to assume a fish sees the same way we do—it should be presented to the side, where vision is best. The fish may have to turn to bring the fly into the binocular section of focus, but it won't see the line moving across in front.

As I mentioned, fish do indeed see colors. However, this occurs during daylight hours; during the night, the images appear as black and white, due the physical change in the eye at that time. As expected, some species can distinguish colors better than others. Still, nearly all fish do see color to some degree; the presence of cone sensors in the retina indicates a basic capability for seeing color. One big exception is sharks, whose eyes have only black-and-white rod sensors.

It's important to understand that water clarity and depth affect the colors fish see. Without going into all the scientific information on the wavelengths of light energy, in the basic terms of the book, "Water absorbs the radiant energy of light as heat, altering it rapidly as it passes through the depths. It's really a filtering process in which certain wavelengths are selectively removed at specific depths." In other words, as a fly goes deeper in the water column, certain colors disappear sooner than others. Red is the first to go; in even clear water, at 20 to 30 feet, any red in a fly will look black. As the depth increases, the next color affected is orange, followed by yellow and finally green. In murky or riled water, these changes occur at lesser depths. This is why I often opt to use a fly with some yellow and green in it during low-light situations, or when the water is roiled.

Through the Fish's Eye is a unique book. This is not a surprise given the background of the authors. Mark Sosin is a well-known angler and outdoor writer. John Clark, a prominent ichthyologist, was associated with the Woods Hole Oceanographic Institute and the Sandy Hook Marine Laboratory, which he helped found. Equally as good is *The Fisherman's Ocean* by David A. Ross. David, who is a good friend, is a scientist emeritus at Woods Hole Oceanographic Institute and one fine angler. His book is based upon his expertise as a scientist and angler. Read these books and you will be far ahead in your understanding of fish behavior, and will be a better angler.

PART III

The Tools of the Trade

CHAPTER 6

Basic Tackle and Gear

We come to understand anything in one of two ways. One is the process of trial and error, learning on our own through experience. The other is to learn from others who have gone before, passing on what they have found to be the better way to do things. So when I knew that I wanted to become serious about saltwater fly fishing, I sat down and read what I consider to be two of the best books on the subject. I was especially interested in learning more about tackle and rigging. Those two books are Lou Tabory's *Inshore Fly Fishing* and Lefty's Kreh's *Fly Fishing in Salt Water*. If you are at all serious about this sport, you should read these books.

I read both books during one winter and then tried their suggestions during the next fishing season. I found that I gained valuable information from both books that helped me with my fly fishing. The information that I culled from both has formed my approach to saltwater fly-fishing gear and how to rig it. I believe that you need to find what works best for you and what you feel you are most comfortable doing. You then develop your own style and approach to saltwater fly fishing, which will add to your success.

Rods

Fly-fishing gear is expensive, so unless money is no object to you, start out building your fly-fishing arsenal carefully. Get the advice of a competent person at your local fly shop and tell him what type of fishing you intend to do. Then test-cast different rods he'll suggest and buy the one that you feel most comfortable casting. It is key to try out different rods, if you can, before deciding on that first fly rod. After using it for a while, you'll begin to get an idea of the type of action that is best for you when you purchase additional rods. The objective of this chapter is to give you some suggestions for avoiding bankruptcy as you begin to assemble what you need to fly fish the salt. Later on I'll cover some time- and labor-saving tips to make your fishing easier.

The weight designation of a fly rod will dictate the reel size and line weight you will use. The conditions you fish will usually determine the rod weight that you should use. Where you're fishing, wind conditions, size of flies, and the size of the fish you could potentially catch all come into play. But above all, make sure your rod is intended for saltwater conditions. The reel seat and guides should be able to withstand the rigors of the environment to which they'll be exposed.

Additionally, you are going to be faced with the problem of what type of action, or flex, a rod possesses. The faster-action rods are a bit stiffer than others, flex the least amount, with the action restricted to the upper portion of the rod. A medium-action rod may have more flex and be a bit less stiff, while a slower-action rod will flex with a greater curve that involves more of the rod than the other two types, and be the least stiff in feel. For me, I prefer rods of fast to medium action because it helps me with my cast. They suit my style of casting and type of fishing better than slower-action, less stiff rods.

My best advice is to try a rod before you buy it. Many fly shops have an area nearby that's large enough for casting, allowing customers to test-cast a rod before purchasing it. I believe that if you're going to spend several hundred dollars for a rod, you should know that what you're buying will meet your needs.

If you have to start your saltwater fly fishing with just one rod, I believe the most versatile choice for the shorebound angler is an 8-weight outfit. It will handle a large number of fishing situations, and do it well. The other rods sizes you would need as you fish the marshes and surf of New England are a 6-weight and a 10-weight rod. These three rods will cover just about every fishing situation you should encounter.

While on the subject of fly rods, I do want to touch on Spey rods. Some saltwater fly rodders are starting to use Spey rods as a way of gaining greater casting distance, particularly when they want to get the fly out over the breakers of a rolling surf. Spey rods also have the advantage of being able to cast larger flies and poppers. I have a Spey rod but I am far from being an expert on its use. I'm just learning how to use it.

Research indicates that the Spey rod's origin is the River Spey, one of the best salmon waters in Scotland. The River Spey is also noted for its pure water quality, one of the prime ingredients needed for the production of Scotch whiskey. A number of famous distilleries are located on the Spey. There aren't many locations that can boast of both great fishing and fine Scotch whiskey.

The rod and the Spey-casting technique were developed on the River Spey because the shoreline, which has steep banks, is covered with small trees and shrubs. It was therefore difficult to cast in the regular manner of fly rods—with the line in the air, behind the caster. However, those using Spey rods in salt water are seeking greater casting distance, casting in the standard manner, with the line in the air behind the caster. This is not to say that the casting methods developed in Scotland cannot be extremely helpful under certain conditions.

For those unfamiliar with Spey rods, they are much longer than a conventional fly rod; those used by saltwater anglers are normally between 12 and 15 feet in length. The rod is held and cast two-handed, with the reel positioned between the hands. But the differences don't end there, and I will highlight some of them, with a little help from my friends.

As I noted, I am far from being an expert on Spey rods. To get more information on their use, I consulted with a couple of fly-fishing friends who have used Spey rods for saltwater fishing. The first of these experts was Captain Doug Jowett.

Doug is a full-time licensed Master Maine Guide who specializes in striped bass and false albacore on Cape Cod and stripers in Maine. He is also an outdoor writer and lecturer. Though Doug uses Spey rods primarily from a boat, especially in areas where he has to sit a distance off rocky shorelines and cast to the rocks, he has had time to evaluate what does and doesn't work when it comes to Spey rods.

Doug noted, "The timing of the cast is most important, and requires practice and patience. I tell everyone to cast soft and slow, and they still try to cast like they have a single-handed rod. You must wait for the cast to develop with the large amount of line off the rod tip. Let the rod do the work and don't force the cast."

I asked Captain Jowett if there were any similarities between conventional fly rods and Spey rods. His answer was, "Fly-casting with Spey rods, using either the traditional Spey-rod method or overhead casting with two hands, is very different from conventional fly rods. Practice is the only similar requirement."

On the subject of advantages and disadvantages, Doug stated, "Casting large flies a good distance using a 625-grain sinking-tip line in rough and windy conditions without strain on your wrist, elbow, and shoulder is an advantage. The only disadvantage I notice is dealing with such a large fly rod. The learning curve of acceptance is also a long one."

I also spoke to my fly-fishing buddy Nick Curcione about Spey rods. Nick, besides being a university professor for 35 years, is an internationally known outdoor writer and lecturer with more than 40 years of angling experience. In 2000 Nick returned to his native waters in the Northeast; he resides in Connecticut with his wife, Kathy.

Nick has a great deal of experience fishing with Spey rods from the shore. His advice in many ways was similar to Doug Jowett's. When it comes to casting a Spey rod, Nick said, "The key to casting these rods is not to overstroke on the forward cast; you want a very brief speed-up and stop. The rod is long to begin with, and if you exaggerate the stroke, the effect is multiplied, the resulting loop will be very wide, and the distance is significantly compromised. To avoid overstroking, apply minimal power with the rod hand. The haul is achieved with the hand grasping the rod butt. The timing is basically the same as that for single-handed rods with shooting heads. Sinking heads do not slow down on the back cast, so you want to make the easiest backstroke possible. If you stroke violently, you lose control and timing."

What lines to use with a Spey rod is a universal question. I have experimented with some types of lines, but my success has been limited. I asked Nick what type of line he uses and his answer shows the time he has spent investigating this area. He told me, "Presently many people are confused about lines, and it took me a while to get this sorted out. First of all, we're not Spey casting, so forget about Spey lines. You want shooting heads. Because of their length, to properly load these rods you need comparatively heavy grain weights. For example, the Thomas and Thomas 14-foot 10-weight would take a 450-grain head. The 12-foot 12-weight will handle 600- to 700-grain heads. As with single-handed rods, you'll find that heads under 30 feet are the most user friendly."

What did amaze me was what Nick told me about the distance he can cast with the lines he builds himself. He uses the 26-foot Versi Tips from Rio fly lines and attaches them to floating running line produced by Rio or Scientific Anglers. They come in 120-foot lengths, but Nick splices in another 20 feet. That's because under normal conditions with no headwind, he will hit distances of 160 to 165 feet. Nick feels that an average caster should be able to attain 100 feet with the proper technique and practice.

One important point Nick makes is that you need a good stripping basket because you are handling so much line. His stripping basket is 17 inches deep with a good number of flexible spikes to prevent tangles.

Lastly, when I asked Nick what was the biggest disadvantage of a Spey rod, he gave me two. As expected, he noted, "The rods are long and heavy, so that's why it's important to let the rod do the work on the cast, otherwise you'll soon tire." The second problem with Spey rods could only come from someone who has extensive experience. Nick said, "They are not the most efficient fish-fighting tools; the fish has the leverage in its favor."

I have devoted space in this chapter to Spey rods because I believe they will become more popular with saltwater fly anglers. Their advantages when used for the right situations far outweigh their disadvantages, and they can add to your angling success. The biggest problem with their use is the average angler's lack of experience with them and the small number of experienced instructors who can teach us how to use a Spey rod. I am lucky to I know Doug and Nick, and I plan to spend some time learning firsthand how to use a Spey rod.

Reels

Today's saltwater fly reels are bigger and stronger than their freshwater ancestors. Reel manufacturers are constantly working to develop reels that can hold more backing and yet not be too heavy during long periods of casting. New materials and their finish have made these reels far less susceptible to corrosion. The drag systems on reels for salt water now feature smooth performance plus the endurance to withstand the long and swift runs of large game fish.

Another area where saltwater fly reels have changed is in price. The increase in line capacity, performance, material quality, and the ability to withstand the severe elements of the salt has meant an increase in cost over freshwater models. A good saltwater fly reel can cost anywhere from $200 to $600, or even more. Recently I had a tackle shop owner proudly show me a reel that had a base price of nearly $600. He then pulled out the manufacturer's literature and showed me that for a mere several thousand dollars more, I could be the proud owner of that reel, manufactured in titanium. Things have certainly changed since I purchased my first freshwater reel for $25.

There are two basic types of fly reels for saltwater use: direct drive and anti-reverse, available at varying prices. The anti-reverse reel is the type where the handle does not revolve if a fish is taking line off the reel. Some anglers don't like this feature, since you can be turning the handle but not reeling in any line. The direct-drive reel means just that: When you turn the handle, the line is wound onto the reel. However, the handle spins as line is taken from the reel. This means that if you aren't careful, the handle will whack your fingers.

Just how fast can a handle spin on a direct-drive reel? Several years ago while fishing for tarpon, a large fish made an unexpected run on me. I didn't pull my hand away quick enough, and the pain didn't subside even after the fish slowed down. Then, when I reached for the handle to begin fighting the fish once more, I discovered that the handle had broken off. The force had been so great that it broke the handle's shaft at the spool. We did manage to get the fish to within 10 feet of the boat using ballpoint pens and the plastic dowels from some large fishing floats to turn the reel. But the tarpon—which the guide estimated to be about 125 pounds—was lost due to a chafed leader.

When you purchase a fly reel for saltwater use, make sure that it's meant for that environment and is corrosion resistant. The reel should have a smooth drag that will handle the run of large saltwater fish, and it should be able to hold a sufficient amount of backing, plus the fly line. The literature for every reel will state its backing capacity. Also, make sure that the size range of the reel is that of the rod that you're going to use it on. Most reels are made to cover one or two rod weights.

There has been a lot of interest lately in large-arbor and wide-arbor reels. Large-arbor reels can retrieve line quicker because the spool is larger in diameter than a standard fly reel; each revolution of the spool retrieves more line. Wide-arbor reels, though the same diameter as reels for the same rod weight, are wider and therefore hold more backing. You must, however, be careful to lay the line down evenly while fighting a fish using a wide-arbor reel.

If you are a fly angler who's fishing the salt for the first time, be aware that this environment can be tough on your gear. That's why you should only use equipment made for saltwater fishing. Sand can cause as much damage as salt water. If you drop your reel in the sand, get it to a place where you can rinse it with fresh water. Remove the spool and rinse the sand from the internal workings. But don't use a high-pressure water stream—it will just drive the sand and salt deeper into the workings. If, when you replace the spool, there is any grinding sound or the reel seems to move less freely than it should, don't use it. Clean the reel thoroughly when you get home or take it to a tackle shop that can do the work.

When fishing around salt water, corrosion is a continual problem. At the end of every trip you should, at a minimum, use fresh water to rinse off your reel and rod. The best solution to corrosion is to take the reel apart and wash it in warm, soapy water and then rinse it. Also, don't forget to rinse all the flies you've used after a trip; they will last longer.

When fishing the surf, it's not only the salt water but also the sand suspended in the water from the surf's action that creates problems. Besides causing corrosion, salt water can carry fine sand into your reel. Again, if you hear gritty, grinding sounds in your reel, stop use and clean it as soon as you can. Given the price of fly reels these days, it is important to take care of them. And remember that if and when you do have a problem with a reel, having a backup along can save the trip.

During the winter, take some time to thoroughly clean and lubricate your reels. Just lubricate them lightly; quite often people will use too much lubricant, which is as bad as not using any at all. If you're not sure about how to maintain your reels, take them to a tackle shop that does such work or check with the reel manufacturer to see if it will do the work. Peen Reels, for example, services all its reels and does a bang-up job. But don't wait until late March to send in your reels and expect a turnaround in a couple of weeks. Even when you send in reels around the first of the year, it may take a month or two for the manufacturer to complete the service.

When cleaning your reels during the season and in winter, don't forget the backing. It should be washed and then left to dry before you put it back on the reel. The backing is a braided line that will absorb salt water and then over time will corrode the reel spool.

Let me say that I like reels that don't have an outer rim or frame after the spool is removed. Reels that have just posts sticking out from the back plate are easy to use when changing spools. Changing spools with this type of reel, even in the dark, is easy because when you place the spool onto the reel, the butt leader section or the leader itself (if on the line) does not get caught. Reels with an outer frame or rim, because of the small tolerance between the rim and spool, have a way of grabbing anything that's sticking out, jamming it between the spool and the rim. Also, when fighting a fish with a reel that does not have an outer rim shielding the spool, you can palm the outer edge of the spool for added drag.

I've found an easy way to determine the right combination of rod and reel for me and my casting ability. With the reel on the rod and loaded with line, I try to balance the whole outfit on my index finger, which I place at the cork grip just above the reel. If it balances there on my finger, I feel that the reel has not overpowered the rod; nor is it too heavy for it. I should be able to cast such a rod-and-reel combination easily for long periods of time.

Here's one last suggestion about the care of your fly reel that's very important. It's often hard to remember this, but when you're done fishing for the day, back off the drag on your fly reels. Do this to remove the compression on the springs and washers in the reel's drag system. If you don't, the drag will eventually lose its effectiveness. It's also vital to check all the drags at the end of the season. A tightened drag that sits over the winter will definitely weaken and lose its capability.

Lines

Though fly lines may cost less than either a rod or reel, they are an important, if not the most important, part of your fishing equipment. It's the line that you cast, not the fly. The fly merely follows the line. It's therefore key to match the size of your line to the rod you're using, but it is also the line that has the most to do with where your fly moves through the water column.

For salt water you'll normally use weight-forward lines, either floating, intermediate, or sinking densities, for the majority of your fishing. There are also weight-forward lines that are saltwater sinking tips; these lines have the sinking weight in the first section of the line, which can be up to 32 feet in length. Still, the one line that you will use the most is an intermediate line. It's the most versatile of the line types and can be used in a variety of fishing situations. I use intermediate lines for about 80 percent of my fishing. I also prefer the clear intermediate lines that have come on the market in recent years.

There are fly anglers who use shooting heads for saltwater fishing. Shooting heads are the forward section of weight-forward lines that are available in different densities. Some anglers make their own shooting heads of different lengths and densities. Most are set up with a loop-to-loop connection to the running line or shooting line. This makes it easy to change the type and density of your fly line without changing reels. It's simple and quick to change from a slow-sinking shooting head, for instance, to a fast-sinking one.

Running line or shooting lines are available in many forms—and there are just as many opinions as to which types are the best. There are monofilament running lines in regular, braided, flat, and oval. I have tried the braided nylon running line but had trouble with it tangling; while one angler I know swears by it, I swear at it. I suggest that you read Lou Tabory's and Lefty Kreh's books for additional information on shooting heads and running lines, and then if you're interested, experiment with the different types and find what works best for you.

Rather than shooting heads, I prefer to fish saltwater sinking-tip lines that are like a shooting head but with an intermediate running line as an integral part of the line, with no loop or connection. These all-in-one lines are available in densities of 500 grains or more, with weight-forward heads in 28- to 32-foot lengths. Teeny Lines made the first ones I used; several other companies have recently started selling them, as well.

One of the best things that you can do to improve your casting is keep your lines clean. Periodically during the fishing season, take time to clean them. It will make a difference because a dirty line reduces your casting distance. If you don't have time to remove the line and wash it, use one of a number of fly-line cleaner-and-pad systems that are sold in most fly shops and catalogs. There's even one that hooks onto your fly rod; you simply run the line out, put cleaner on the pads, insert the line into the cleaning unit on the rod, and then reel in a clean line.

During the winter, do a thorough job of cleaning your fly lines. Soak them in warm, soapy water and then rinse and dry them. Line dryers, which resemble large, open spools with a handle, are invaluable for this process. I built a large line dryer so I can load all my lines on it at one time; this is easy to do because I've rigged my fly line with a loop in the butt leader and also in the end that attaches to the backing. (I'll discuss this rigging in the next chapter.) Each line is attached to next. I put them on the dryer with a small twist-tie joining the loop of one line to the next. When the lines are dry, I run them through a cleaning pad and fly-line cleaner as I take them off to get at any dirt that may have been missed. This puts a nice finish on the line, as well, which helps with casting distance. I then put them on the spools used to store them. When done right, the lines are on their storage spools with the rear end of the line last onto the spool, ready to be loaded directly onto a reel.

It's also a good idea to rinse or wash the backing on your reels. Most backing is a braided material that will hold salt. The salt will corrode the inside of your reel's spool if not attended to on a regular basis.

I use 20-pound- and 30-pound-test backing on my reels. The 20-pound backing goes on my 6- and 7-weight outfits, while the 30-pound backing is used for all weights above that. I really like the white Cortland Micron backing; there are other good backings out there from other manufacturers, but this one has served me well. It's so durable that I also use the 30-pound Micron on my conventional surf reels for casting. It works like a charm.

Depending upon use and storage, all fly lines will eventually wear out, but sunlight and heat can accelerate the process. All forms of fishing line are affected by direct sunlight and heat to different degrees. Fishing lines other than monofilament may tolerate longer times of exposure to the sun and heat before being seriously impacted by these elements. When I spoke to the people at Cortland Line about this, they told me that heat will do serious damage to fly line—and it doesn't have to be excessive heat. Temperatures like that found in a closed vehicle during the summer will seriously harm fly lines by causing premature cracking and breakdown of the line coating. Fly lines used in tropical climates do not last as long as those used in the Northeast for this very reason.

As you begin to buy and use more fly line, it will become difficult keeping track of line sizes and types. Initially, to help identify lines, I used a product that was a shrink tube with the line weight imprinted on it. It went on the front end of the line before I tied on the butt leader. This worked very well but unfortunately, this product is no longer available. I've now switched to black permanent marking pens. I use the system described in Lefty Kreh's book, in which one wide mark is equal to a 5 and a short mark to a 1. Therefore one wide mark and three short ones would designate an 8-weight line. The one problem I had was with sinking lines, which are usually dark in color. That hurdle was recently taken care of when I found white permanent marking pens.

Flies

I can remember my initial feeling of confusion the first time I surveyed the saltwater fly section of my local tackle shop. The number of different flies to choose from can be a bit overwhelming. Besides the many standard patterns, which are offered in different sizes and colors, there are the local patterns to consider. Over the years since that first pass through the fly section, I've been lucky to have angling buddies who have either given me samples of successful flies or told me of patterns that are good fish producers. Like wine, good fly patterns are learned through personal use and the advice of others.

Still, there are some standard patterns that seem to work no matter where you're fishing. If I had to limit myself to just a few fly patterns, I would definitely make sure I had some Clouser Minnows, Lefty's Deceivers, and Half-and-Halfs of various sizes and colors. These are good patterns to begin your fly collection. I say fly *collection* because if you become a serious saltwater fly rodder, you'll eventually amass a good number of flies, particularly if you fish different areas of the coast.

Some basic colors for these patterns have proven to be successful. For the Clouser Minnows, olive and white, chartreuse and white, blue and white, and all black will handle most situations where you want a fly that gets down in the water column. Your Deceivers should be white with dark backs of either black or dark blue. As for the Half-and-Halfs, which are a blend of Clouser Minnow and Deceiver, the colors noted for the Clousers are a good start.

Your best bet as you build your fly arsenal is to match the bait that is present in the area you regularly fish. This is usually the most successful approach, but I will say that I've seen flies that looked nothing like the local bait, yet, on occasion, outfished the more popular patterns.

Additional Equipment and Safety Gear

When I first thought about this section of the book, I planned to tell you that the most important piece of gear after your rod, reel, and line was a stripping basket. And indeed, you cannot fish salt water without a stripping basket.

A stripping basket is a must when fishing salt water. Many anglers make their own using a plastic basket, bungee cord, and heavy mono fingers secured to the bottom.

Whether you're standing on a beach or the rocks of a jetty, your line will become tangled or covered with sand. Even if you're fishing a quiet estuary, the amount of line you'll be casting precludes letting it coil on or sink below the surface of the water. A stripping basket is a must when fishing the saltwater shoreline.

Having said this, I should add that a recent event changed my priorities. Over the past few years there have been several occurrences of fly fishermen drowning here on Cape Cod. In each case the angler had been fishing the opening to an estuary and stepped off an edge into swift-moving water. His waders filled with water and he drowned before anyone could get to him. While writing this book, another fly angler died, this time on Martha's Vineyard. He was not a rookie; the gentleman was a guide and familiar with the shoreline of the Vineyard. No one knows for sure what happened. I have fished that same area; the last time I was there it was a foggy night, but we were careful to move toward shore as the tide moved in.

I believe that anglers should wear some kind of personal flotation device (PFD) in any situations where a misstep puts you in deep or fast-moving water. There are several PFDs that are ideal for the fly angler. I have one that resembles a pair of suspenders. These units are not bulky; they inflate either automatically or manually with a pull of the lanyard. They inflate by way of CO_2 cartridges, which are replaceable, if used. The prices for these units start at around $100, and they are worth every cent because these PFDs can save your life.

Another alternative is the flotation vest that is also a fly-fishing vest. Sterns manufactures the one I'm most familiar with, which is Coast Guard approved as a Type III PFD. The beauty of this vest is that it's like a regular fly-fishing vest, though slightly bulkier, but still holds all those small items you want to have with you when standing waist deep in the water 100 yards from shore. The Sterns flotation vest is sold in many catalogs.

Don't take chances, especially at night, in areas that have deep or swift-moving water nearby. Even if you think you know the area and its structure, it can get confusing in the dark, and fog just adds to the problem. *Buy and wear some form of PFD when fishing potentially dangerous waters.* It may take some time to get used to wearing it, but at least you'll be around to complain about the minor inconvenience.

Let's take a look at some additional gear for fly fishing the shoreline of New England. Waders or hip boots are necessary since you'll encounter water that's normally too cold to wade for any length of time without their protec-

Bob Mitchell models the personal floatation device (PFD) he uses when fishing potentially dangerous sections of shoreline. They cost much less than a fly reel and can save your life.

tion. There are some isolated locations where the water during the peak of summer will be warm enough to fish without waders or hip boots.

Hip boots will work for many locations that have no surf. I have a friend who uses hip boots most of the time here on Cape Cod, and he does catch his share of fish. I prefer bootfoot waders to those with felt soles or stocking-foot waders. The bootfoot type meets all my different fishing requirements. If I am fishing rocky beaches or jetties, metal cleats or ice creepers fit over these boots easily. Two of the more popular cleats sold are Korker and Stabilicers. I like the latter brand because they have Velcro straps, which makes them easy to get on and off.

Felt-soled waders may work on some rocky conditions, but these soles will not last when used on a sandy beach for any length of time. If you do use felt-soled boots around rocky beaches, I recommend those that feature small metal cleats. Stockingfoot waders do not do well in the surf. The fine sand will eventually work its way into the wading shoes and abrade the wader material in the shoes; leaks will quickly develop.

Lastly, use a waist belt with your waders, especially in the surf; a short, waterproof jacket worn over the waders also helps. A wader belt is a must for the unexpected wave that washes over you. It will prevent the water from filling up your waders and holding you under.

Though maybe not a complete list, here are some other items that will make your fishing easier and more successful:

- **Tide schedule** A tide schedule for the area you're fishing is a must. Most tackle shops provide tide schedules free of charge; this is the best bargain you'll ever get on fishing information.

- **Polarized sunglasses** Not only will a good pair of polarized sunglasses protect your eyes from the sun's harmful rays, but it'll be invaluable in helping you see fish in the water, as well. You'll be able to see the bottom and associated structure when wading. Glasses also protect your eyes from flying hooks that fish occasionally send your way.

- **Waist-length, waterproof jacket** These jackets are not only good in the rain but also make great windbreakers. When worn over your waders in the surf, they go a long way toward keeping you dry.

- **Shoulder bag, chest pack, or backpack** Since my early days of surf fishing, I've preferred a shoulder bag to haul whatever gear I want to carry. If need be, I can push it around to my back, out of the way. Whatever's your style, you'll need some way to carry your extra spools, flies, pretied leaders, compass, measuring tape, penlight or small flashlight, small first-aid kit, long-handled pliers to remove hooks from fish, and small camera.

- **Hat** Fish with a hat that has a dark underside on the brim. This will reduce the glare that comes off the sand and water. It's also better to have a fly from a windblown cast embedded in your hat than your head.

- **Fishing pliers** These pliers should have a cutter on them that will cut through a hook's shank. They are usually about 6 inches long but very versatile in the things they can do. Besides hooks, they're also great for cutting leader material of all sizes.

- **Insect repellent** You'll be happy you carry this as part of your equipment when you encounter one of those windless nights that bugs just love. However, let me give you a big warning: If you have residual insect repellent on your hands and you handle your fly line, it will start to break down the coating on the line. Make sure your hands are free of insect repellent before you start fishing. A package of Handi-Wipes or Wet Ones in your vehicle comes in handy for cleanups like this.

CHAPTER 7

Putting It All Together

When I first became serious about saltwater fly fishing, I spent the winter with two of the best anglers around: Lou Tabory and Lefty Kreh. I read *Inshore Fly Fishing* and *Fly Fishing in Salt Water* to educate myself on the areas of the sport that were new to me. Though I had a good background in saltwater fishing, I was new to the game of setting up my fly lines, tying my own leaders, and such. My objective was to read about and then try different things throughout the next season to find a system that suited my style of fishing. In addition I reviewed my copy of *Practical Fishing Knots II*, by Mark Sosin and Lefty Kreh. By the time the fishing season was halfway through I had worked out how to rig and store my fly lines, how to tie my own leaders, and what knots would do the job for me.

Rigging Up: Knots

One of the biggest problems for me was how to easily change fly lines on my reels. Not only did I want a way to change lines quickly, but I was concerned about storing the lines when I wasn't using them. I knew I didn't want to tie the lines directly to the backing. There was no flexibility there. I had read of preformed loops that could be attached to the line, but they seemed to be too bulky. Then I read in Lefty's *Fly Fishing in Salt Water* about how to create a loop-to-loop connection with the backing by whipping the end of the fly line into a small loop. It was exactly what I was looking for.

With a little practice you can whip a loop in the end of the fly line; just read Lefty's book. When you complete the loop, coat it with about three light applications of Pliobond, allowing for drying time between each coat. The glue soaks into the wrap, and is waterproof and flexible.

If you're concerned about these loops not being strong enough, you can forget about it. If done right, they are as strong as any connection you can construct. I've fought several 125-pound-plus tarpon that were into the backing for long periods of time and never have had this loop fail.

My next concern was what knot to use in the backing to complete the loop-to-loop connection system. *Practical Fishing Knots II* had the answer to the knots I would need to accomplish this, plus the majority of all the knots I would use. The knot combination I selected for the backing was a Bimini twist and surgeon's loop. Now, I've seen the expression that people make when the Bimini twist is mentioned. It's not a difficult knot to tie; it just takes practice. When tying the knot, you need to make a loop that fits over your two knees so that you can open your legs slightly to maintain pressure on the loop and aid in the process whereby the tag end spiral-wraps back over the twisted portion of the line. When finished, I end up with a double section of line that's about 2 feet long. In the middle of that double line I then tie a surgeon's loop. As you tie this knot, make sure the double line between it and the Bimini twist remains of equal length for strength purposes. Both knots are then treated with Pliobond like the whipped end of the fly line.

You now have a double section of line formed by the Bimini twist with a surgeon's loop halfway on the double line to form a loop of about 12 inches. You need a loop at least that big to make it is easy to change lines, which I will explain in a minute. You can also tie a smaller Bimini twist that fits over just one knee while tying and forget the surgeon's loop. The key is to have a loop big enough for the fly reel or the spool that you store your line on, to pass through it.

When making a loop-to-loop connection, all of the line associated with one of the loops must pass through the other loop or back over itself. This means that when you're connecting the backing to your fly lines at the start of the season, you have the choice of passing the loop on the backing over either the reel or the storage spool holding the fly line, after the loop on the backing is first inserted through the loop in the end of the fly line. However, once the reel is mounted on the rod and the season is under way, your only option is to pass the loop over the line storage spool, unless you remove the reel from the rod.

In Lou Tabory's book you'll find an excellent diagram on page 176 that shows the proper way to make a loop-to-loop connection. If it ends up looking otherwise, it will compromise the strength and integrity of the connection.

I prefer to use the Pliobond that comes in a small 1-ounce tube. Not only is it easy to squeeze out the right amount during use, but it also doesn't take up as much room as the bottle size when traveling. Just be sure to keep it in a zip-lock bag to avoid any mess, if there is a leak. When I apply Pliobond to my knots I use one paper match from a book of matches for each coat. The matches are cheaper to use than brushes, work just as well, require no cleanup, and, again, take up less space when traveling.

The final thing I needed to do to complete my rigging was make a loop connection on the front end of my fly lines so it would be easy to change leaders. I opted to use a short butt leader with a loop in it. The obvious answer was to use a nail knot to attach the butt leader to the line, but I was told by one fly shop owner that a nail knot would pull off the outer coat of the line when it was put under any great strain—say, a big striper. Still, most experts feel a nail knot is good choice in this situation. Those tarpon I told you about not only tested the connection between my backing and fly line, but also gave the seal of approval for the nail knot at the front end of my line. I've never had a nail knot pull the coating off a fly line.

Now, I can handle a Bimini twist, but I fail miserably when trying to tie a nail knot. That's why I sought some help on this one. I bought a handy little tool called the Tie-Fast Knot Tyer; some catalogs call this a basic knot tool. Whatever you call it, it works, and I use it to tie all my nail knots. In fact, I've been able to easily tie nail knots using 40-pound mono with the tool.

I tie the butt leaders onto my fly lines using a nail knot that is tied about $1/4$ inch from the end of the line; I then trim the fly line back, close to the knot. Though I don't coat the knot with Pliobond, I know some anglers who do. The key is to go slowly and work the knot so that as you tighten it, the wraps remain even and do not overlap.

I use 30-pound mono for the butt leaders on the lighter-weight fly lines and 40-pound monofilament for line weights of 9 and above. The length of my butt leaders is about 6 inches. At the end of it I tie a perfection loop, which allows me to quickly and easily change pretied leaders. The perfection loop is another knot that stands up well to the rigors of saltwater fishing.

When it comes to knots, my best advice is to practice tying them during the winter. If you're having trouble, find someone who knows knots and ask him to work with you and show you how it's done. Perhaps the worst scenario imaginable is that you're on the beach, it's dark, the fish are hitting . . . and you're struggling with a knot. Also, if you are forced to tie knots in the dark, use a flashlight to check the knots and make sure they're tied right, and tight. Otherwise you'll lose a fish when the knot unravels; ask me how I know this. Sometimes these lessons are learned the hard way, but the good news is you don't forget them.

Leaders

I tie all my own leaders because I can make up the lengths and tippet strengths that I use the most. Most of my leaders are 6 or 8 feet in length, with a few a bit longer for use on lighter-weight outfits. The tippets on these longer leaders are usually either 6- or 8-pound test; I use them mainly for squeteague. The majority of the leaders that I tie have either 10- or 20-pound tippets. I use fluorocarbon for all my tippets. The rest of the leaders are tied with a quality monofilament leader material.

I start out tying a leader by putting a perfection loop in the end that will connect to the butt leader. Usually, that first section is tied with 30-, 25-, or 20-pound-test mono. If the overall leader is to be 8 feet long, the first section is about 30 inches in length. If the first section is 30-pound mono, I will tie it—using a simplified blood knot—to a 30-inch section of 20-pound-test mono. To that I tie a 3-foot piece of 10-pound fluorocarbon, again using a simplified blood knot. Here are instructions for tying one:

1. Place the tag ends of the two sections of mono that you are going to join so that they point in opposite directions. Grasp them between thumb and forefinger at a point where you have about 10 inches of mono free for each piece to tie the knot (as you get better at tying this knot that length can be shortened). Begin wrapping one tag end over the other line. Wrap in a different direction, going away from your body. The number of wraps depends upon the mono size and stiffness. Use 6 or 8 for lighter lines and maybe 4 for heavier, stiffer mono. Bring the tag end back, pass it between itself and the tag end of the other line, and hold with your two fingers.

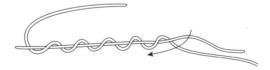

2. You may have to switch hands to hold the pieces as you start the

second part. Now wrap the other tag end around the other line but in the opposite direction, toward you. When you have completed enough wraps, pass the tag end through the opening where you are holding the other tag end, except that it should be going through in the opposite direction.

3. Without letting the knot come apart, begin to tighten it by initially pulling on both of the tags' ends. This is to ensure that when you pull on the standing ends of the mono, the knot will not pull apart. Do not pull so tight that the wraps overlap.

4. Moisten the knot and begin to tighten it by slowly pulling on the standing ends of the mono. If it appears that the tags' ends might pull out, stop and tighten from the tags' ends, then pull again on the standing ends until the knot is tight. If tied properly, the wraps are even and do not overlap, and the tags will stick out of the knot at right angles and in opposite directions. Trim the tag ends close to the knot.

I try to tie a good supply of leaders of different lengths and tippet strengths during the winter. Then I coil the leaders and put them in a leader wallet labeled with the length, plus the strength of the regular monofilament sections and tippet. Be sure to stretch and straighten your leaders before you use them to remove the memory of the coils.

You'll go through a number of leaders on the days when you have to keep changing flies, especially when the fishing is slow and you're searching for that one fly that'll turn things around. A good supply of leaders in the wallet will get you through such days.

While on the subject of tying flies to leaders, I don't use a knot that cinches the fly to the tippet. I believe that this type of knot often kills the action of the fly. Regardless of the fly or line type I'm fishing, I use the nonslip mono loop to tie all my flies to the leader. This may bring me flak from some longtime fly rodders, but as I said, it's what works for me. Try it, and if you don't like it, go back to something like the improved clinch knot or Trilene knot. If I were to use a clinch knot, I'd use the Trilene knot. I used it for years to tie swivels and snap swivels for my surf outfits.

The non-slip mono loop is also good knot to learn because it is strong and allows flies greater movement even if a heavy tippet is used.

1. Tie a loose over-hand knot approximately 6 to 8 inches from the tag end of the tippet.

2. Run the end of the tippet through the hook eye and back through the overhand knot. Make sure that the tag end passes back through the overhand knot the same way it left it.

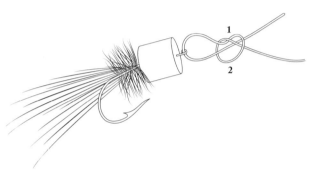

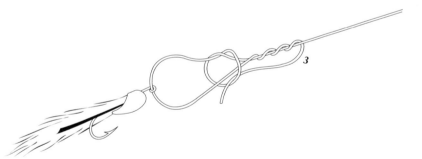

3. Wrap the tag end around the standing line and run it back through the overhand knot. The number of turns or wraps depends on the pound test of the monofilament line being used. Stren Fishing Lines suggests seven wraps for 6- to 8-pound line, five wraps for 15- to 40-pound test line, and four wraps for 50-pound test line. Also, keep the overhand knot as small as you can and close to the eye of the fly when tightening. This will help form a small loop.

4. Moisten the knot and tighten evenly.

The Fishing Log

It's Friday evening and you finally have time to try a spot that you've been told has had some good striper fishing. The information is right and you have a great evening. You can hardly wait to get back to try the location again. About a week later, you're able to leave work early and fish the new hot spot again. For the next several hours you work the water with different flies . . . without getting even a hint of a fish. What has happened? What's different from the successful trip of a week ago?

Old surf rats have a saying: "You have to put in your time and pay your dues." That means far more than just putting in fishing time. It also refers to learning from your experiences and understanding what's happening when the fishing is good, and when it isn't. It means learning from those experiences about what is the best tide, at what time of day, and what weather conditions will produce the best opportunity for catching fish. It is also, given those conditions, knowing why one location will be better than another at providing angling success.

Many things can affect your fishing, and the key is to sort them out into recognizable patterns relative to the success or failure of your fishing trips. There is structure, both in the water and along the shoreline; tides; weather, including current, past, and impending weather, all of which impact the fish and your fishing; and finally, the availability of prey that the fish would be pursuing. All of these elements are part of the mix that influences when and where you can expect to catch fish.

Initially, all this may seem to be a bit complicated and difficult to keep track of, and especially remember. This is where an angler's logbook comes into play. Very few of us can keep track of all of the fishing trips we have had, what occurred, and what the conditions were. Keeping a logbook will assist you in understanding what made one trip a good one or another not so successful. Maintaining and using a fishing log will help make you a better angler.

A logbook doesn't have to be something fancy. A standard form that you can duplicate and keep in a looseleaf notebook works quite well. Bob Mitchell gave me a 4- by 6-inch card that he uses, which is printed on both sides. I like it so much that I may start using it in lieu of my own log sheet. The key, though, is not how fancy your logbook is, but rather that you religiously keep track of your fishing trips, review the information, recognize the patterns, and use them. The elements of both successful trips and ones that were a bust are important to note. If you do this, you will soon instinctively recognize the patterns and know when and where to find fish. I say this because every successful angler I've known has kept a logbook to record trips, and referenced the information regularly.

Let's look at some basic entries that should be part of your logbook. The illustration on the next page shows a sample log sheet that can be duplicated and kept in a notebook. Keeping information in a logbook that has blank pages is okay, but there's the possibility that you might forget something pertinent.

Additional Helpful Hints

As fly-fishing books recommend, you should put candle wax or beeswax on the ferrules of your rods when you put them together. You should take them apart at least once a year, as well. Otherwise when you want to take a rod apart, it may be a difficult task. When do take your rods apart and store them for the winter, if you can, stand them upright. I found an old tie rack that was basically a board with dowels sticking out of it. I nailed the rack on a wall of my basement, 3 feet from the floor. I set the rod sections between the dowels and use rubber bands stretched across the dowels to hold the rods in place.

For years, even before getting into fly rodding, I was looking for a way to both clean cork grips and keep them from drying out and becoming brittle. Most of my surf rods have cork grips; I like the feel of cork, and it's lighter than a number of other materials used to make rod grips. Cork is a wood product; it is the outer bark of an oak tree that grows in Mediterranean countries. Being wood, it does dry out, crack, and break. I talked to people about it but no one had any good suggestions. A couple of people told me that I could lightly sand the grips as a way of cleaning them. But repeated sanding will reduce the size of the grips.

Since cork is a wood product, I began to experiment with different furniture polishes and finally found one that kept the cork from drying out and it would clean all but the most severe dirt off the grips. Now at least twice a year—at the end of the season and before it starts—I wipe the grips down with Old English furniture polish that contains lemon oil.

Use a soft rag to apply the Old English polish, rubbing the cork surface well to clean off the dirt. You must make sure the cork is damp from the polish. It will soon soak in and you will see that the cork does not have any slippery feeling to it. I have surf rods with cork grips that are 40 years old and have been treated with Old English; the fiberglass rod blanks will probably-give out before the cork grips do.

FISHING LOG

Location: _____Date:_____

Time of Day Fished: _____

Weather Conditions: Sunny _____Cloudy _____Overcast _____

        Drizzle _____Rain_____Showers _____Other _____

Wind Direction:_____Wind Speed: _____Calm

_____Light 0–10_____Moderate 10–20_____Strong 20+

Comments _____

_____

_____

Previous Weather Conditions:_____

_____

Impending Weather: _____

_____

Air Temperature: _____Barometer:_____

Tide: _____Water Temperature: _____

Water Conditions: Flat_____1 Ft Waves_____2–3 Ft Waves _____

      3–5 Ft Waves _____5 Ft Plus Waves_____

Comments: _____

_____

_____

Water Clarity: Clear _____Cloudy _____Very Dirty_____

Water Depths Fished: _____

_____

Structures Fished: _____

_____

Flies: _____

Line Types & Weights: _____

Fishing Techniques:_____

Fish Caught: _____

Average Size: _____Largest: _____

_____

_____

Comments: _____

_____

_____

Another tip I would like to pass on is about spool tenders—those elastic straps that fit over your spare spools to keep the line in place. Buy spool tenders that have a space on them where you can write the line type and weight. They are inexpensive enough that you should have one for every fly line you use. When you go on trips and take spare spools, knowing which spool has what line saves time. Also when you switch spools on a reel, put the right spool tender on the one taken off. If you don't do this, it soon becomes a shell game as to what line is where.

Line storage is always a problem. You can try to keep your lines on those plastic spools the manufacturer uses to package them, but there are some problems with this. First, some of the spools come in two parts and must be glued together for use. Second, it's very difficult to wind the line onto these spools. Your line soon becomes twisted and tangled when winding it on by hand.

When I started buying different lines for different rod weights, I soon realized that I had to come up with a method that could keep them organized. I wanted a way whereby I could easily store the lines in winter, after cleaning, yet have an easy and simple way to put them back on in the spring, plus change lines during the season. I also needed a practical way to carry extra lines on fishing trips without being limited to just the reels and spare reel spools.

I discovered a product called the Fly Line Winder manufactured by Rio Products. It was exactly what I needed. Each unit is a small square box with a removable spool in it. To wind your fly line onto the spool, you inserted the front end through a hole in the lid of the box and secured it to the spool. Then you placed a small crank handle through the sides of the box and spool, and used it to turn the spool, winding on the line. In spring it was a simple operation to attach the line to your backing and load the reel.

This was a great system. I could label each box as to what line it held. I had a storage box for every fly line I owned. These Fly Line Winder boxes traveled well and took up less room than a spare reel spool. If you've noticed, though, I've been describing them in the past tense. Rio no longer makes these units. To say I was upset when I found this out is an understatement. But through some searching of catalogs, I came up with an alternative that works almost as well.

It is the Reel-E-Good Line Winder offered in the Feather-Craft Fly Fishing catalog. Though there are no storage boxes for the spools of line, it does make a good winter storage system. The unit costs more than my old technique, and it does require the stand to load line onto the spools. I must admit that I have lost the ability to easily change lines when on a trip using these storage spools; however, I am using some of the Fly Line Winder boxes to carry the lines I take on fishing trips. That way I will still have a simple way to change fly lines in the field.

Every good fly-fishing book will tell you that before fishing, you should stretch and straighten your fly line. When the line sits on the reel, the line will start to develop the curves of the reel spool. I used to do what most anglers do and try to stretch it between my hands, a few feet at a time. Then the first night I ever fished with Chip Bergeron on Martha's Vineyard, he taught me a great way to stretch my fly line—one that was so obvious I couldn't believe it when I saw him do it. He simply attached his fly line to the back of his pickup and backed up, letting out the line. When he got to the end, he grabbed the fly line firmly and gently stretched it. When done, he walked back to the truck, reeling in the line; then off we went to fish. For the shorebound angler, this is a great way to stretch and straighten your fly line.

Today catch-and-release is a popular conservation ethic among fly-rodders. Photographing your catch is one way to preserve the memory of your fish before you return it to the water. If you're going to take a picture of a fish to be released, try to have the camera ready beforehand to minimize the time the fish will be out of the water. Also, when taking the picture, hold your fish horizontally, supporting it under the belly. Do not hold the fish vertically, because that puts a great deal of strain and pressure on its internal organs. Also, keep your hands out of the gills to avoid any damage to that delicate area. Use wet gloves or a wet towel when handling a fish to prevent removing the slime coating its scales; this slippery film is the fish's protective barrier against infection.

There are several models of cameras on the market that do quite well in the saltwater environment. I have two such cameras; one is the Pentax IQ-Zoom 90-WR, which is no longer made, with a 38mm to 90mm zoom lens. The other is the Pentax IQZoom 105-WR, with a 38mm to 105mm zoom lens. They are both weather-resistant cameras that can withstand the elements around salt water better than any standard camera. Small enough to fit into my shirt pocket, both have a built-in flash and autofocus, and can take close-up shots.

The picture quality these cameras can produce is excellent, and a number of pictures I have taken with them have appeared in magazines, to go along with my articles. These cameras are very good for the saltwater environment since they can be washed off with slow-running water or in a shallow basin with a sponge. When fishing, I have at least one of these cameras with me at all times.

Here's an idea I've used since my early surf-fishing days. It's always handy to have a rag to wipe your hands after handling a fish or to dry them to take a picture. But I was forever losing rags that I had stuffed in a pocket, or forgetting to take one with me, or having it slide into a boot leg where I couldn't reach it.

Then I hit upon an idea whereby I could have a good supply of rags that I couldn't lose and would always be handy. I went to a store that sold towels, blankets, and such. These larger chain stores usually have different-quality and -priced items. I purchased the least expensive hand towels they sold. In a marine supply store I bought a grommet kit whose brass grommets can be put into material with just a hammer. I put a grommet in one corner of each towel. I then used metal shower curtain hooks that I purchased at a hardware store to attach the towels to one strap of my waders.

This arrangement allows me to tuck the towel inside my waders but still have it accessible. When one towel gets dirty, I replace it with a clean one and wash it. There is always a rag attached to my waders so I never have to worry about forgetting it.

The tips I've offered in this section of the book are the result of my experiences, including trial-and-error effort over time, in finding a way to outfit and rig my gear, plus make my fishing easier and more enjoyable. No two anglers are the same, and each will be comfortable with different approaches to fishing. The suggestions and ideas presented are starting points. This is the objective of this book: to help you become a better angler.

PART IV
Fly Fishing Boston and Beyond

CHAPTER 8

Boston Harbor

Boston is a city with a rich history. It's a modern metropolitan complex, a major port on the Atlantic seaboard, and the capital of Massachusetts, named after the Massachusetts, a Native American tribe that inhabited the region in 1630, when Boston was first settled. From its earliest years, a number of people have played a part in the city's historical development. The names of such famous Bostonian patriots and authors as John Adams, Paul Revere, John Hancock, John Quincy Adams, Henry David Thoreau, and Ralph Waldo Emerson are known by every schoolchild. But Boston also played a part in a less patriotic endeavor.

Today Boston is fondly called Beantown, a name that refers to its famous beans baked in molasses. It is a dish that had its beginnings during Boston's colonial era. However, there is a darker connection between Boston and molasses. It dates back to when Boston was a major producer of rum, which is manufactured from molasses, and was a part of the "triangle trade"—the infamous business whereby sugarcane was harvested by slaves in the West Indies and shipped to Boston and other New England locations, where it was made into rum. The rum was then sent to Africa to be used in the purchase of additional slaves, who were sent to the West Indies. Boston continued to be a prime producer of rum even after the abolition of slavery. As a matter of fact, that industry played a part in what has to be one of the oddest disasters known.

In 1919 Boston was the site of the Great Molasses Flood, a tragedy that killed 21 people and injured some 150. This odd catastrophe occurred when

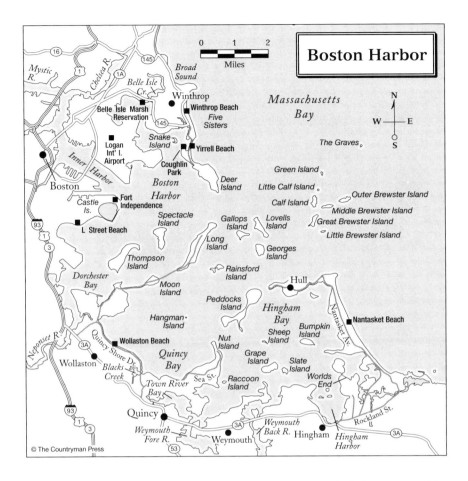

a tank holding molasses intended for rum production exploded or ruptured in Boston's North End. The molasses then flooded and destroyed the surrounding area.

Disproving the widely used description "slower than molasses in January," this accident occurred on January 15, 1919; however, the reported weather was mild, with temperatures in the 40s. A tank holding two and a half million gallons of crude molasses, located about 50 feet above street level, let go, causing buildings in the area to collapse, trapping people. The molasses buried other people as they tried to outrun it. The black, sticky mass was said to have flowed through the area at a speed of 35 miles per hour, creating a wall of molasses 8 feet high. The devastation took more than two weeks to clean up. It is said that even today, on warm summer days, the faint, sweet odor of molasses can still be detected in that section of Boston.

Fishing Boston Harbor today is far different than it was during colonial times. The shoreline of colonial Boston is now a number of city blocks inland from the current waterfront. Since 1630, the land area of Boston has tripled. The three large hills that dominated the landscape of colonial Boston are not recognizable today. Pemberton, Beacon, and Mount Vernon are all but gone, reduced by 60 feet or more from their original height. Most of the material was used as landfill. Areas of Boston like Back Bay, Charlestown, and the Fenway all came to be by way of this landfill effort.

The maps of Boston, as it was in 1630, show it located on a peninsula, with a narrow approach to the main portion of the city. The first major construction, as the city began to evolve, was Long Wharf, which extended nearly half a mile out into the harbor. To understand the scope and magnitude of the effort required to produce the Boston shoreline of today, you need but look at the size difference between colonial Boston and more modern times. In 1630 Boston's total size was a mere 783 acres, as compared to 1,904 acres in 1910. The Boston waterfront of 1630 is located several city blocks from where today's waterfront sits.

During those early days of our country, saltwater fishing meant commercial fishing. Fish from the sea has been and still is a New England industry. Saltwater fly fishing in New England has a long history, as well. In his book *Profiles in Saltwater Angling,* George Reiger tells of the first American to write about saltwater recreational angling; more importantly, he used fly-fishing tackle. This pioneer was Jerome V. C. Smith, a medical doctor and amateur naturalist who, in 1833, authored *Natural History of the Fishes of Massachusetts.* As Reiger notes, Dr. Smith was primarily a freshwater angler who was using the fly tackle of the day to pursue trout and salmon. Fishing back then was a leisure-class activity and almost exclusively a freshwater sport, since the pursuit of saltwater fish was solely a commercial endeavor. However, for some years in the early 1800s, Dr. Smith lived on a small island in Boston Harbor and caught striped bass while fly fishing for sea-run brook trout at a location he called Poket Point. Dr. Smith even suggested that the Atlantic mackerel, which was plentiful in his day, could provide some angling sport on fly tackle. Anyone who has hooked a mackerel on a 5- or 6-weight outfit knows Smith's observation to be a slight understatement.

Over the years the growth and development of Boston and surrounding communities took their toll on the waters that Dr. Smith once fished. By the 1980s Boston Harbor had gained an unwanted reputation worldwide as one of the most polluted bodies of water in the country. The primary source of the problem was the antiquated Massachusetts Water Resources Authority (MWRA) sewage treatment facilities at Deer Island. Every time there was heavy rain or the plant had a breakdown, which was frequently, raw sewage overflowed into Boston Harbor. Everyone agreed that something had to done, and done fast.

A plan was developed that called for the replacement of the existing effluent discharge lines in Boston Harbor and the construction of a new, modern sewage treatment facility at Deer Island. The replacement for the old discharge lines was a new pipe that can pump up to 1.2 billion gallons of treated sewage or effluent per day, from 43 communities, into the Stellwagen Basin section of Massachusetts Bay. The new line or pipe is an engineering marvel, but when you read the word pipe, it may be misleading. It is 24 feet in diameter or nearly the size of the Callahan Tunnel, which connects downtown Boston with Logan Airport.

The new Deer Island plant was completed and went into operation just a few years ago, and in just that short time a big change has occurred in Boston Harbor. The water in the harbor cleared, and it didn't take long for the marine life to respond. Soon the fishing in and around Boston Harbor was getting a lot of press. The word was out that the fishing in Boston Harbor had become some of the best in New England.

If you are at all familiar with fly fishing Boston Harbor, then you know that no one knows more about these waters than Jack Gartside. Jack is a well-known fly tier, fly fisherman, and author of the best guidebook to fly fishing the area, *The Fly Fisherman's Guide to Boston Harbor.* As a youngster, Jack's love of fly tying began with a lesson from none other than fly angler and Red Sox slugger Ted Williams. Jack's book is a must read for anyone wanting to fly fish Boston Harbor.

I have known Jack for some time but wanted to sit down and talk with him about fly fishing Boston Harbor and his thoughts about the area. Since he has been fishing the 186 miles of Boston Harbor's shoreline for nearly 50 years, who better to ask about it? Jack agreed to meet me in Winthrop for lunch, discuss Boston Harbor fly fishing, and then fish some spots in the afternoon and early evening. It turned out to be a day I'll remember for quite a while.

Driving into Boston I wondered if the afternoon was going to be an exercise in futility. It was bright and sunny, with the temperature already near 90 and expected to hit 95. It was not my image of a day to catch striped bass. Jack was to prove me wrong.

One of the first questions I had for Jack related to the weather and chances of getting any pictures of fish that day. Jack just gave me his well-known grin and informed me that one of the largest striped bass he had ever taken, which was better than 40 inches in length, was caught on a bright, sunny afternoon, somewhere between noon and 2 o'clock, and in shallow water.

I was very surprised at his answer and expressed some doubt. However, Jack explained why this was so. He asked, "Are fish more active in low light? Of course they are, because the baitfish are more active in low light. But that doesn't mean they are inactive during the bright, daylight hours. They [striped bass] are opportunistic. If they have the deep water, they can move into the shallows and feed when it is best for them and then retreat very quickly to the deeper, cooler water." He went on to remind me that this is one of the main characteristics of many locations around Boston Harbor.

To underscore his lunchtime statement, later that afternoon at the first location we stopped, and within 15 minutes, Jack landed a nice bass. I stood there after taking some pictures and shook my head. Here we were at low tide, on a summer's day so hot that most people were hiding with a cool drink, and I was looking down at a nice striper. Jack Gartside made me a believer.

During our lunch, Jack offered good advice for the angler new to a location. "Learn an area and how it fishes. You can transfer that knowledge to another location with the same characteristics."

We talked about the various species of baitfish that are in Boston Harbor and the flies to use. Jack felt that you don't have to closely imitate the local baitfish to catch striped bass. He noted, "Smelt, herring, mackerel, and menhaden are schooling-type fish. It is just mere chance that you come across them while shore fishing in Boston Harbor. Therefore, I do not use flies that imitate them."

I was a bit skeptical about that but I also knew that Jack was consistently successful when it came to fishing Boston Harbor. His many interviews in magazines and newspapers were testimony to that. My face may have shown some doubt, however, because he added, "Bass will feed on the mussel beds, and the shrimp, crabs, and worms there, but they will still take the right fly presented in the right way, even though it might not resemble a crab, shrimp, or worm. They are opportunistic feeders." I fully agree with him.

I wanted to know what was the best indicator in determining a locale to fish in Boston Harbor. Jack gave me a very simple yet informative answer. He said, "If you have mussel beds and deep water nearby, then you have a good location to fish."

We also talked about the numerous places worldwide that Jack has fished, in both fresh and salt water. I knew he was also a very experienced trout fisherman so I asked him if a trout fisherman makes a good saltwater fly fisherman. He replied, "Yes, but let me qualify that by saying a good trout fisherman will make a good saltwater fly fisherman." He added that to have positive results when saltwater fly fishing, first and foremost the fish must be present; second, you can't spook them, you must use the right fly; and lastly, you must make the proper presentation and retrieve. This sure sounds like someone who has also done some trout fishing.

Another of Jack Gartside's general rules for Boston Harbor is that estuaries and their mouths are the best places to fish in spring. During the summer and fall, look for cooler, deeper water that is close to a shallow area. If there are mussel beds in the area, all the better. Overall, Jack likes to fish the last two hours of a dropping tide through the first two hours of the rise.

There was one more thing that added to that day with Jack Gartside, besides proving to me that you can catch bass on a sunny, hot afternoon. During our lunch he noted that you should pay special attention to the last 30 feet of your retrieve. He went on to tell me that he catches most of his bass when his fly is less than 30 feet from the tip of his rod. Once again I was skeptical, but said nothing. While fishing later that afternoon, he made me a believer again, and a member of the Jack Gartside fan club. Not only did he hook striped bass less than 30 feet out, but I watched him catch bass as close as 12 feet from the tip of his rod, not once but several times.

The fishing season in and around Boston Harbor begins about mid-May when the striped bass show up. The first fish are the smaller schoolies, which are soon followed by the larger fish. The bass will be around all summer and into fall. Look for them to leave around the first to the middle of November. Some bass do winter over in the harbor, as they do in other New England locations. Look for bluefish to show several weeks after the bass. They will be around until the first of October or later if the weather remains mild. However, bluefish are rare in the inner harbor because the water is normally too cold for them. But they will, on occasions in late summer or early fall, venture into the inner bays chasing schools of bait.

Though not considered a fly-rod game fish, you can occasionally catch a cod when fishing around deepwater structure. Early and late in the season are when the chances of this happening are the highest.

Striped bass and bluefish have a large and varied food source in Boston Harbor to please them. Some are seasonal visitors, while others are resident year-round. Herring arrive in spring and will be present until fall. Their heaviest concentration is in spring, during their spawning runs into local estuaries. The blueback herring is the most abundant of the herrings.

Silversides are the most prevalent bait in Boston Harbor. They are around throughout most of the fishing season. Sand eels are also found in the sandy areas of the harbor, primarily the shallow bays. Mackerel, which will feed on both the silversides and sand eels, show up in May. They are found in the deeper water, and for the most part in the outer harbor. If you come across a school of mackerel, you're in for a grand time catching them on a fly rod.

You will start to see schools of menhaden toward the end of summer, and they will be the number one item on the menu until October. Striped bass have a particular fondness for peanut bunker.

You do have the opportunity to catch pollock in Boston Harbor. Like cod, they will be in the deeper water. The smaller sizes of this fish are not only a food source for blues and bass, but also a great fish to catch on a fly rod. If you think they're around, try using white-and-yellow or green-and-white flies.

Crabs and shrimp are year-round residents and a staple of striped bass. One of the primary places that bass look for these goodies is around mussel beds. Shrimp are also in and around the marsh areas of small bays and estuaries.

Boston Harbor Islands

Before discussing specific fly-fishing locations around Boston, I want to reiterate that Jack Gartside's *Fly Fisherman's Guide to Boston Harbor* is a must for anyone wanting to learn more about the numerous fishing destination around Boston Harbor. The book covers the area from Winthrop to Hull, including the Boston Harbor Islands.

The islands of Boston Harbor are a national park area; it is officially known as Boston Harbor Islands National Recreation Area. It is a unique arrangement whereby the 30 islands are managed by a partnership of 13 members. Some of those include the National Park Service, U.S. Coast Guard, Massachusetts Water Resources Authority, Massachusetts Department of Environmental Management, Massachusetts Port Authority, Metropolitan District Commission, City of Boston, The Trustees of Reservations, Boston Redevelopment Authority, Thompson Island Outward Bound Education Center, and Boston Harbor Islands Advisory Council.

It was bright and sunny, with temperatures pushing 95 degrees. It was not my image of a day to catch striped bass. Jack Gartside was to prove me wrong.

Ferries that run from downtown Boston, Hull, Hingham, and Quincy, plus Salem on the North Shore, provide access to a number of these islands. In-season there are regularly scheduled ferries that connect to Georges Island, and from there, water shuttles take visitors to some of the other islands. During the day there is ferry service available to Georges, Lovells, Peddocks, Grape, Bumpkin, Gallops, and Great Brewster Islands, whose shorelines you can wade and fish. These services can change from year to year, so it's best to check by calling the park information at 617-223-8666. Another way to learn more about these beautiful islands is go online to www.BostonIslands.com.

Certain islands do permit tent camping from early May through the Columbus Day weekend, in October. As of this writing, camping was available on Lovells, Grape, Peddocks, and Bumpkin Islands. Some sites are free, while there is a nominal fee to use others. To find out which islands are open for camping and the numbers to call to secure your camping permit, again, call 617-223-8666 for park information.

For planning purposes, when fishing the shorelines of these islands you'll encounter either rocky structure, cobblestone beaches, gravel beaches, coarse sand beaches, or combinations thereof. The only true sandy beach is on Lovells Island. There is no drinking water available on the islands, so make sure to bring your own. There is also a carry-in/carry-out policy since there are no trash receptacles on any of the islands.

Two islands that have camping and good fishing are Lovells and Peddocks. There is no charge to camp on Lovells Island; you can secure reservations by calling Boston Harbor Island State Park at 617-727-7676. One of the best locations to fish on the island is the southern end. A bar or spit of land extends out quite a ways at low tide there. However, this is one of those places where you have to be very aware of the tide times. It is best fished from two hours before low to two hours into the rising tide. Staying out there any later means you could become cut off, with a strong current to deal with. Fish both sides of the point, depending upon the wind, when going out and coming back. This location can be very good in June and July on a dropping tide in the early morning or evening.

To request a camping reservation on Peddocks Island, you need to call the same number as above to get your camping permit; camping is free here, as well. This is one of the larger islands in the group, and like Lovells Island is the site of an old fort. The forts on the islands were built to defend Boston Harbor.

With the amount of shoreline that Peddocks has, there are a number of locations to fish and a variety of shorelines. The good news is that maps of the islands are available; this will help a first-time angler to explore and find the better fishing spots. At the north end of the island, where the old fort is located and where you'll arrive by ferry, are some nice mussel beds, and to make it even better, they're close to deep water. When you arrive by ferry and before you head for those mussel beds, spend some time fishing the deep water near the pier. A sinking line that will take your fly to the bottom of this large, deep hole would be the choice here.

You will find both striped bass and bluefish around this island, with the summer months providing the best chance to catch both species. In spring look for mackerel and herring to be the target of both; often this bait is gone by July, as the water warms. But there is enough other bait to keep the predators happy. In late summer and early fall the bass and blues will turn their attention to the peanut bunker when they show up.

At the southern end of the island is Prince Head, which is a long, gravel point. You'll want to fish the end of the point at low water. Besides a steep drop-off within casting range, a rip often forms here. This spot will have fish hanging in the deeper water, even at dead low.

The Boston Harbor Islands are excellent destinations for the fly fisherman—close to the city and very easy to reach. There is not only the opportunity to fish some great locations, but also much to explore and see on these islands. For the camping enthusiast, you have access to several islands where you'll be able to fish at any time of the day or night. So whether a day visitor or a camper, as a fly angler you'll have access to some unique fishing.

Winthrop

Back on the mainland, and to the north, the town of Winthrop sits between Logan Airport and Boston Harbor, and the open waters of the Atlantic. Jack Gartside introduced me to this area; if you fish here on a regular basis, you stand a good chance of running into him somewhere along the shoreline.

To reach Winthrop, leave downtown Boston via the Callahan Tunnel as if you were going to Logan Airport. However, stay on MA 1A past the airport and take the exit for MA 145 north. Follow MA 145 and the signs for Winthrop. Just before you enter Winthrop, you will come upon the bridge for Belle Isle Creek. The marshes to your left, up from the bridge, can be a good spot, especially early in the season. You'll have to park on the street, where space is available. Striped bass will move in and out of here with the tide, and this is one of those locations where a grass shrimp fly can pay off.

Going into Winthrop, continue on MA 145 through Winthrop. Pleasant Street will become Washington Avenue, and at the stop sign, when you cross Shirley Street, it will be Sturgis Street; this short block leads you to Winthrop Shore Drive. Once there, you can't miss the most obvious structures along that part of the shoreline. Just offshore are five stone breakwaters that run parallel to the beach. These are called The Five Sisters.

The Five Sisters are situated parallel to the shore as protection to that beach. They're also great structures that attract a variety of fish. These breakwaters can be reached at the lower stages of the tide by traveling over a number of gravel bars. Key in on the ends of these breakwaters where the water moves in and out with the tides, as well as the large pockets of water behind the structures. The combination of gravel bars, pockets of deep water, and mussel beds makes this a good fishing destination. Don't ignore the deeper holes where the bass may be holding during the lower stages of the tide, waiting for the incoming water.

Though mackerel, pollock, and bluefish may venture into these waters, the primary fish here is striped bass. This an ideal environment for them to hunt and find a meal. The two hours before and after low tide will give you access to some fine fishing. One word of caution: Keep an eye on the tide. Don't get caught by a rising tide.

Heading south toward Deer Island you'll find a small, sandy beach called

At the first place we stopped, it was a long walk out just to get to water above my knees. Within 15 minutes, Jack Gartside landed this nice bass and made me a believer in how good the Boston Harbor fishing is.

Yirrell Beach. You can reach this beach by parking on Shirley Street at the seawall or by parking at the end of Winthrop Shore Drive and walking from there. This beach is bounded on the north by some gravel bars that are just off the water tower on Cottage Hill and to the south by the beginning of Deer Island.

Yirrell Beach is easy to wade, and with mussel beds nearby, there's a high probability that you'll find feeding bass in this location. A light easterly wind will push bait into this spot and still allow some wading; but a stronger wind from that direction will produce some good waves. If you can work a fly into that wind, you'll often find the fishing pretty good.

Continuing in a southerly direction on Shirley Street, look for Bayview Avenue and take a right there. On your right will be Coughlin Park, which has some tennis courts and a baseball field. Coughlin Park has a limited number of parking places, so as a second choice, you may have to park on the street when fishing there. If you continue on Bayview, it becomes Grand View Avenue, where you may find parking along the street. You are just across the water from Logan Airport and Boston.

Just offshore from Coughlin Park is a channel that separates the mainland from Snake Island. This is a deep channel with a good deal of boat traffic in summer, but the territory from Coughlin Park to the channel can be very productive. Wading is solid here, and at low water you can get very close to the channel—but watch out for the drop-off. The bottom here is firm with many mussel beds throughout the area; however, be cautious of the deeper holes that are scattered throughout the area. A wrong step can fill your waders.

The beauty of this spot is that you can also work your way toward Deer Island on a dropping tide, and then back on the rise. When Jack Gartside and I were last at this location, he told me that some very large bass have been taken in this section from Coughlin Park, along Grand View Avenue and toward Deer Island. I think that comment alone would make this a must spot to fish in Winthrop.

Castle Island

There are a number of good fishing spots in and around Boston Harbor for the fly angler—and in his book, Jack Gartside has fished and documented every one of them. Therefore, I asked him to select his two top fly-fishing locales for the first-time angler planning to fish the Boston Harbor area. His answer was Castle Island in South Boston and, just down the Southeast Expressway, Blacks Creek in Wollaston.

It's quite simple and easy to reach Castle Island. Driving either north or south on the Southeast Expressway, take the Columbia Road exit. If you were coming out of downtown Boston and going south on the Expressway, at the end of the exit ramp, turn left onto Columbia Road, going over the Expressway to the rotary. Approaching Boston from the south, when you exit the Expressway, turn right at the top of the ramp to the rotary. William J. Day Boulevard will be the second road leading off the rotary. From there you follow the William J. Day Boulevard for just a couple of miles to Castle Island.

On your way to Castle Island, which isn't an island anymore, you will pass the well-known L Street Bath House on the right, as well as several beaches that are situated on Dorchester Bay. Castle Island has a large parking lot at the base of the hill that is the site of Fort Independence. The island received its name from the fact that every fort located here—and there have been more than one—was always known as "The Castle." The first was an earthen fortress with just three cannon. The current pentagon-shaped fortress is made of granite and took 17 years to finish; it was completed in 1851.

Castle Island is a popular place for walkers, joggers, skaters, and people just wanting to get away from the hustle of the city. It's also a very popular destination for fly fishermen. As indicated, Jack rates this destination, which is just a stone's throw from downtown Boston, as one of the best in Boston Harbor. *The Fly Fisherman's Guide to Boston Harbor* provides excellent details on fishing the numerous spots at Castle Island.

Two locations that I think are very good are also the closest ones to the parking lot. The first is the mussel beds, which can be seen at low tide at the beginning of the causeway that curves out and around from Castle Island to City Point and forms Pleasure Bay. You passed City Point on the way to Castle Island, while on Day Boulevard. The mussel beds are just off the shoreline and below the fort. This area is the eastern point of Castle Island, and it has a large area of rocks and mussel beds. What makes this area so good is that it's adjacent to a deep channel—one of the prerequisites for good fishing in Boston Harbor.

Jack's book includes a caution about the boats that travel the channel adjacent to the mussel beds. They often run close enough to produce a good wake. I have witnessed this and, as Jack cautions, don't wade any farther than having the water halfway between your knees and waist. Fish this location

The first culvert on the causeway at Castle Island is a prime striped bass location—and it is within a very short distance of downtown Boston.

on a dropping tide, from near low to just after low since the tide will fill in this area quickly once it starts to rise.

The second location on Castle Island that I like is at the first culvert, out on the causeway. Since this is one of the openings where the water flows into and out of Pleasure Bay, it's an excellent spot for striped bass. Fish the inside of the culvert on the incoming tide and the outside on the drop. The area around the inside section of the culvert is excellent, and the deep hole there is where striped bass will hang, waiting to ambush bait entering on the flow of the incoming tide. Jack refers to this location as the "sugar bowl." The best times of the season to fish the first culvert are in spring and fall.

On an outgoing tide, fish on the opposite side of the culvert, on the outside, facing Boston Harbor. There can be a very strong flow here as the water rushes out of Pleasure Bay. On the higher tides of the full and new moons is when the water will be rolling swiftly through the culvert. When the tide drops down enough to allow wading along this outside section, fish the edges, as well as in the middle of the outflow's current, until you find where the bass are holding. Drifting flies like Jack's BeastMasters, Deceivers, or similar patterns seems to work the best here.

Blacks Creek flows into and out of a pond on the west side of Quincy Shore Drive. Striped bass will pursue herring and silverside into this side of the creek.

Blacks Creek

Jack's other choice for the best fly-fishing destination in Boston Harbor is Blacks Creek. Be prepared to have company when you fish here, because it's a very popular place for anglers. To get to Blacks Creek, drive a bit farther south on the Southeast Expressway and take exit 12; there are signs there for Quincy and Neponset Avenue. As you come down the exit ramp you'll need to bear right and travel under the Expressway. Bear to the right and follow Neponset Avenue over the bridge. Look for the signs for Wollaston Beach and bear to the left off Neponset Avenue, and then onto Quincy Shore Drive.

Stay on Quincy Shore Drive; it will curve to the right along Wollaston Beach. This long beach is a good wade-fishing spot, with parking along the beach side of the street. Working this beach at night on the high tide can provide some good fishing. However, the most popular spot in the area is Blacks Creek, which is at the southern end of Wollaston Beach. The parking lot for Blacks Creek will be on the right, just before the creek itself. You will see the marshes and back part of the creek just before the parking area. The parking lot is mainly for people using the small park adjacent to Blacks Creek, but anglers use it, as well.

The park, whose official name is Caddy Park, is where you can access Blacks Creek and its associated marsh. The park will also have just as many people enjoying the outdoors as those fishing. The park is a historical site of sorts; a rock here holds an inscription that reads, "Black's Creek. Once owned by Edmund Quincy IV. This body of water supported two gristmills in the early 1700's. These tide mills stored water in millponds when the tide was high. The water was slowly released to turn large stones, which crushed grains to make flour. Sold to Black Molasses in 1788, the creek became known as Black's Creek."

This location can be crowded with anglers in May and June when the bass are following herring and silversides into the creek on a rising tide. There will, however, be stripers in the pond all season long, from spring into summer. Wading along the pond's edge is easy since it has a firm bottom. I urge you to scout the pond at low tide to see where the channel and drop-offs are located. A visit at low water will allow you to note where and what structure is covered at high tide. On the flood tide, I would also fish the upper ends of the pond, and work that area from the banks of the marsh. The best times to fish Blacks Creek are early morning and evening.

You can also fish on opposite side of the road from the park where Blacks Creek empties into Quincy Bay. There is a nice hole here that attracts bait, which attracts the striped bass, which in turn attract the anglers. In May and June this location becomes crowded with anglers fishing bait and artificial lures, as well as the fly casters. If you like to fish in a crowd, then enjoy. During the summer, bluefish will be in this area chasing bait like silversides and sand eels. In late summer and early fall the peanut bunker will bring additional action.

Worlds End

Just a bit to the south and east of Quincy is my favorite fly-fishing location on Boston Harbor. This is Worlds End, a picturesque place with a variety of shorelines and fishing possibilities. To reach this spot, which is in Hingham, drive south on MA 3A from Quincy to Hingham. At the rotary in Hingham, just past the harbor, take Summer Street, which will quickly become Rockland Street. A sign at the rotary indicates that this is the way to Nantasket. There will be a traffic light just a short distance down this road; you should turn left at this light. You are now on Martin's Lane and should continue on this road to the end, and the entrance to Worlds End; it's less than a mile from the traffic light to the entrance.

*To the left of the small parking lot outside the gate to Worlds End is Martins
Cove. Stripers will move onto flats here on an incoming tide.*

To reach Worlds End from the south, take the exit for MA 228 off MA
3 and follow the signs for Hingham. This road has many turns as you head
north toward Hingham, so pay close attention to the signs along the way.
When you come to MA 3A in Hingham, turn left there and follow the road
to the rotary. Take the first right off the rotary, where the sign directs you to
Nantasket, and follow the directions above for Worlds End.

This beautiful peninsula is owned and operated by the Trustees of Reservations and is also a part of the Boston Harbor National Park Area, even
though attached to the mainland. Worlds End is just 15 miles from Boston,
and if you like good fishing in picturesque surroundings, this is an outstanding choice.

Just outside the entrance to Worlds End is a small parking lot that will
accommodate three, maybe four cars. This is where you would park after
hours if you wanted to fish here. During operating hours—sunrise to
sunset—a fee is charged to park inside the gate; the last time I was there it
was $4.50. When paying to enter, be sure to ask for the map of Worlds End;
it will be very helpful since it shows the trails of the 251-acre reservation,
with its estimated 5 miles or more of shoreline just waiting for you to fish.

The beauty of this spot is that you can get out of the wind, regardless of its direction. It also has a variety of shoreline and structure to please any angler: rocky structure, sandbars, coarse gravel beaches, channels, clam flats, and mussel beds, all of which are prime striper haunts.

One of the closest locations to fish is just beyond the fence at the small parking lot outside the main gate; this is Martins Cove. The flats here should be fished on the incoming tide as bass move in to see what might be available for food. In his book Jack Gartside notes that this spot is a clamming area; striped bass will move onto the flats with the tide after the diggers have left. So if there are clammers on the flats when you arrive, be patient and fish it when they are done.

Worlds End is a peninsula made up of two major sections of land, separated by a narrow section joining the two. On the official map, the outer section is called Worlds End even though the complete reservation is known by this name. The 251-acre peninsula divides Hingham Harbor from the Weir River. On the Weir River side look for the fishing to begin in late April or early May, when herring are moving up the river. You can bet the bass will not be far behind. This is when patterns that mimic the herring work best.

This is an area that will take time to learn. When working this shoreline in search of fish, it's not a bad idea to make note of when and where you found fish. There is good structure here along with moving water and deeper-water locations, such as the narrow channel of the river, where the bass can move in and out with the tide.

As the season progresses, the diet for the striped bass will change to silversides and other small baitfish that inhabit the Weir. My advice is take some time to explore this shoreline at low water. Considering the amount of shoreline present, it may take several trips to accomplish this. Take notes and observe the location of key structure. This is a spot that is worthy of your time. If you take a few scouting trips in very early spring, you will be ready when the stripers arrive.

Before he passed away, Percy Gilbert gave me one of his shrimp flies, which is shown in this book's color insert. He noted that estuaries like this are prime places to use such a fly. It is a pattern that's often overlooked but can very productive in estuary and marsh environments. You should give the fly very little or no movement; instead, let the current carry it along, with maybe a few small twitches. Depending upon the water depth and speed of the current, use an intermediate or floating line. In locations where the current is swifter and the water deeper, you might want to try a slow-sinking or a sinking-tip line with a shrimp fly.

At the outer end of Worlds End, you can wade out to the edge of channel of the Weir River for bass—but be sure to do this on a dropping tide. You'll also need to keep a close eye on the tide since you'll want to retreat toward the shore as the tide begins to rise. Don't forget to fish the water between the bars that extend from shore both going out and returning. As the tide fills, fishing over these bars can often be productive.

Worlds End has so many fine fly-fishing spots that you may be hard pressed to learn them all in a season. But take the time to learn about as many as you can. This gem of a spot offers outstanding fishing opportunities in a most picturesque setting. This is what fly fishing is all about.

CHAPTER 9

The North and South Shores

In Massachusetts, the coastline that extends from Boston to the north and south is known as the North Shore and South Shore, respectively. These two regions have become bedroom communities for Boston's workforce. The towns in these coastal sections have seen their populations grow at a rapid rate. The North Shore is a bit ahead of the South Shore in its expanding urban sprawl. With this growth came the demand for development of more and more land. Prime property, especially that with a water view, has been snapped up at a rapid rate. One direct result of this coastal development is that shoreline access for anglers has dramatically decreased along both the North and South Shores.

There are some fine locations for fly fishing along the North Shore, but not as many as you might expect given the amount of coastline that runs from Revere to Salisbury. Over the years the development planning didn't take into account the need for such facilities. Therefore, areas with access are often restricted to town residents; other, public sites can only support one or two anglers. There are spots that I've been asked not to include in this book, given concerns that the publicity might create an increase in anglers and cars parking nearby. This situation usually results in neighbors complaining and then the town putting greater restrictions on fishermen.

Access should be the concern of every shorebound angler. As locations are lost, there are fewer and fewer places to fish. There are a number of things that we can do to maintain what few accesses there are. First, be courteous and obey the local parking laws. Keep the locations clean; that means even picking up trash that the fisherman before you may have left. Though your predecessor was inconsiderate, all anglers will suffer from his actions, so picking up the garbage he left is helping not only yourself but all of us, as well. And lastly, get involved in organizations that are working to preserve coastal access for angling and other outdoor activities.

I was involved in a fishing trip a while back that brought home to me how difficult it can be to find access to the shoreline on the North Shore. One day Bob Mitchell and I were having coffee and doughnuts before heading out to fish along the North Shore. While discussing options, Bob mentioned a spot that had been an outstanding striper producer. He admitted that he hadn't fished it in some years but felt that this rocky point would be worth the drive. So off we went to fish Bass Point, a location in Nahant.

Bob couldn't believe what we saw when we got there. The whole rocky point had been developed, with a fence between the private property and the street. As we continued on we came across a small park that was on a point with a view to the south and the Boston Harbor Islands. This was an ideal angling spot, with convenient parking and outstanding fishing structure. However, signs indicated that I needed a town sticker to park there. The next day when I made some calls to Nahant, I found out that Nahant residents were the only ones who could use this location.

The North Shore

Still, there's some good news for shorebound fly rodders fishing the North Shore. Let me tell you about some excellent fly-fishing locations here—spots where you *will* catch fish and you *won't* be looking over your shoulder for local authorities asking you to move. The first is in Marblehead; in fact, there are several good fly-fishing locations there, all within a short driving distance of each other.

Driving north on MA 1A from Boston, you will take a right onto MA 129 in East Lynn, just before entering Swampscott. This is Atlantic Avenue; continue north on it to Marblehead. At Ocean Avenue, turn right, and in a

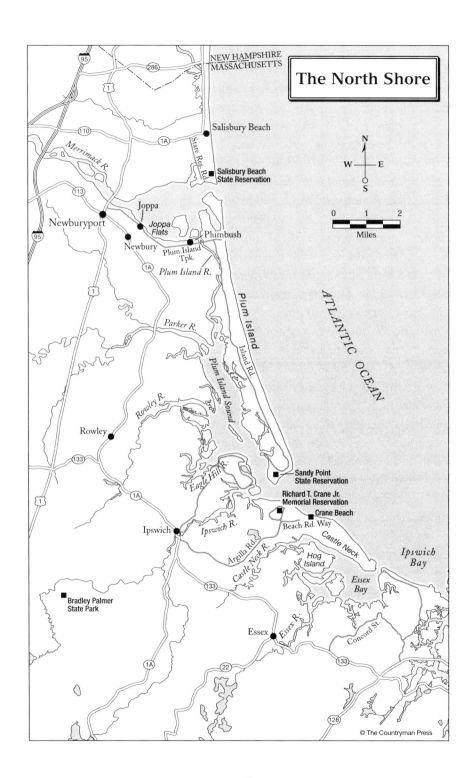

The North Shore

NEW HAMPSHIRE
MASSACHUSETTS

Salisbury Beach

Salisbury Beach
State Reservation

Joppa
Newburyport
Joppa
Flats
Plumbush
Newbury
Plum Island
Tpk.
Plum Island R.

Merrimack R.

Plum Island

Island Rd.

ATLANTIC OCEAN

Parker R.

Plum Island Sound

Rowley R.

Rowley

Eagle Hill R.

Sandy Point
State Reservation

Richard T. Crane Jr.
Memorial Reservation
Crane Beach

Ipswich
Ipswich R.
Beach Rd. Way

Castle Neck

Hog
Island

Ipswich
Bay

Argilla Rd.

Castle Neck R.

Essex
Bay

Bradley Palmer
State Park

Essex
Essex R.

Concord St.

N
W E
S

0   1   2
Miles

© The Countryman Press

very short distance you'll come to Devereux Beach. The entrance to the beach and its parking lot will be on your right. Devereux is a large, sandy beach just before the causeway to Marblehead Neck. During the summer months you will have to pay to park here.

Devereux Beach is an excellent striped bass location with a lot of fine structure. The best spot to fish is to your left as you face the water, toward the causeway and the rocks. There is a bar just offshore that you should fish at low tide. Work your way out as the tide drops, fishing as you go; then, as the tide turns, fish your way back. Fishing along the front of the causeway and farther to your left, you can make your way to Marblehead Neck and its rocky shoreline. You should fish that first point at low water. It is private property along this section of shoreline, but if you stay below the high-water mark you can fish such private shorelines.

Leaving Devereux Beach and driving to the other end of causeway on Ocean Avenue and into Marblehead Neck, you'll find street parking to fish this same point. You can then walk back toward the causeway and gain access to the rocky shoreline of the point. That access point is between the first house on the street and the end of causeway. As noted, you should fish this area at low tide. A key piece of information is that the street parking has a two-hour limit, but that should be enough to get in some good bass fishing.

Stripers are regularly caught in this section of water from Devereux Beach to the beginning shoreline of Marblehead Neck. In spring, fish sand eel patterns and small Deceivers. As the season progresses, throw poppers in the early morning and evening, when the water surface is the calmest.

While in Marblehead Neck, you should also fish Castle Rock. Just continue on Ocean Avenue for about $1^{1}/_{2}$ miles from the causeway, and look for a small brown sign with white lettering on the right side of the street, indicating the location of Castle Rock. It's just past a large house with a wrought-iron fence. This is a residential neighborhood, and the only parking is on the street. Castle Rock is at the end of a path that goes between private homes, so be quiet, leave no mess, and respect the neighbors. These are always good practices for the responsible angler.

Castle Rock is a good bass location but with limited fishing space available. You can fish on either side of point, though the left side is the better one; there is a steep descent and climb back on right side. On the left side of the point is a beach of small stones that forms a small cove with large rocks to the right and left. On low tide, a second small cove will form to the left of the beach. You can walk to it, but you need to keep an eye on the incoming tide.

Top to bottom: Sand Eel tied by Jack Gartside; Shrimp Fly by Percy Gilbert; Soft Hackle Streamer, "Secret" Soft Hackle Deceiver, Gartside Gurgler, and Blue/White Beastmaster flies created by Jack Gartside.

*Top to bottom: Two Clouser Deep Minnows; Half & Half tied by Captain Tom Koerber;
Lefty's Deceiver; Two Rat's Arse flies originated and tied by Harry Koons;
Four Penny Fly originated by Tony Penny, tied by Al Brewster; Fuzzy Bugger
originated and tied by Chip Bergeron.*

Top to bottom: Grocery Fly (yellow, green, and black) tied by Brock Apfel; Grocery Fly (white with dark back) tied by Brock Apfel; Bunker Fly tied by Bob Mitchell; Bunny Fly tied by Bob Mitchell; Jim's Grocery Pollock Fly tied by Jim Bernstein; Surf Candy originated by Bob Popovics, tied by Bob Mitchell; Lobster Fly tied by Dr. M. Wiener.

Top to bottom: Razzle-Dazzle originated and tied by J. Kenney Abrames; Gibbs Striper Fly originated by Harold Gibbs, tied by Steve Cook; Papie's Special originated and tied by Al Brewster; White-Water Witch originated by Ray Smith, tied by Captain Eric Thomas; Rhody Flatwing by Bill Peabody; Ray's Fly originated by Ray Bondorew.

You will find a strong surf pushing in and around the point, creating a backwash that attracts feeding stripers. This is an excellent spring location, and some nice-sized bass have been caught here. Though a prime location in May and June, you'll find striped bass here all season long, with October being a strong month.

As you proceed north and approach the New Hampshire border, several outstanding destinations for the fly angler offer a variety of fishing opportunities. The first such place is Crane Beach. Besides having the distinction of being one of the best beaches in New England for swimming, it also has a reputation as a fine fishing spot. I have seen a picture of a 40-pound striper that was taken on a fly rod from Crane Beach a couple of years ago. Every year some nice fish are caught here.

Crane Beach is a very easy location to reach. As you are driving north on MA 1A from MA 128 in Beverly, you will pass through Hamilton; as you enter Ipswich, look for Argilla Road on your right. Turn there and take this road to the Richard T. Crane Memorial Reservation. If you are coming south on MA 1A from Rowley, you'll turn left onto Argilla Road as you leave Ipswich. Argilla Road will become Beach Road Way and take you to the entrance for Crane Beach.

Crane Beach is not only one of the best bathing beaches in New England, it is also a top fishing location.

There is a fee to park at the beach, regardless of what time of year it is. When I was last there the charge was only $5 to park in a very large lot, which is needed for the summer crowds. The gates to the lot close at sunset, but you can still fish here at night. You first need to go to the Ipswich Town Hall—it's located at 25 Green Street—and get a fishing permit, which will allow you to fish at night. You then can park in the small area on the circle just outside the main gate after they close. The gate attendant assured me that the police would not ticket anyone with a permit. For more information, contact Ipswich Town Hall at 978-356-6600 or the Richard T. Crane Memorial Reservation at 978-356-4351.

One of the biggest problems you will have at Crane Beach is where to fish. There is a long, sandy beach that runs north and south from the parking lot. Essex Bay is to your right and south of the lot. To your left, as you cross the dunes, you can see the tip of Plum Island and the strait between Crane Beach and Plum Island.

That water between Plum Island and Crane Beach is fine fishing. There is good, moving water, created by Plum Island Sound, the Parker, Ipswich, and Rowley Rivers, plus some other smaller estuaries that all come together and empty into the Atlantic at this point. This is an excellent area to fish, particularly on the dropping tide.

Essex Bay, which is about 3 miles to the south, is a long walk but worth it. The Essex River, Castle Neck River, and some other smaller estuaries all feed into the bay. At low tide there is a very narrow channel at the tip of Castle Neck, which is where Crane Beach is located. You can fish this channel for striped bass throughout the season, with spring and fall being the best times. When fishing here, watch the tide closely, since it floods into the bay quickly. The rising water can fill in behind you and cut off your route back to the beach if you're not careful. Caution is the key here, because you're dealing with the current, holes, and drop-offs; it can be a dangerous spot. My best recommendation is to fish this channel and bay at least once at low water and in the daylight to see the hazards. Also wear some sort of flotation device like the suspender-type that anglers are beginning to use.

Crane Beach has a great amount of area to fish, from Essex Bay to Fox Creek, which is to your left and around the point. Don't ignore the beach out front, though; not only does it offer good striped bass fishing, but blues often show up, chasing schools of bait. The beach has good structure with a series of bowls and small points formed by the currents from both north and south, plus the surf. In fall peanut bunker will get pushed into the surf on light easterly winds. When this happens, bass like that 40-pounder will make an appearance.

Fishing this area does require a good bit of walking. It's 3 miles south to the tip of Castle Neck and the opening of Essex Bay, and a mile or so north to Fox Creek. You should be prepared to take a minimum amount of gear but still be able to handle the different fishing situations. Take extra flies, pretied leaders, and spare spools with different line—one with intermediate line and one filled with sinking line.

As noted, you can see Plum Island from Crane Beach; this is another outstanding North Shore destination. To get there, drive back into Ipswich and then turn left onto MA 1A, heading north to Newburyport. As you are entering Newbury, turn right at the first traffic light, which is Rolfes Lane; you will see a sign for Plum Island and the Parker River National Wildlife Refuge. The road will end in less than half a mile and you'll turn right onto Water Street, which comes from the center of Newburyport. Water Street will become the Plum Island Turnpike and take you onto Plum Island.

Just before the bridge that crosses over the Plum Island River you'll see a small parking area on your right. If you pull off and park there, you have an easy access to fish the banks of the river. Give this spot a try—it's good estuary fishing and an excellent striper location.

This location was recently opened through the hard work of the Coastal Conservation Associations of Massachusetts and New Hampshire, plus the Plum Island Surfcasters and other organizations that included the Parker River National Wildlife Refuge and the U.S. Fish & Wildlife Service. The last time I was there with Bob Mitchell—one of those who worked on this project—he noted that this location will remain open for fishing only if it's kept clean. We as anglers should not only keep this spot clean, but also all the places we fish. We're already losing access to fishing through development; let's not lose access through our thoughtlessness and disregard for the environment, and other people's property.

Once you reach Plum Island, take your first right. This road, after a short drive, will bring you to the gatehouse for the Parker River National Wildlife Refuge. The refuge is open from sunrise to sunset, but you can get a permit to fish at night as well as one to travel the beach. There are allowances for beach access that depend upon bird nesting; contact the Parker River NWR at 978-465-5753 for the latest regulations for beach use and fishing.

There is a fee to enter the refuge—$5 when I was last there. However, I have been told that if you have a valid federal duck stamp, you can avoid this

Though heavily populated and developed, there are locations on the North Shore that have been preserved for public use, including fishing.

fee. You should also be aware that if you are seeking a permit to drive the beach, it must be a conventional four-wheel-drive pickup truck or sport-utility vehicle with the proper safety equipment, plus you must possess a rod and reel. In other words, these permits are strictly for fishing purposes. Also, while at the gatehouse, make sure you get a map that shows all access trails and parking lots, which are numbered.

Though this is primarily striped bass territory, you will find bluefish along the ocean side during the summer and early fall. In late spring and fall you'll find good striper fishing in the surf. In autumn schools of small bunker will attract the predators. That action will be easy to find; all you have to do is look for the birds—and enjoy.

The water behind the island also has good bass fishing. At Parking Lot 3, there is a spot that the locals call "high sandy"; there in the river on the backside are some worm beds. Striped bass will often be in there, rooting around on the flats and feeding during low light and at night. Farther down the island, between Parking Lots 6 and 7, is Emerson Rocks. There is great fly fishing around the rocks from the last few hours of the dropping tide through the first hours of the rise.

At the southern end of Plum Island is Sandy Point State Reservation.

From this point you are looking south, across the water to Crane Beach. Sandy Point is open from April 1 through October 15; no access fee is charged at the gatehouse if you proceed directly to Sandy Point and do not stop in the Parker River NWR. You have beach access via two trails except when birds are nesting on beach. The fishing here is quite good, especially on the outgoing tide.

When you leave Plum Island and head back to Newburyport on Water Street, you'll pass an outstanding fly-fishing location. Joppa Flats is a well-known destination with access to the Merrimack River. To fish Joppa Flats, park along Water Street at the seawall. This location is best during the last few hours of the dropping tide and first few of the rise. Check out the flats at low water so you can see what type of structure you are fishing. Look for and fish the drop-off that runs in a wide arc from the yacht club to Woodbridge Island. This is an early-season location, with the best striper fishing in June.

There is one more North Shore location that I want to tell you about: Salisbury Beach. From the Joppa Flats, continue on Water Street into Newburyport and turn right onto US 1, which will take you north over the bridge that spans the Merrimack River. When you reach Salisbury, turn right onto MA 1A, which is also Beach Road, and head east toward Salisbury Beach. At State Reservation Road turn right and drive south into the Salisbury Beach State Reservation.

Salisbury Beach State Reservation is more than 500 acres in size, with nearly 4 miles of beach that faces the Atlantic Ocean and the mouth of the Merrimack River. If you're interested in doing some camping along with your fishing, this destination, with nearly 500 sites, has very good facilities. However, because it's such a popular camping location, you'll need to make your reservations well in advance. I have been told that people reserve spots a year or more ahead of time. For more information and to secure reservations, call 877-422-6762.

You can purchase a seasonal pass to Salisbury Beach; if you want to fish there just for the day, there is a daily fee. Early in spring and in fall you can fish the ocean side, but during the summer the number of people using the beach can make this difficult. For the best striper fishing, concentrate your efforts at the mouth of the Merrimack River. Fish from just inside the jetty to the large pyramid marker called "The Toothpick." You cannot fish on the jetty itself because it's very dangerous, even on the calmest of days. Take the time to carefully work this shoreline from the jetty to the marker, and even beyond the launch ramp into Black Rock Creek.

The South Shore

Often it's the people we meet while fishing that play the biggest part in our fishing memories. Such is the case when I think of the South Shore. My thoughts are of a gentle man who gave me a fly that he had tied, not long before he passed away. Percy Gilbert, whom I met at the Rod Builder's Workshop in Kingston, had tied a shrimp fly for me to use in this book. It wasn't an expensive gift, but to me it is priceless because I remember the advice he gave me about how to fish it. I will also remember the light that shone in his eyes as he held the fly; it was his love of fly fishing that sparkled there as he explained when and where to fish his fly. I received not only a fly that day, but also the kindness of someone who had been sharing his love of fly fishing with anglers in and around Boston for many years.

Not that far south of Worlds End is one of the first locations on the South Shore that I'd like to tell you about—Peggotty Beach in Scituate. You can get there either by traveling south on MA 3A from Hingham or—if you're on MA 3 traveling either north or south—taking exit 13 in Hanover. Drive north on MA 53 for half a mile to the traffic light and intersection with MA 123. Turn right there and travel on MA 123 through Norwell and to the traffic light at MA 3A, which will be a distance of about $5\frac{1}{2}$ miles. Driving on MA 3A from the rotary in Hingham, it's 8 miles to the point where MA 123 ends at MA 3A.

If you're traveling south on MA 3A, turn left at the traffic light for the intersection where MA 123 ends at MA 3A; if you're on MA 123, go across MA 3A. As soon you do this, you must make an immediate right onto Driftway. This road will take you past the Widow's Walk Golf Course, which will be on your left. In a bit over 2 miles, you will approach Scituate Harbor and come to a stop sign. At this point Driftway is called Kent Street.

At the stop sign, turn right onto Edward Foster Road and go over the bridge to a small, triangular traffic island. At that traffic island bear right onto Peggotty Beach Road. Almost immediately, there is a right turn for the parking lot at Peggotty Beach. Though this is a town beach, you shouldn't be bothered if you're fishing. Leave a note on your dashboard for the police, telling them you're fishing.

As you reach the top of the walkway to the beach, stop for a second and survey the area. This is a fine striped bass location. You will see a sandy beach that forms a large bowl and has rock seawalls at each end. This is the type of structure where predators love to trap bait. In late summer and early fall look

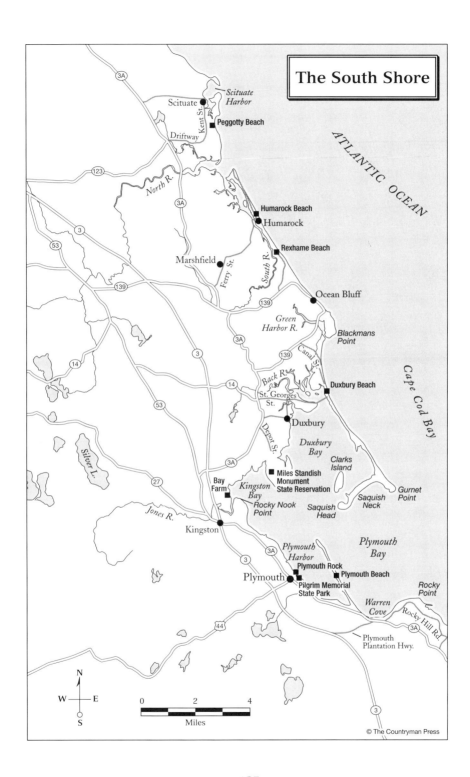

The South Shore

Scituate

Scituate Harbor

Kent St.

Peggotty Beach

Driftway

3A

ATLANTIC OCEAN

123

North R.

3A

Humarock Beach

Humarock

3

53

Rexhame Beach

Marshfield

Ferry St.

South R.

139

Ocean Bluff

139

Green Harbor R.

3A

Blackmans Point

3

Canal St.

14

Back R.

14

Duxbury Beach

53

St. Georges St.

Duxbury

Cape Cod Bay

Depot St.

Duxbury Bay

Clarks Island

3A

■ **Miles Standish Monument State Reservation**

Silver L.

27

Bay Farm

Kingston Bay

Rocky Nook Point

Saquish Head

Saquish Neck

Gurnet Point

Jones R.

Kingston

Plymouth Bay

3A

Plymouth Harbor

3

Plymouth Rock

Plymouth Beach

Plymouth

Rocky Point

Pilgrim Memorial State Park

Warren Cove

Rocky Hill Rd.

44

3A

Plymouth Plantation Hwy.

N

W—E

S

0   2   4

Miles

3

© The Countryman Press

The South Shore has a variety of shorelines to fish. The varied structure along this section of the coast is what makes the angling so good.

for menhaden along this beach. At that time, Deceivers or similar patterns that mimic the bunker are your best choice. Even if you see no signs of these schools of menhaden, work the area until you find the bass. Time your trips to fish Peggotty Beach for the early morning and evening. During the summer, this beach will be crowded during the day.

To reach the next spot on the South Shore tour—Rexhame Beach in Marshfield—retrace your route back to MA 3A. When you get back to the traffic light, turn left and head south on MA 3A for 7 miles and the junction of MA 139. At that traffic light, turn left and drive east on MA 139. Within 3 miles, look for the sign for Rexhame Beach on the left-hand side of the road, at Winslow Street. Winslow Street isn't too far past the entrance for the Marshfield Airport. Turn left onto Winslow Street and follow it to Rexhame Beach, which is less than 2 miles from MA 139. This is a narrow road that goes through a residential area and has a low speed limit.

On the ocean side of Rexhame Beach, you can fish for bass and blues along the beach. This is a long and wide beach, comprised mostly of sand and cobblestones. It faces the Atlantic and will have a sizable surf when the wind is blowing strong from a northerly or easterly direction. Lighter onshore breezes will push the bait into the surf. This is a good location in fall, when the fish are fueling up for their migration south.

On the opposite side of the parking lot and over the dunes is the South River, which also has good striped bass fishing. There are deep holes and flats in the river; you should survey it at low water to see all the structure. Clouser Minnows would the first choice here.

There is an added feature at this location: In spring the South River can have some good American shad fishing for the fly rodder. Kent Jackson, who has fished here in spring for shad, told me of an old American Indian saying: When the leaves on the trees are the size of a mouse's ear, the shad will be in the river. For those of you who don't have time to check the leaves, this is sometime around the early part of April. You should use very small flies, similar to the shad darts, to catch these shad. Some fly anglers will actually use the shad dart as a dropper fly in conjunction with a slightly larger fly. My choice is a very small Clouser Minnow. But regardless of what fly you use, I've found that the shad seem to prefer ones with bright or fluorescent colors.

The parking lot for Rexhame Beach is open from 6 AM to 9 PM, and during the summer there is a charge to park. You will also see a sign stating that Rexhame Beach is for residents only. However, when I checked with the Marshfield Police before fishing there, they told me that if I was there fishing, I would not be ticketed. I was instructed to park on far side of the lot, farthest from the beach, and leave a note on my dash indicating that I was fishing. They also did warn me that the gate to the lot is locked at about 10 PM and not unlocked until about 5 the next morning.

Let me suggest that when you are fishing a new location and you aren't sure of the regulations, check with the local police. I've found that if they know you're fishing, they will usually be accommodating. It's amazing the number of fishing stories I have swapped in police stations when I asked about fishing a location in their town. Remember, many members of the police also fish, and are understanding.

When you return to MA 139, the next location is Ocean Bluff, which is only 2 miles south on MA 139. You'll know when you reach there because you'll be driving on a street with the ocean close to it on your left. To fish Ocean Bluff, park on the ocean side of the street, but note that there is a two-hour parking limit from 8 AM to 10 PM.

Ocean Bluff is typical of a number of locations on the South Shore, with a street and houses right next to the water and only a seawall to protect things. Since this is a bathing beach, it will be crowded during the summer, and especially on weekends. Therefore, I suggest fishing here early in the morning or in late evening. Coincidentally, this is when you'll find the best fishing.

The beach at Ocean Bluff faces onto the Atlantic Ocean and has very good structure. It's a narrow, sandy beach with small stones, and stone jetties that are there as beach protection. These rock structures are not in the kind of condition that makes for a good fishing platform. I suggest that you not fish from them. What you should do is fish along the sides of these jetties. Bait will often be schooled up in the corners between beach and jetties. This is the ideal scenario where a fly drifting in the current and washing alongside the rocks will do very well for stripers.

It is very deep water off the beach, and with onshore winds the surf can really roll in here. With a strong surf it's possible for the beach to be gone and the waves to be washing against the seawall. You will notice an occasional large rock showing here and there in the water. This tells me that there may be more rocky structure below the water that doesn't show, even at low tide. This type of structure just screams *striped bass.* Fish your fly as deep as you can without hanging it up in the rocks. During the summer and early fall, you may also find blues feeding on the bait that congregates around the jetties. Don't forget the wire leader when they're around.

After leaving Ocean Bluff and continuing on MA 139, there is a sign for Duxbury Beach, which is open to the public. Look for Canal Street, which is a left turn off MA 139. This intersection is wide, with grass islands separating the different lanes. Continue on Canal Street, which parallels the shoreline for $1^{1}/_{2}$ miles as it goes through a residential neighborhood. This road becomes Gurnet Road and ends at the Duxbury Beach parking lot.

This is the public section of Duxbury Beach; there's a $5 charge to park here during the summer season. The lot is open from 9 AM through 8 PM during the season; the gate is locked at night. This lot will give you access to the Atlantic and the marshes of the Back River. There is also an entrance for four-wheel-drive vehicles that leads south. This is for that section of Duxbury Beach that allows beach driving but requires a permit. I will shortly tell you more about this section of Duxbury Beach and how to get a permit to drive and fish that part of the beach.

I recommend fishing both the Atlantic side and the upper end of the Back River and its marshes in the off-season. This beach, because it's public, is a very popular place during the summer. The good news is, excellent bass fishing occurs in spring before Memorial Day—and after Labor Day look for both stripers and blues on the ocean side. I have seen the gate unlocked early in the morning and late in the evening when they were not charging to park.

If you are looking for a beach on the South Shore that you can fish using your four-wheel-drive vehicle, then head for the other section of Duxbury Beach. Just continue south on MA 139 from Ocean Bluff, past the entrance for the public section of Duxbury Beach, until you come to MA 3A; turn left. In a short distance you will come to a traffic light, which is the intersection of MA 14 and St. Georges Street. MA 14 ends at this intersection, and St. Georges Street will continue east. Turn left onto St. Georges Street and follow it until you go past the high school and arrive at a flagpole, where you should bear left onto Powder Point Road. Stay on that road as it goes over the Powder Point Bridge to the entrance for Duxbury Beach.

You can also get to Duxbury Beach by taking exit 11 off MA 3 and driving east on MA 14 toward Duxbury. In a short distance you'll reach a small rotary or roundabout; just go halfway around it and continue on MA 14. This is also Congress Street. On MA 14 look for the Duxbury Police Station on your right. Immediately after it is a split, with MA 139 going left and MA 14 bearing to the right. Stay on MA 14 until you come to the traffic light at MA 3A. Cross MA 3A onto St. George Street and follow the directions previously given.

The vehicle beach permit for Duxbury Beach, which is purchased at the Duxbury Town Hall on MA 3A, is rather expensive. The last time I checked, a yearly permit cost $100 for residents and $200 for nonresidents. Your cost justification will depend upon how often you plan to fish Duxbury Beach.

This is a nice, sandy beach that is ideal for the four-wheel-drive angler. The two primary targets of anglers here are bass and blues, though I've heard of some nice flounder taken on the inside, in Duxbury Bay. If you want to try for flounder, use Clouser Minnows on the bottom, and fish them with a jigging motion in your retrieve. The fly should lift off the bottom and then settle down as you make your retrieve, with the flounder often taking the fly as it settles to the bottom. Not only are flounder good eating, but they can give you a good tussle on a lightweight outfit, as well.

This is also a good wading location for stripers. However, take note that at certain stretches along the beach, you cannot drive on the bay side; you'll have to walk over. When wading and fishing the bay side, watch out for any deep holes or drop-offs.

If you don't have a four-wheel-drive vehicle, just before the Powder Point Bridge is a spot where a few cars can park. From there you can fish the Back River area, the marshes and the upper bay. It's the same area that you can access from the parking lot at the public section of Duxbury Beach, off MA 139.

Bay Farm is my favorite location on the South Shore because it is a very scenic spot to fish, and you do catch fish. To reach Bay Farm from Duxbury Beach, continue south on MA 3A for about a mile to Depot Street. Turn left onto Depot Street and drive into South Duxbury. In the center of town, turn right onto Bay Road, which will take you to Landing Road, where you turn left.

At the Kingston/Duxbury town line is a small parking lot on your left, with access to the water, which is about a quarter mile across a field. A sign indicates that this is an access to Kingston Bay. You'll also see a small kiosk that is painted brown and has a message welcoming you to Bay Farm.

This location is also very close to exit 9 on MA 3; exiting from either direction on MA 3, go right on MA 3A at top of the exit ramp. In 1 mile there is a split in the road where MA 3A and MA 53 bear off to the left. Stay to the right; you're now on Landing Road. You will go under a railroad bridge and under MA 3, and in a short distance on your right is the parking lot for Bay Farm.

It's about a 10-minute walk across the meadow to the water; just follow the path across the field. On the far side of the field, and just before the woods, there is a split in the path. Both paths lead to the water, but you'll find easier access if you head to your left along the edge of the woods. The shoreline you'll be fishing is grassy banks and rocks, with a shallow flats area and small rocks scattered throughout the area. The bottom is a bit soft, so wade carefully.

Striped bass are the standard here, with the usual drill of fishing early morning and evening. The better fishing is early and late in the season because this shallow water does get warm in summer. There is a channel that you can wade out to and fish. During the summer, you can see the markers or buoys marking its location; they're absent in the off-season, however, so watch for the drop-off. It would be advisable to visit Bay Farm at low water to determine exactly where the channel's drop-off is located. There are also two estuaries a bit of a distance to both the right and left of the area that feed into Kingston Bay.

This is such beautiful location to fish. The scenery and quiet are an added bonus. It's the kind of destination where you have a smile on your face as you drive home, even if you didn't catch any fish. Bay Farm is an all-around enjoyable fishing experience.

The next two locations on our tour of the South Shore are in Plymouth, but at opposite ends of the town. The Nelson Street Beach is at the western end of Plymouth and $2^{1}/_{2}$ miles from exit 9 on MA 3. It's a small park with access to the flats of Plymouth Harbor and Kingston Bay.

From exit 9, travel south on MA 3A through Kingston and into Plymouth, past the Cordage Park complex, which will be on your left. Look for the sign for the Nelson Street Memorial Playground on the left, at Nelson Street. Turn left onto Nelson Street and drive to the end. The playground will be on the right as you pull into the park; drive past it to the dirt parking lot next to the water.

This is primarily a striped bass location, but on occasion small bluefish will venture into Plymouth Harbor. The water off Nelson Street is shallow and features a large area that is easy to wade and fish. It has a firm bottom with some soft spots here and there, so if you're fishing this spot for the first time, proceed with caution until you're familiar with the environment. Since it's such shallow water, it's fairly warm in summer, making this an early- and late-season fishing destination for stripers. Concentrate on the mornings and evenings when the bass are on these flats looking for food.

On the other side of Plymouth is an area that has as much varied structure as any location on the South Shore. Plymouth Beach and Warren Cove are 4 miles south on MA 3A from Nelson Street. If you are traveling on MA 3, take exit 6 and drive to the center of Plymouth and the intersection of MA 3A. At that traffic light, turn right onto MA 3A; in $2^1/_2$ miles, just after you cross the Eel River, you will see Bert's restaurant on the left. Turn left into the entrance just before Bert's. This is the entrance to Plymouth Beach.

The unpaved parking lot is very large; during the summer season there's a charge of $10 on weekends and $7 during the week. Since it's such a large lot, park at the end farthest from the road if you intend to walk the beach out to the end. You may see four-wheel-drive vehicles going out onto Plymouth Beach, but that access is limited to Plymouth residents only.

This whole area is good fly fishing for both stripers and bluefish because there is a good deal of structure to attract predator and prey. Wading and fishing the long spit of land called Plymouth Beach will be a hike since it's more than 2 miles long. You may also hear this beach referred to as Long Beach. Though it's a good distance to cover, you'll experience some very good fishing for both bass and blues. To minimize the amount of gear I need to carry in situations like this, I use an intermediate line and carry an assortment of weighted and unweighted flies so I can fish at various depths without changing line. Just be patient, since it will take some time for a weighted fly to sink your line; through experience you will learn how many seconds it takes for the fly to get to the desired depth.

Plymouth Beach is a sand beach with areas of cobblestones and a series of small jetties located near the parking lot. This is a gradually sloping beach, so it's advisable to scout it during low water for any structure hidden by high tide. There are also some rock seawalls along the lower portion of the beach.

To your right, or east from the parking lot, is a very large cove known as Warren Cove. There is a lot of rocky structure here mixed with some sand, running from Bert's to the east along the shoreline of the cove. You'll see large rocks in the water at high tide, telling you that there's much more structure not seen, even at low water. Again, get your fly down to this structure to find the bass that are in among the rocks, looking for food. This is excellent striped bass water so don't be surprised to see the boats working the cove, as well.

Eel River empties into Plymouth Harbor on the backside of Plymouth Beach. I suggest fishing here on the dropping tide for stripers. You can expect to find some fish if you can match a morning or evening with a dropping tide, especially early or late in the season.

I believe that fishing is much more than just the act of catching a fish. I once heard a saying about the stages of fishing that an angler passes through. It went something like this: When someone first starts to fish, all he wants to do is catch a fish. After catching that first fish, he wants to catch a lot of fish; then he wants to catch the biggest fish. Eventually, many anglers move into the last stage, where all they want to do is just go fishing.

Anglers move through the various stages, sometimes lingering longer in one or another before moving on. Some spend their whole life seeking to catch the biggest and most fish. For me, I moved in the latter stage a while back but can't say when it actually occurred. I get excited if there are a lot of fish to catch, and a big fish will sure get my heart pounding. But in the final analysis, I just love to be fishing. It is the places we experience while fishing, and more importantly the people we fish with and whom we meet while fishing, that make angling what it is.

My friend Bill Burke used to fish with me before he moved to Florida. We fished mostly from my boat then, working the waters of Cape Cod Bay. Many mornings in summer we would be leaving Barnstable Harbor just as the sun was coming up over the eastern horizon. And to this day I can remember what Bill would reply whenever I asked him where we should fish that day. He'd smile, look off over the water, and say, "You call it. I'm just happy to be out here." I guess that sums up what fishing is all about.

Chapter 10

Maine

Mention Maine and pictures of a rockbound coast and crashing surf come to mind. That image reflects both the state's history and its people. The first settlers who attempted to establish a colony here in the early 1600s found impossible conditions. After nearly another 100 years there were still fewer than a dozen settlements in Maine, which was still under the control of Massachusetts. It wasn't until more than 200 years after that first try at settling that Maine became a state.

Maine's early inhabitants were Native Americans of two major nations. The Micmacs were primarily warlike in nature, while the more prevalent Abenakis were a peaceful nation that farmed and fished to survive. Where once a large number of tribes populated the land, there are now only two. The Passamaquoddies and Penobscots, who now live on reservations and number less than 3,000, are but a shadow of what was once a great tribal nation.

It's unclear who among the Europeans initially discovered Maine. A couple of explorers are supposed to have come across the area. Half a century before Columbus, Leif Eriksson is believed to have explored this region and even tried to set up a settlement. The other contender is John Cabot, who in 1498 briefly visited the coastline of Maine, stopping there for repairs. The first attempt at settling in the region didn't occur until 1607, when the Plymouth Company established the first settlement at what is today Popham. The settlement at Jamestown, Virginia, was started at the same time but because the colony at Popham didn't survive the first harsh winter in Maine, Jamestown received the honor of being this country's first permanent settlement.

At the beginning of the 18th century there were but half a dozen settlements in Maine. By that time, any land claims for this rugged region were owned by Massachusetts. That control would last until 1820 and is why Maine was never listed as one of the original 13 colonies. But changes were on the way. Soon after the French and Indian Wars, Massachusetts began to offer 100-acre lots in Maine to anyone willing to settle in this rugged wilderness. The growth of Maine had begun, and between 1743 and 1763 the population of the region doubled to 24,000. By the end of the 1700s that number had swelled to 150,000.

Statehood for Maine came as a result of our country's dispute over slavery. In 1820 Congress passed the Missouri Compromise, which allowed Maine to be the 23rd state. The object was to allow Maine to join the Union as a free state and Missouri to join a year later as a slave state, thus preserving the numerical balance between free and slave states.

Maine has another tie to slavery and the Civil War: The book *Uncle Tom's Cabin*, which stirred up a great deal of antislavery feeling just prior to the war, was written here. The author, Harriet Beecher Stowe, was the wife of a professor at Bowdoin College, and the book was written right in Brunswick.

Lastly, for all you who enjoy your evening cocktail, Maine is the home of the temperance movement. The world's first Total Abstinence Society was started in 1815 in Portland. By 1834 there was a state organization, and it soon developed enough political strength to force the enactment of the "Maine Law." That law, which prohibited the sale of alcoholic beverages except for "mechanical and medical purposes," would remain in effect, in various forms, until 1934 and the repeal of National Prohibition.

So after a day of fly fishing along Maine's coast and when you are relaxing with that evening cocktail, give a toast to all those rugged individuals who came before you. Just imagine what it must have like, after a cool, fall day chasing stripers along Popham Beach, to toast your success with some warm tea. Ah, the good old days.

Still, nothing in life is ever what it seems. The standard portrayal of the rockbound coast of Maine is only a partial picture. Anglers who have fly fished Maine's coastline know that there is also excellent fishing along sandy beaches, quiet coves, and in estuaries and rivers. However, it wasn't always that way, specifically in its rivers. At one time, pollution drove most species of fish from Maine's rivers. The state has worked hard to change this and there are a number of success stories, but none is more special than the Kennebec River. Striped bass are once again spawning there; this major accomplishment is the direct result of the vision and dedication of two people. John Cole and Brad Burns played key roles in making that happen in the Kennebec River.

I first met Brad Burns when I was working to form the New England Coast Conservation Association, a part of the Coastal Conservation Association. Brad's love of striped bass is exceeded only by his tireless dedication to their conservation. That love and dedication on behalf of stripers came into focus just prior to his meeting John Cole. Brad had learned from a friend, whose family had lived for generations on the Kennebec, that striped bass once spawned there. The man's great-grandfather told of netting 2- to 3-inch young-of-the-year bass from under the ice. Hearing this, Brad checked with Lou Flagg, a marine resources scientist with Maine's Department of Marine Resources, to confirm the story. With that confirmation, Brad believed that he could return spawning fish to the Kennebec. Having read *Striper*, Brad contacted author John Cole, who was living in Maine, and sought his help.

John, who has written many fine books, including two of my favorites, *Striper* and *Fishing Came First*, met with Brad in 1980. Together with Lou Flagg, they would, over the next several years, work to return a native striped bass population to the Kennebec River; just one of several species of fish that had disappeared from the river by way of humankind's abuse. There were many who told the pair that this was an impossible task. I'm sure that thought often crossed their minds, as well. John handled the fund-raising effort while Brad worked through the maze of state and federal agencies whose help was required to get the job done. If you ask who was responsible for their success, each will say it was the other.

In 1982 they had 319 wild, young-of-the-year striped bass seined from the Hudson River; these were the first fingerlings to reach the Kennebec. The next year was even better with 572 young bass being seined from the Hudson and transported to Maine. Then in 1984, with more donated funds, they bought 2,506 young bass from a private source. These fish were reared by the U.S. Fish & Wildlife Service in its Attleboro, Massachusetts, hatchery. Lou Flagg arranged to have Maine's Department of Marine Resources, which enthusiastically supported this project, transport the fingerlings that autumn to the Kennebec. Such cooperation of state and federal agencies was unheard of until that effort.

From then until 1991, young striped bass were obtained from the Verplanck Striped Bass Hatchery on the Hudson River, raised by the U.S. Fish & Wildlife Service, and transported to the Kennebec River for release. Brad and John's dream was now in high gear. As an example, in 1985, 46,759 fingerlings were stocked; in 1988, the number was 66,623. Only in 1987 were no bass released, due to a production deficit at the Verplanck Hatchery. Still, Brad, John, and Lou were to have a major victory that year: The Maine Department of Marine Resources captured 2- to 4-inch young-of-the-year juvenile bass in Merrymeeting Bay, where the Kennebec and Androscoggin Rivers meet. This represented the first verified proof of striped bass spawning success in the Kennebec River in more than 50 years. Other than these men, few people truly understood the significance of that event.

To appreciate what Brad and John had accomplished, you must look at the history of Maine's rivers. Brad and John's vision was an understanding of what was, and what could be. Maine's rivers had seen the best and worst of times; they once were alive with fish, and then nearly devoid of them.

In colonial times the rivers supported vast populations of salmon, shad, alewives, smelt, eels, small cod, sturgeon, and striped bass. Their numbers were so great that commercial fishing operations could be found along the banks of all major rivers. This fishery supported local markets plus those in distant Boston. The clear, swift waters were perfect for these fish; many of them traveled hundreds of miles up the rivers and their tributaries to spawn. The Kennebec, which runs some 164 miles from Moosehead Lake to the sea, was a premier habitat for these fish. Unlike many of the other rivers in Maine, which broaden at their mouths, the Kennebec runs swift and deep all the way to the sea. Before the establishment of the dams on the river and their serious impact upon the river's quality, the tidal effect was felt nearly 55 miles upriver, above Augusta. Striped bass were known to ascend the river to Waterville, 20 miles above Augusta, some 65 miles from the sea, but the dams changed all that.

The striped bass population of colonial times was enormous, with both large and small fish. A report in *The Fisheries and Fishery Industries of the United States,* published in 1887 by the U.S. Commission of Fish and Fisheries, tells of a striped bass caught years earlier in Middle Bay that weighed 100 pounds. Bass of more than 50 pounds were common, and many of these fish were year-round residents. How great was the striped bass population prior to the introduction of dams and the pollution that followed? That 1887 report stated, "On the Kennebec at Abagadasset Point, as late as 1830, bass were so plenty that the fishermen were troubled to dispose of those taken in the weirs. A single weir has been known to take 1,000 pounds at one tide.

There was no demand for them. Sometimes hired men would take them in pay. When plentiest they were given away."

This same report tells of an impending problem. By 1887 dams had been erected on every major river in Maine. The dam built at Augusta in 1837 restricted the migration of salmon from hundreds of miles to 45 and shad from 100 miles to 50. The breeding grounds of these fish, plus the alewife, had been cut off. Adding to the problem was pollution, as documented in that same 1887 federal report: "The artificial alterations in the condition of the rivers are very considerable. They arise in part from the cultivation of the soil, but mainly from the erection of dams and the throwing of refuse from the sawmills into the water. The exposure of the bare earth to the action of rains, as in all cultivated fields, especially in hilly districts, results in the washing of great quantities of soil into the rivers, where it settles in all places not swept by strong currents, but more especially near the mouths of rivers. From the first occupation of the country, until recent times it has been the general custom to throw into the river all refuse from sawmills, including not only sawdust but shavings, edgings, and in many cases even slabs." Though many consider river pollution to be a modern-day problem, it was well established in the rivers of Maine by the 1880s.

The situation did not get better. With the advent of the paper mills along the rivers, pollution became severe. Maine's rivers were considered to be the most polluted in the nation. The sulfates and other chemical by-products from the paper mills, septic system leakage, barnyard runoff, plus nutrient overloads—typically nitrogen and phosphorus from fertilizer—combined with the heavy algal blooms of rotting and decaying wood to create an environment most fish could not survive. The smell was often overpowering. There is a well-known story of college students who threw up from the odor while trying to canoe on one river.

By the early 1960s, Maine realized that something had to be done, and done quickly. The state began passing legislation to clean up its rivers; this was prior to any major federal action. Paper mills upgraded their facilities, reducing their discharges into the rivers, while sewage treatment facilities were also improved. The change in the condition of Maine's rivers was impressive.

By 1979, as water quality was improving, striped bass began to return to the rivers, migrating north each spring; however, they did so *after* spawning in the Hudson River and Chesapeake Bay. The native, spawning population of the Kennebec had been lost. This was when Brad Burns learned of the native stripers that once made their home in the Kennebec and became determined to reestablish a spawning base in this majestic river. With John Cole's help, they wrote a bright new page in the river's history.

Some folks point to the actions of the Atlantic States Marine Fisheries Commission as the reason for the improvement in the Kennebec's striper fishing. It was, however, the establishment of striped bass that recognized the Kennebec River as the place of their beginning that changed things. This reestablished the cycle of fish returning to spawn and perpetuate a population of native Kennebec River stripers. I believe that at one time many of the rivers on the East Coast supported populations of spawning bass, but they are now gone. If programs like the one carried out by Brad Burns and John Cole were conducted in other major estuaries in New England, they too might see striped bass returning to spawn.

The friendship, alliance, and hard work of Brad Burns and John Cole changed the history of the Kennebec River and left a priceless legacy for future generations of anglers. If ever there was an example of people who cared and, regardless of the difficulty, made a positive difference, this is it.

However, there still remains one obstacle to returning the rivers to what they once were. A number of the original dams still block many of the rivers. Their removal is far from simple; if not done properly, it will unleash the pollutants that have lain dormant, below layers of sediment above the structure. But it can be done properly, as witnessed by the Edwards Dam.

The Edwards Dam, which stretched more than 900 feet across the Kennebec River, was successfully breached in the summer of 1999. For the first time in 162 years some 10 species of fish—including striped bass, shad, alewives, several species of herring, Atlantic salmon, shortnose sturgeon, and Atlantic sturgeon—can now travel from the mouth of the Kennebec River to Waterville, through the access to another 17 miles of the river. The testimony to the worth of the dam's removal is the exceptional striped bass fishing now occurring in that 17-mile stretch of the river.

As this book goes to press the Smelt Hill Dam on the Presumpscot River, which is located just north of Portland, is scheduled for removal. It is hoped that the success associated with the Edwards Dam project will be repeated on the Presumpscot. If so, another of Maine's rivers will take a step toward what they once were before all the dams and pollution. Still, with so many rivers and dams in Maine, the work is far from done.

When you examine a map of Maine, you'll see the irregular coastline with its many estuaries running to the Atlantic Ocean. As with most of New England, the glaciers of the Ice Age sculpted Maine; its rugged coastline, with 2,000-plus islands, is the hallmark of the Pine Tree State. But there is much more than that awaiting the saltwater fly rodder in Maine. Though the fishing season may be slightly shorter than what other states in New England enjoy, the quality of the fishing is by no means diminished.

Kennebec River Area

Before the arrival of stripers and blues each year, certain key baitfish start to move into the coastal waters and estuaries of Maine. Alewives begin entering the rivers to spawn in the latter part of April through the first of June; they will begin to swim back down and out of rivers in August. Mackerel spread from the south along the coast in the latter part of May, and will be present throughout the summer and into fall. They are great sport to catch on light-

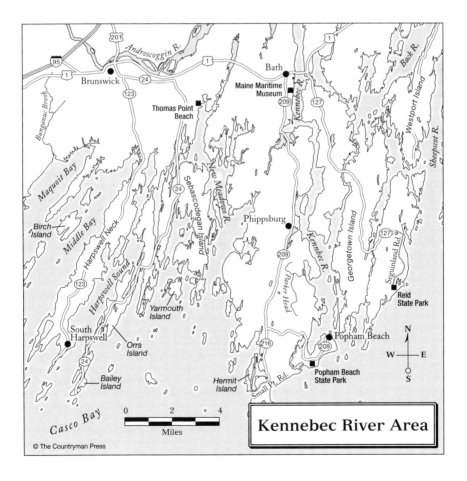

Popham Beach, looking east from Fort Popham toward the mouth of the Kennebec River. With deep water close to the beach, this is an excellent fly-fishing location.

weight outfits. A prime place to look for them is around the mouths of estuaries. The herring arrive around second or third week in June, and are from 3 to 6 inches in length. Herring and mackerel patterns are two key choices of fly rodders in spring.

Eels are found in the rivers year-round, with elvers or juvenile eels coming from the Atlantic into the rivers in spring. You'll find sand eels in sandy areas all along the coastline from the early spring until the end of the fishing season. Another bait that will be around for the complete season is silversides. Menhaden are making a comeback; they were once very plentiful in Maine's coastal waters. Bunker will normally reach Maine in early July, and remain through the end of August or the first part of September.

Striped bass arrive on the scene the second or third week of May and move into the rivers. In the Kennebec they will be spawning in shallow bays and backwaters. Some of these fish will move back out into the ocean in late June and July, spreading along the coast. There is evidence that some of these fish travel as far south as Boston Harbor and Cape Cod for the summer. However, many hold in the rivers until the first part of October, when they begin their long migration south.

Bluefish usually show no later than the first of July and remain around through the end of August, into early September. They will precede the bass heading south, fueling up at every opportunity as they head for North Carolina.

I had planned to use the Kennebec River as the northernmost boundary of coverage for this book. But when I discussed my intention with Chris Grill of the Kennebec Angler—a fine tackle shop in Bath—he convinced me to include Reid State Park, which is just north of the Kennebec River, on the northern side of Georgetown Island. Though I haven't fished there, Chris assured me it's an excellent fly-fishing destination for stripers and an occasional bluefish. It's one of the places he recommends to people who come into his shop.

To reach Reid Sate Park, you must cross the Kennebec River from Bath on US 1. Once you're across the bridge and are in Woolwich, go right on ME 127. Continue on the road through Arrowsic Island and on to Georgetown Island. Keep an eye out for Seguinland Road, which leads to Reid State Park. It's approximately 13 miles from US 1 to the park.

At Reid State Park there is a small river, the Little River, to the south of the beach area. When fishing for bass here, you should drift your fly on the outgoing current from three-quarters down to low tide. Mile Beach and Half Mile Beach are sandy beaches, and the park has another rarity for Maine—sand dunes. The shoreline in the park is a combination of sandy beaches and rocky areas. Chris Grill noted that fishing the water below Griffith Head can be productive. Concentrate on fish that may be in the backwash. During the summer months, you can also catch an occasional bluefish here, along with the bass.

Reid Sate Park was Maine's first state-owned saltwater beach. There is a minimal daily fee charged to enter the park. For more information on Reid, call 207-371-2303.

To the south of Bath are Popham Beach, Popham Beach State Park, and Hermit Island, all of which are fine fly-fishing destinations. All three can be reached from Bath by taking ME 209. This road parallels the Kennebec River and is a scenic drive. There are several places along the way where you can pull off the road and fish the coves and marshes of the Kennebec. Even if you don't catch a fish, the scenic beauty is worth the time.

It's approximately 14 miles from the center of Bath and US 1 to Popham Beach State Park. The complete trip is made on ME 209. However, do watch for ME 209 to take a left turn; at that point ME 216 goes straight and to Hermit Island. Just watch for and follow the signs for Popham Beach State Park. The entrance will be on your right.

Popham Beach State Park, which is a 529-acre facility, has some features that are similar to Reid Sate Park. To the right of the parking lot and beach area is the Morse River; this is a small river and within easy walking distance of the parking lot. The standard drill for stripers here is to drift a fly in the current on a dropping tide. This is a reasonably easy spot to fish; since you can cast from the bank of the Morse, you can wear hip boots instead of waders. If you're planning to fish the beach, however, there can be a good surf at times, and you'll encounter tides of up to 10 feet or more, which isn't unusual for Maine. Waders with a belt are standard gear in the surf.

You should take note that dogs are not allowed in Maine's state parks. My dog, BJ, has a real problem with this rule since he travels with me. Popham has a very large parking lot and is open from 9 AM to sunset. A small daily fee is charged; when the attendant isn't present, there is a collection box and the honor system is used. Popham Beach State Park is open from April 15 through October 30.

Less than 2 miles beyond Popham Beach State Park is Fort Popham and Popham Beach. This location has parking for only about a dozen cars, but it's no more than a few steps from the beach. Popham Beach, with historic Fort Popham, sits at the mouth of the Kennebec River. Fort Popham and the rocks on which it was built are at the beginning of Popham Beach, which runs east toward the Atlantic.

Begin your fishing near the rocks, walking along the beach and using a fan pattern of casting every 10 feet. The set of wooden pylons that is a bit down the beach is a good spot to spend some extra casting time. Near the seaward end of the beach is a point and nice hole. I have seen bass pin bait against the beach here, resulting in some excellent fishing. You will, on occasion, find mackerel working in this lower section of the river, as well. Popham Beach is an excellent night fishing location throughout the season. Many people are aware of this, so expect company—and if you want a parking place, get there early.

Chris Grill passed on some sound advice about fishing locations like Popham Beach. He noted that wading into the water too far has several drawbacks. First, the beaches are steep in many sections of Maine, not gradual like some beaches you may be used to fishing. As the tide drops, the high bank can hamper your cast. Second, because water is deep close to shore, the bass are usually moving and feeding close to the beach. Lastly, the steep banks and strong current, as at Popham and many other locations, can make for a dangerous situation. One step too many and you can be swept away in the current.

Hermit Island is a great camping and fishing site of 255 acres, with more than 5 miles of shoreline. It's a very popular campground, and anyone planning to stay there needs to get their reservations in as early as possible. Hermit Island has both sandy beach areas and rocky shorelines to fish. The primary quarry for fly rodders here is striped bass or mackerel, with occasional visits by bluefish.

When driving from Bath on ME 209 to Popham Beach, you were traveling in the same direction for Hermit Island. However, where ME 209 makes a left turn, you should continue straight on ME 216 and follow the signs; Hermit Island is about $2^1/_2$ miles down the road. This is an excellent location to combine some fly fishing with a family vacation. For information on the Hermit Island campground, you can write them at 42 Front Street, Bath, ME 04530, or call 207-443-2101. They also have a web site whose address is www.hermitisland.com. The Bath Chamber of Commerce at 207-443-9751 can provide information on Hermit Island, plus other locations of interest in the area.

One of the top flies for this area is a Deceiver-like pattern that I first saw tied by Brock Apfel; it was initially intended for use in Kennebec River. In Lefty's *Saltwater Fly Patterns*, it is shown on page 147 and described on page 145 as Brock's Bulky Deceiver. Locally it has gained fame as the Grocery Fly. This fly is very good in mackerel, herring, and bunker patterns—the bait found in this area of Maine. I have used this fly in other sections of New England with very good results. It's an excellent striper fly. Other flies that you should try are Deceivers, Clouser Minnows, and the Half-and-Half, which is part Deceiver and part Clouser Minnow. Top colors for these flies are olive and white, chartreuse and white, green and yellow, and black, if you're fishing at night.

Portland and South

Down the coast from the Kennebec River is the city of Portland, and from there southward are a large number of good locations to fly fish. Mackerel are plentiful in the area and are great sport for fly rodders. The mackerel show up about the last week of May to first of June in the Portland area, and are around until the end of October. They are always around unless the bluefish run them off. This fish is great sport on a lightweight rod, either a 5- or 6-weight. This type of fishing is a good way for the freshwater angler to start fishing the salt. Mackerel can run 2 pounds or more.

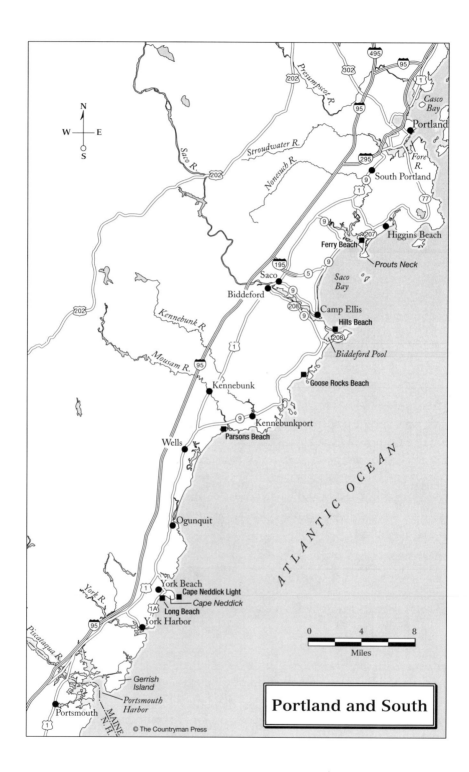

Portland and South

0   4   8
Miles

© The Countryman Press

The hallmark of Maine's saltwater fly fishing is the numerous estuaries along its coastline.

What locals call harbor pollock, a smaller size of American pollock that average about 1 to 2 pounds, are also the targets of fly anglers. Like mackerel, they are great sport on lightweight outfits. You can find these smaller pollock around rocky ledges that have deep water nearby. Besides being pursued by fly fishermen, mackerel and pollock are also the favorite food of striped bass and bluefish.

You'll find some small menhaden around, but not like the vast schools that swarmed the Maine coast in the early 1990s. There are also sand eel and silversides for baitfish, and fly patterns to imitate them are a good choice; chartreuse-and-white and brown-and-white Clouser Minnows work well where these baitfish are present. The Grocery Fly that imitates mackerel, alewives, or herring is another good pattern in this area. I've been told that squid patterns have also taken a good number of stripers here.

Since Portland is a bit farther south than the Kennebec River, the striped bass will normally arrive here the second week of May and depart on their migration south near the end of October. The blues appear in June, hang around the whole summer, and begin moving out by the first week of October.

One of the better fly-fishing locations close to Portland is Mackworth Island. It's easy to reach by driving north out of Portland on I-295 and US 1, and continuing on US 1 north where it bears to the right and goes over the Martin Point Bridge. After crossing the bridge, turn right onto Andrews Avenue. There will be a blue sign for the Governor Baxter School for the Deaf. You should follow that road over the bridge onto Mackworth Island. You'll need to stop at the guard shack and tell them you're planning to fish there. You will then be directed to parking; once you're there you'll see a path that goes around the shoreline of the island, with paths leading to the water.

Mackworth Island can only be fished during daylight hours and provides access to the north side of where the Presumpscot River empties into Casco Bay. This is an area of primarily mudflats and stone beaches. It's close to Portland and yet has a very natural setting, with only the school on the island. You should fish this location from midtide through the drop, concentrating on the section from the river side of the island to the front and the stone pier.

Moving down the coast, past Portland, the next area to highlight is Higgins Beach in Scarborough. Driving south on US 1 and ME 9, turn left onto Black Point Road at the traffic light. At this point you are on ME 207 and will go through Scarborough. Within approximately 3 miles of the traffic light, look for ME 77, which is a left turn. Take that left onto ME 77 and in less than 1 1/2 miles, Ocean Avenue will be on the right. There is a green sign on the corner for Higgins Beach, but unfortunately it's facing the other direction. After turning right, continue through the stop sign onto a one-way street that leads to the water. There is a turnoff across the street from the Higgins Beach Market, which will be on your left. A fee is charged for parking during the summer.

When standing on the beach and facing the water, to your left is the Spurwink River. This is primarily striped bass water; they will go up the river to feed on the rising tide and then drop back on the falling tide. The best spot to concentrate your effort is around the mouth of the river on the dropping tide. Higgins Beach is a gradually sloping, sandy beach with some rocks. The evening and into the night is the best time to fish here. You can also work your way south, fishing toward the rocks at that end of beach. Many of these rocks will be covered at high tide.

Not that far to the south is Ferry Beach, which faces onto the north side of the Scarborough River. As at Higgins Beach, striped bass are the primary fish sought by anglers at Ferry Beach. You'll have access to fishing located just inside the mouth of the Scarborough River, which empties into Saco Bay. You should fish this water on either side of low tide; this is when it's most productive, since at low tide the stripers will concentrate in the deeper holes. It's all sand here with a nice bar and a deep channel on the other side of it; keep a watch on the tide since there can be a 9- to 10-foot difference here. You don't want to get cut off with no way back to shore. It's best to fish Ferry Beach in the early morning and evening; I'm told that if you want to fish there at night, you should notify the Scarborough Police.

To reach Ferry Beach from Higgins Beach, go back the way you came, to ME 207, and turn left. This section of the road is a notorious speed trap—locals have warned me about the strict enforcement of speed limits along this stretch of the road. So when you see the sign indicating a 35 mph speed limit, do not exceed 35 mph. After the 35 mph zone, the speed limit drops to 25 mph; this is just before the golf course and where motorists get ticketed the most.

After the golf course, begin watching for Ferry Road and the signs for Ferry Beach and boat ramp. Turn right onto Ferry Road; it's less than half a mile to the parking lot at Ferry Beach. This is a large parking lot, and a fee is charged to use it during the summer.

A bit farther south, down the coast in the town of Saco, is a very popular destination for fly rodders. The Camp Ellis breakwater is also a favorite of other anglers, so this location can get crowded at times. I suggest fishing this long jetty in spring, when the bass and mackerel are there. It can be very good fishing then.

To get to Camp Ellis from Saco, take ME 9 off US 1, just before the Saco River. This will be Beach Street, which eventually turns into Ferry Road. At the intersection where ME 9 turns left, take the right onto Camp Ellis Avenue, and then your first left onto Main Avenue. Drive all the way to the end, turning right onto North Avenue and then left on Beach Avenue. You can look for parking on the street, but pay close attention to the signs. There is also parking, for a fee, at Camp Ellis Center.

You will get to fish what is probably the longest rock jetty you've ever seen. Therefore, even though there may be a lot of anglers, there's usually enough room, and the fish often move in and out along the breakwater. Spring is the best time for catching stripers and mackerel on the breakwater, while bluefish will often show up there in summer. There is a debate as to whether the incoming or outgoing tide is best to fish; this leads me to believe it can vary from day to day, and to what part of the day, be it morning, evening, or midday.

Across the Saco River and near Biddeford Pool is Hills Beach, another good striper location. Leaving Camp Ellis, get back to ME 9 and take it back into town and then south over the Saco River. ME 9 will parallel the

Saco River along its south side, heading toward Biddeford Pool. Do not be confused with the signs that say this is ME 9 west; it says that all the way to Kennebunkport and Cozy Corners, where it joins US 1. You are on ME 208 as well, and ME 208 will also take you to Biddeford Pool, but on the south side.

When you reach the University of New England, take the road that forks left through campus. In less than a mile you should turn left onto Hills Beach Road. Biddeford Pool will be on your right and Hills Beach, on your left. It can be difficult parking here, with limited available locations. Depending on the time of season, you might want to try the ends of side streets that go to water for parking. Always be respectful of any owner's wishes, and be courteous. Fish this beach on the dropping tide for bass and bluefish.

Following ME 9 along the coast toward Kennebunkport, not far down the road is Goose Rocks Beach, which is very good location to fly fish. Look for the sign for Goose Rocks Road, which is no more than 5 or 6 miles down the road from the University of New England. Turn left onto Goose Rocks Road; in less than a mile you'll come to the end of the road. Go left for a very short distance and park along the side of the road. From here it's just a brief walk to the beach.

Goose Rocks Beach is a long, sandy beach that faces Goosefair Bay. It's a gradually sloping beach with large rocks and small islands just offshore. This is a great beach for the wading angler. You can expect to catch both striped bass and an occasional bluefish here. The prime time to fish for bass at Goose Rocks is on the incoming tide, after dark. To your left, or at the north end of beach, is the mouth of a small creek; there's a second estuary at south end of beach. You should fish the opening of both of these on the dropping tide when the stripers are most likely feeding there.

Traveling south on ME 9, and after passing through Kennebunkport, you will come to a unique and picturesque location. The road for Parsons Beach is just before the intersection where ME 9 joins US 1 at Cozy Corner. As soon as you pass over the Mousam River, a sign on the left marks Parsons Beach Road. It's just a short ride down this road to a small parking lot that sits on the south side of the Mousam, which empties into the Atlantic Ocean not 100 yards from where you're parked.

This is a very scenic location with the river flowing into the sea, sand dunes, and the beach. I believe the land here is one of a number of parcels belonging to the Rachel Carson National Wildlife Refuge. These sections of land—what the refuge calls divisions—consist of salt marshes and estuaries that are scattered along 50 miles of Maine's coastline, from Cape Elizabeth to York.

As noted, there is limited parking, but the river and beach are both within an easy walk. You should note that no parking is allowed from 11 PM to 6 AM. The appeal of this area is that it's so easy to fish either the river, the mouth of the river, or along the beach. The beach is sand but with good structure, having both rocks and some nice holes within casting range. On the dropping tide, there is a rip at the opening to the river that is a great striper location. Parsons Beach is considered one of the best striped bass spots along this part of the coast. It's also one of the rivers that has good fishing for sea-run trout.

Yes, there is a very special fishery in Maine, and that is sea-run brown trout. The Mousam is one of the estuaries noted for sea-runs. The fish in these estuaries are stocked by the state. Even some of the brown trout that are stocked farther upstream in various rivers will drop down to the salt water.

Initially the brown trout that were being stocked at the lower end of the rivers were small, and it seemed that the sea-run program wasn't that successful. It was determined that not many fish were surviving, so the state decided to try larger fish—and it worked. The brown trout now being released for the sea-run program are 14 to 16 inches in length. The result was the inception of a great sea-run fishery in Maine.

Sea-run browns are an excellent way to extend your season after the striped bass have departed the Maine coast for warmer waters. During the time when bass and sea-run browns may be present, use small sand eel patterns; they will catch both species of fish. Small Clouser Minnows are also good flies to use in this situation. Preferred fly colors are olive and white, white, and yellow and olive. The key is that the fly should be small. You can fish for sea-runs from fall until spring, as long as there is no ice on the water and you can tolerate the weather conditions.

When I was last at Eldredge Bros. Fly Shop in Cape Neddick, Jimmy Bernstein showed me a picture of a sea-run brown that weighed just over 12 pounds. The fish had been taken at the mouth of the Ogunquit River. Even though it had been caught on a spinning gear and not a fly rod, I was still impressed with the size of the fish. Jimmy feels that this sea-run was probably one of a number of broodstock fish released by the state.

Some of the estuaries that have been stocked with sea-run browns in the past by the Maine Department of Inland Fisheries and Wildlife are the Scarborough, Spurwink, Ogunquit, Androscoggin, Mousam, and York Rivers.

For additional information on current stocking operations, contact the department at 207-657-2345. There is a daily bag limit and minimum length requirement for these fish, so check with the local tackle shop nearest to where you intend to fish as to the current regulations.

Besides sea-run trout like the one mentioned earlier, the Ogunquit River has fly-angling action for bass and blues. The Ogunquit and adjacent beach are only a short driving distance from Parsons Beach and the Mousam River. Just continue down ME 9 maybe a mile or so to US 1 at Cozy Corners. Drive south on US 1, going through Wells and into Ogunquit. At the center of Ogunquit, look for Beach Street on your left; turn onto Beach Street, and in very short distance you will cross over the bridge that spans the Ogunquit River.

As soon as you cross the bridge, you'll see a large parking lot on your right. During the summer season, you'll have to pay to park there. There is also no overnight parking in the lot, so if you're planning to put in an all-nighter, you may want to park on the street before crossing the bridge, and then walk over.

This location is a fly-fishing triple treat. You have the ability to fish the Atlantic and its surf; the mouth of Ogunquit River, which has a large, sandy shallow or flats area and a nice rip on the dropping tide; or up in the river itself. All of this fishing borders or is within a short walking distance of the parking lot. Bluefish will frequent the ocean side as well as feeding in the mouth of the Ogunquit River. The whole area, from the ocean around to the marshes upriver, is prime striped bass fishing territory.

Starting at the oceanfront, if the surf is too heavy, you can move to the right and fish the mouth of the river, where there is a large shallow area where you can wade out toward the channel. Take care as you fish here: Current and unseen holes can be a danger. Your best bet is to scout this area at low water.

If you continue to fish to your right, it will take you into the river itself and deeper water. A short distance upriver is the bridge that you drove over, which is a good structure to fish. Beyond the bridge is a marsh area accessible from the parking lot side of the river. This whole area from the ocean to the marshes can be fished both during the day and at night.

Remember that image of Maine that most people have? Well, Cape Neddick, the next destination down the coast, is the epitome of rockbound Maine. It's where the state's most photographed and painted lighthouse sits. It's also a good fly-fishing location.

Anglers should concentrate on the section of water between the parking lot and the island on which Cape Neddick Light sits.

Traveling south on US 1 from Ogunquit, within just a few miles you will enter Cape Neddick. US 1A will be a left turn toward Cape Neddick Light; this road will take you into the town of York Beach as it winds its way to the lighthouse. Though it may seem a bit confusing, you're heading for a point of land that juts into the Atlantic and is known as Cape Neddick, even if you are in York Beach.

The key here is to watch for the signs for Nubble Lighthouse, which in fact is the Cape Neddick Light. You will be turning left onto Broadway Avenue, which will turn into Nubble Road. Keep an eye open for the sign for Sohier Park and Nubble Light. That left turn will take you to a very small parking lot with a view of the lighthouse. This lighthouse is only 40 feet tall, but it's nearly 90 feet above the water thanks to the rock island on which it sits, less than 100 yards from the mainland.

From the parking lot you can see the areas on both sides of the point where you can fish. This is primarily striper water, but you can occasionally pick up a bluefish here. If you're fishing your fly on the bottom, don't be surprised if you catch a flounder, as well. You will be fishing from the rocks with deep water right at your feet; the standard line for this spot would be a sinking line. Plan to fish here in the early morning or evening because during the day the lot will be crowded with tourists, especially during the summer.

Long Beach, the next stop on this fly-fishing tour, is a very short ride from Cape Neddick Light. There are a couple of ways to get there, but I like the picturesque route along the water. When you leave Sohier Park, turn left onto Nubble Road, follow that street to the stop sign at US 1A, and turn left. You will immediately see Long Beach, which local anglers call York Beach. There is parking along the Long Beach Avenue, which is also US 1A; the parking is on the ocean side of the road, and during the summer it's metered.

This section of the coastline is another very good striper location, and anglers have taken a number of large bass from this spot. During the summer and early-fall months you'll find bluefish making an occasional run along the beach, chasing bait. York Beach is a long, sandy beach with a gradual slope that runs from the rocky shoreline of Cape Neddick, at its northern end, to rocky structure on its southern end, with small, sandy coves interspersed. There is a good bit of water to fish along this beach so it will take time to learn where, what tides, and what times of day are the best. However, this is one of those locations that's well worth the effort to learn. Your reward will be some quality stripers on a fly.

Just a few minutes down US 1A, in the town of York Harbor, is a place on the York River called Mill Pond that is yet another favorite of fly rodders. Drive south on US 1A to York Harbor and turn left onto ME 103. Follow the road down the hill and leave your vehicle in the small dirt parking area on the left side of the road. Across the road is a short path leading to Mill Pond, a large body of water formed by a dike running parallel to the York River.

There is an opening to Mill Pond about two-thirds of the way to the other end of this dike. The water pours in and out of the pond with the tides at this inlet. This is strictly a striped bass location. Fish the pond itself and the opening onto the York River on a dropping tide. As the tide drops, the waters of Mill Pond pour out into the river. You can also fish along the shoreline of the river, which is an area of mudflats running to the channel of the York River.

It was interesting to discover on one of my trips to this area that the bridge spanning the opening to Mill Pond is the oldest suspension bridge in the country—though it's not that long. The locals call it the Wiggly Bridge because of its movement when you cross it.

The last time I stopped in Eldredge Bros. Fly Shop, Jimmy Bernstein and I discussed what flies work well along this part of the coast. Jimmy noted that the primary baitfish around the region are alewives and herring in spring; they move up the rivers and then return to the ocean in early fall. Mackerel are around from spring through fall, while silversides and pollock are present year-round. When fishing any of the deepwater locations, I like to use Jim's Grocery Pollock Fly, which is pictured in the color plates. If you're looking for bigger bass, this fly will certainly get their attention. Jim also suggests that a green crab pattern around rocky areas and in estuaries is another good choice. Lastly—and you also heard this from Jack Gartside—the fishing in this lower section of Maine is good even throughout the daylight hours. As Jim Bernstein told me, "I've had some of my best fishing then."

CHAPTER 11

New Hampshire

Inever gave New Hampshire much thought when it came to saltwater fishing. That all changed when I started fly fishing and was introduced to the opportunities that are along its short coast.

Few people equate New Hampshire with any type of shorebound saltwater fishing. When they think of the Granite State, folks imagine the White Mountains, Lake Winnipesaukee, and winter skiing. And indeed, New Hampshire is a beautiful state where, until 1603, only the Native American tribes of the Abenaki and Pennacook roamed the land. It was in that year that Martin Pring, whose mission was to map the area and set up trade with the Indians, sailed up the Piscataqua River. He was in search of sassafras, a tree prized for its roots, which were used for medicinal purposes.

Records indicate that the first settlements in New Hampshire were started in 1623. There were two, with one near the mouth of the Piscataqua River; it was called Little Harbor and also Pannaway. Today it is the town of Rye. The second settlement was located farther up the river in the area where Dover is today.

New Hampshire, which was the northernmost of the original 13 states, was initially a part of an area called New Virginia. Then the northeast section became New England. There is some dispute as to who made that change in name, King James or Captain John Smith. It was Captain Smith who discovered the Isle of Shoals, which sits some $6^{1}/_{2}$ miles off the coast of New Hampshire.

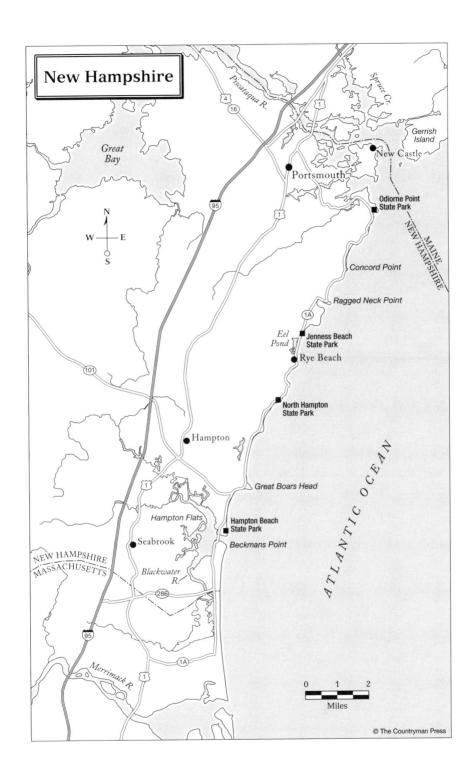

New Hampshire

Great
Bay

Piscataqua R.

Spruce Cr.

Gerrish
Island

New Castle

Portsmouth

Odiorne Point
State Park

MAINE
NEW HAMPSHIRE

Concord Point

Ragged Neck Point

*Eel
Pond*

Jenness Beach
State Park

Rye Beach

North Hampton
State Park

Hampton

Great Boars Head

Hampton Flats

Hampton Beach
State Park

Seabrook

Beckmans Point

NEW HAMPSHIRE
MASSACHUSETTS

*Blackwater
R.*

Merrimack R.

ATLANTIC OCEAN

0   1   2
Miles

© The Countryman Press

New Hampshire, which was named after the county of Hampshire in England, played a large role in the Revolutionary War. For example, nearly all the soldiers at the battle of Bunker Hill were from New Hampshire. Many other famous names from that era spent time in Portsmouth—a major hub of anti-British government activity. John Paul Jones lived there for nearly two years, while other revolutionary notables including Paul Revere, George Washington, Benjamin Franklin, and John Hancock spent time there, as well.

Prior to our country's break from England, all the white pines of New Hampshire that were 2 to 3 feet in diameter belonged to the king of England. This valuable resource was highly prized and used as masts for the sailing ships of the king's navy. Shipbuilding became a major industry in New Hampshire during those early years, and is still a valuable industry.

New Hampshire was also part of the triangle trade, as was Boston. *Triangle trade* refers to the unsavory business whereby sugarcane was harvested by slaves in such places as Barbados and Haiti then shipped to New England locations, where it was manufactured into rum. The rum was then shipped to Africa to be sold, with the profits used for the purchase of additional slaves, who were taken to the West Indies.

New Hampshire is a fairly large state that is about 180 miles long, and between 50 and 90 miles wide. Many people overlook the coastline, which is a mere 17 miles in length. I was guilty of this myself for many years. To me, New Hampshire was the 20 minutes of driving on I-95 between the borders of Massachusetts and Maine, with only the interruption of a tollbooth. After I began to spend more time fly fishing, however, I learned what I had been missing thanks to my friend Bob Mitchell. Bob, who is a fresh- and saltwater guide and senior editor for *Fly Fishing Magazine,* introduced me to a number of good saltwater fly-fishing destinations along New Hampshire's short stretch of coastline.

The primary game fish for fly rodders along the 17-mile coastline is the striped bass. But as Bob has reminded me on a couple of trips, don't be surprised if you catch an occasional mackerel or pollock while fishing for stripers. The deeper-water locations are where this is most likely to happen.

The foremost forage baitfish are sand eels and silverside minnows. In spring blueback herring move in along the coast and into the estuaries to spawn. Smelt may be around early in spring, but will then move to cooler offshore waters until fall. Bunker or menhaden will be around from late summer into the fall.

Striped bass normally arrive in New Hampshire's waters about the middle of May. They begin the migration south in early fall, and are usually gone by the first or second week of October. They are very opportunistic feeders and, besides the baitfish mentioned, will also eat small lobsters, crabs, pollock, and mackerel. I can attest to how much stripers love mackerel and pollock. They were the live bait of choice when I fished Provincetown for bass in the 1960s. Bob Mitchell informed me this past year that he'd found a good-sized lobster in the belly of a bass he caught. Stripers sure have a keen sense for fine cuisine.

Traveling from north to south along New Hampshire's coastline, the first location I'd suggest to the fly angler is Odiorne Point Sate Park in Rye. The easiest way to reach it and all of the other fly-fishing locations is to get onto NH 1A. Start at the rotary just off I-95 in Portsmouth. It's the last exit driving north before you cross the Piscataqua River Bridge into Maine. Once at the rotary, you'll want to take US 1 south. Driving about 2 miles, look for Elwyn Road and turn left there. In less than $1^{1}/_{2}$ miles you'll come to NH 1A at Foyes Corner, as Elwyn Road ends. Bearing or turning right will put you onto NH 1A; follow that road to Odiorne Point State Park.

If you are driving along the coast in Maine, simply get onto US 1 in Kittery and cross the Memorial Bridge into Portsmouth. You should then take a left onto Miller Avenue, which is also NH 1A. As you drive that south, it will become Sagamore Avenue just before you approach Foyes Corner, in Rye. At this point you are not far from Odiorne Point State Park.

The first sign you will see for Odiorne Point State Park will be on your left and is for the boat-launch ramp. Continue driving past it to the next sign for the park, which will also be on the left. This sign marks the entrance to the park and tells you that this is the location for Odiorne Point State Park, the Fort Dearborn Site, and the Seacoast Science Center.

Odiorne Point State Park, which is some 300 acres in size and the site of one of the 1623 settlements, is open from 8 AM to 8 PM and charges a minimal entry fee. Parking should be no problem since there is a large lot just inside the gate. I've been told that some people drive past the gate to a small, public parking area along the side of the road and then walk into the park.

The park is a scenic location with its rocky shoreline facing the open Atlantic. The striped bass fishing is done primarily from low water through the incoming tide. This allows you to see the structure present and where the pockets or holes are located. As anglers have learned, however, if there's no bait in the area, the fishing results will be very slim. As noted, this a rocky shore, with a large amount of structure to fish. Korkers or similar studded footwear that provide better footing are a must when you fish this type of shoreline.

The point behind the science center is a prime fishing location. There are several large rocks just to the right of the point that make ideal bass structure. A slow retrieve through the water that swirls around these rocks will produce stripers. Also, try drifting a fly through this same water.

Another good location is the bowl to the left of the point. Stripers will often drive the bait into this bowl and, once they have them cornered, feed for some time. It is a bit of a walk over the rocks to fish the complete shoreline since this bowl is fairly large, but it's well worth the effort when the bait and bass are there. If there is only bait present, be patient, for the bass will show. This is a catch-and-release-only site since Odiorne Point State Park is run by New Hampshire Fish & Game.

In addition to having excellent fly fishing nearby, this is one of those spots that the whole family can enjoy. Besides having a picnic, the children will find the science center to be a very interesting place to tour. There are a number educational displays featuring local marine life, with live exhibits.

As you make your way south on NH 1A, the next couple of fishing destinations are nameless; I'll try to be as specific as possible to help you locate them. The first is just half a mile down the road from Odiorne Point State Park. There is a parking area on the left side of the road—the first one you encounter going south. This is probably the public parking that I mentioned earlier.

This location is also very rocky, with water washing around large rocks and great striper structure. Again, you should fish this spot from dead low to high tide. Be sure to keep retreating as water rises at any of these rocky locations. If you don't, you'll be caught on a rock with no access to dry ground. The tide along the New Hampshire coast will have a difference of 8 to 10 feet in height from low to high. A moon tide, onshore wind, or combination of the two can increase this height by at least another foot or more.

The key structure to fish at this location is the bowl to the left of the parking area. Though this is a smaller bowl than the one at Odiorne Point State Park, it can be just as productive. Also, fish around the rocks as they become covered with water. A drifting fly that is slowly sinking along the rocks is often the easy meal that bass are looking for.

Though the next location down the road has no name, I like to call it the green sign pull-off. It's a bit father down NH 1A, and it, too, has a parking area located on the left side of the road. This pull-off has a green sign that faces the road with information about the Isles of Shoals, a group of islands just offshore. This is the last such pull-off on the left side of the road before you reach Wallis Sands State Park. Though the parking area accommodates only a few cars, this can be very good spot if the bait is around. It's worth taking some time at this location and fishing the incoming tide.

Though it may sound like I'm repeating myself, this location also has a bowl to the left of the parking area. As at the other locations, such structure is a key feeding station for stripers along this section of the coast. The bait will gather in these bowls or be driven into them by the bass. Either way, this type of structure allows the striped bass to contain the bait in one area and feed upon them. And if there is bait present, this is one of the best fly-fishing spots along the coast.

It is a 4- or 5-mile drive farther south on NH 1A to Jenness Beach State Park. Look for the large parking lot on your left, which faces a sandy beach and the ocean. A sign in that lot identifies it as Jenness State Park. The parking lot has meters, and unfortunately you have to feed them quarters from 8 AM until midnight. Additionally, there is a four-hour maximum on the parking meters—but that's nearly a full tide, so it shouldn't be too much of a problem.

You may be inclined to fish the beach, but given the constraints of tide and parking meter, head to your left and the better fishing at the rocky point jutting into the Atlantic. You should time it so that you are as far out on the point as possible at the time of low tide, and then begin to work your way back toward the beach as the tide moves in. You'll need studded footwear when working this point. As with the New Hampshire locations previously described, the primary game fish here is the striper. Depending upon the time of the season, though, you can catch an occasional pollock or mackerel at any of these spots.

From Jenness Beach State Park, the next fly-fishing destination that I like is Hampton Beach State Park. To reach it, you'll have to drive on NH 1A south through Hampton Beach. The state park is situated on the left, just before you cross the bridge into Seabrook. Like Jenness Beach, the parking lot has meters that are in use from 8 AM until midnight, with a maximum time limit of four hours.

Hampton's main feature is the large, sandy beach that is situated at the mouth of Hampton harbor. The fly-rodder has the option of fishing the ocean-side, the inlet, or the harbor—all from one spot. Stripers and late summer blues will pursue bait into the inlet and harbor on the rising tide, and then drop back out as the tide recedes. Concentrate your fishing times in the early morning and evening hours at this location.

After leaving Hampton Beach Sate Park and shortly after crossing the bridge in Seabrook, there is a nice fly-fishing spot on your right in Hampton Harbor. You will see an open area of grass and sand on your right; the shoulder is large enough that you can pull off and park. Be sure that you don't pull off too far and end up in soft sand. You'll be directly across Hampton Harbor from the Seabrook Nuclear Power Plant.

It's just a short walk to the water, where a sandy shoreline runs from a bulkhead on your left all the way around to the bridge on your right. This is a good location from spring into October, with a possible lull in the action in August. The structure here includes sandbars all along this shoreline. The best way to fish this section of water is to be on the downcurrent side of a sandbar and cast your fly up onto the bar. Then slowly work the fly off the sandbar and into the deeper water where the stripers are waiting for a meal to be swept over the sandbar. You should fish these sandbars on the outgoing tide, from high water to low. However, be sure to arrive at low tide so you can see the structure you'll be fishing. I like this spot because it has easy access, it's easy to fish, and it's one of the few good fishing locations along the New Hampshire shoreline that isn't rocky.

Another benefit of this location is that if you're looking for bluefish, Hampton Harbor is the place you're most likely to find them. Blues will occasionally chase bait into the harbor, and when they do, you'll have a ball with a popper on floating line. Remember, you can't move it fast enough for a bluefish. But if you're having trouble with a popper or the breeze is killing your cast, use an intermediate or sinking line and a fly to match the bait. Make your retrieve as fast and erratic as you can; and don't forget the wire leader.

Not that far from the shores of Hampton Harbor, and just before entering Massachusetts, there is a first-class location for fly fishing an estuary. About $1\frac{1}{2}$ miles south on NH 1A you'll come to the intersection where NH 286 heads west. Turn right here, and in a very short distance on NH 286 you'll come to a bridge that spans the Blackwater River. As soon as you cross the bridge, you can pull off the road and park on the shoulder, across from Bartlett's Farm Stand. There is another spot to park just ahead and on the left side of the road, as well.

From this spot you can access and fish the Blackwater River, both north and south from the bridge. This is great striped bass water and provides first-rate fishing throughout the season. As good as the fishing is during the day, I recommend that you fish this river at night; it's even better then. Nevertheless, this is quality estuary fly fishing regardless of when you fish it.

One of the better locations on the river—you'll want to check it each time you fish the Blackwater—is the rip just to the south of the NH 286 bridge. Bass love this type of water where they have an advantage over their prey. There is an excellent view of the rip from the bridge. A sinking line and small fly in this rip will produce striped bass. However, do work the river to the north as well as the southern sections, because you will find bass throughout this estuary. The Blackwater River flows into Hampton Harbor at its northernmost end.

From about the last week of May through the summer and into early fall the Blackwater River is a quality fly-fishing destination; after about the first week of October, the action will begin to taper off. The fishing in this estuary is at its best when there is a good supply of sand eels in the river. The appeal of the Blackwater is that you can fish it with just hip boots. But do be especially careful when fishing this location at night; don't stand too close to the edge of the bank, since one false step and you will find yourself in some fast-moving water.

This location has an added pleasure, which is Brown's, an eatery that serves an outstanding fried clam meal. You passed Brown's on your right, just before you crossed over the bridge and parked. Anglers will also park at the back of Brown's and fish that side of the river. As my friend Bob Mitchell has noted to me on several occasions, a stop at Brown's for some clams can really lift your spirits when the fishing is slow. It's an excellent way to take a break from fishing, regardless of how well you're doing.

If you continue west on NH 286, it will connect with I-95 in Massachusetts. Driving north on I-95 in Massachusetts is an easy way to reach all these New Hampshire coastline locations. Farther north on I-95 in New Hampshire, NH 101 east will take you into Hampton Beach and NH 1A. From there you have a short drive either north or south to some great fly fishing.

A key to fishing any location, whether it's a familiar one or a new destination, is to use flies that match the bait that is around. Along the New Hampshire coast, the ever-popular Clouser Minnows and Deceivers are the best choices to try initially. I like a chartreuse and white Clouser Minnow when it comes to a decision of color. Anytime you're new to a fishing location, it's also worth the time to stop and check the local fly shop as to the best flies and colors to use. Also, while fishing, pay attention to what the other anglers are using, especially if they are being successful and you aren't. Most anglers will share such information with you; if not, it costs nothing to ask.

One bit of advice that Bob Mitchell gave me when I first traveled the New Hampshire coastline with him was to use primarily intermediate lines, except for early in the season or when fishing particularly strong currents; then you should use a sinking line. He is also an advocate, as I am, of using a semicircle—working your casts from left to right to get good coverage of an area. If there is no action, then move a bit and repeat the pattern. This casting pattern will cover an area well and will be a more accurate way of locating where the fish are holding. Also, remember to vary your retrieves until you find the speed and movement that interest the fish. When you find eddies in any current, particularly in estuaries or around rock structure, cast your fly into the eddy and let it drift like a helpless baitfish. It's a surefire technique that takes fish.

CHAPTER 12

Cape Cod
and the Islands

M ention Cape Cod, Martha's Vineyard, or Nantucket to a salt-water fly rodder and you'll evoke an enthusiastic and positive response. People have either fished there and want to return, or are planning to go there sometime. It's the vacation destination of many tourists and anglers. Every fishing magazine has a feature article or two yearly on these New England fly-fishing destinations.

Cape Cod and the islands of Martha's Vineyard and Nantucket are the products of the Ice Age. The Great Ice Age began about one and a half million years ago, with sheets of ice advancing into and retreating from temperate zones. In eastern New England the last invasion and retreat of ice occurred some 25,000 years ago. Nantucket and Martha's Vineyard mark the boundary of the ice's farthest advance. During that time, and for some time after the ice's slow retreat, the worldwide sea level was about 400 feet below its current level. Therefore, Cape Cod, Stellwagen Bank to the north, out beyond Georges Bank, and the continental shelf to the south were dry land. But the sea was moving ever closer. As the ice melted over thousands of years, what we know as the Atlantic Ocean claimed the lower portions of the region, shaping and building the sandy beaches, cliffs, marshes, and inlets of New England.

This is why Cape Cod, Nantucket, and Martha's Vineyard are such a favorite of anglers. Not only is there a quality fishery here, but the number and variety of locations that can be fished on foot are numerous. And at various times of the year each location will produce fish. Additionally, wind is less of a concern when fishing Cape Cod or the Islands because you can almost always find a spot where you can get out of the wind—or at least not have it in your face.

Cape Cod and the Islands are popular tourist destinations, and there's no doubt things can get crowded at times. However, an angler can easily find spots, particularly during the prime fishing times from early evening until sunrise. This is when I believe that the fishing is at its best and the most enjoyable. It's also when access to many of these locations is less of a hassle.

Cape Cod

Cape Cod was first settled in 1637, in an area that is now the town of Sandwich. Plymouth Colony records indicate that permission was given to 10 men and their families to settle there. Back then there was no Cape Cod Canal, just two estuaries in that area. The longer of the rivers flowed into Buzzards Bay, while the smaller stream emptied into Cape Cod Bay. George Washington was the first to recognize the need for a canal to move goods quicker to and from Boston, and ports to the south. After many starts, the original canal was not completed until 1914. It was narrow, and the fast-moving tides made navigation through the 17-plus miles of this man-made waterway very tricky. In 1928 the U.S. Army Corp of Engineers took over the canal and enlarged it to its present size. In 1935 the two bridges spanning the Cape Cod Canal were completed. With their completion, the outside world began to learn about the beauty of Cape Cod and the fishing it offered. Following World War II the word began to spread among the saltwater angling community: Cape Cod was the home of trophy-striped bass and bluefish.

If you look at a map of Cape Cod it resembles an arm, bent at the elbow and jutting some 60 miles into the Atlantic, separated from the mainland by the Cape Cod Canal. The mostly uninhabited Elizabeth Islands stretch from the upper arm southward into the Atlantic. Just offshore of the upper arm and to the east of the Elizabeth Islands is Martha's Vineyard, which is visible and just a short boat trip from the Cape's southern shore. East and south of the Cape's elbow lies the smaller island of Nantucket.

Each section of the arm of Cape Cod has its unique characteristics. The

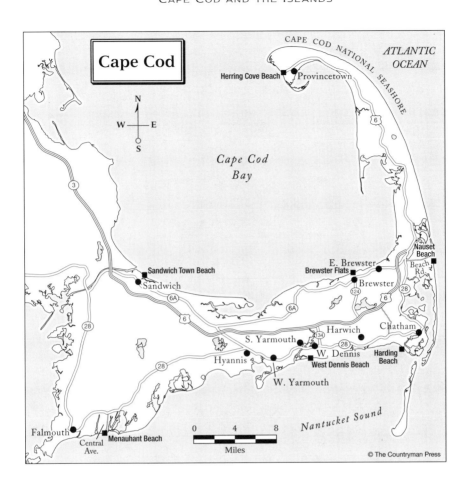

inside or northern portion of the arm faces the waters of Cape Cod Bay. The water here, even in summer, is colder than the more shallow Nantucket Sound, which is bounded by the Elizabeth Islands, Martha's Vineyard, Nantucket, and Cape Cod's southern shore. This is important because at certain times of the season, Nantucket, Martha's Vineyard, and the Cape's southern shoreline will host additional species of fish to pursue. Though striped bass and bluefish can be taken from most locations around Cape Cod, Nantucket Sound—because of its warmer water in summer—is home to bonito, false albacore, squeteague, and Spanish mackerel.

To the east, the outer portion of the forearm faces the Atlantic. This section of the Cape has predominantly sandy beaches and surf. Other sections of the Cape have light surf or none at all. Locals refer to this east-facing section of Cape Cod as "the backside." Though it may be more difficult for the fly rodder to fish the surf here, once it's understood and mastered it can be extremely productive.

There is one minor deterrent to fishing along this ocean-side stretch of Cape Cod during the summer—a reddish brown alga suspended in the water in great clouds; anglers have tagged it with the name "mung." It will build up on your line and plug the rod guides. The stripers love to hide in the mung but it can be nearly impossible to fish when it's present. If you can find sections of water free of the stuff, fish those.

The saltwater fishing season on Cape Cod covers a span of about seven months. The fishing begins around the end of April or early May, depending on spring weather. The first fish to arrive are the striped bass; the initial influx of fish will be the smaller ones. The larger bass aren't too far behind these schoolies. They initially appear on the south side of the Cape, in Nantucket Sound. As they move into the estuaries and bays to feed, anglers from Falmouth to Chatham are taking bass. Within days, fish are also moving through the Cape Cod Canal and spreading throughout Cape Cod Bay. As the ocean's waters warm, bass are in the surf from Nauset Beach to Provincetown.

By about the second week in May, bluefish move into Nantucket Sound, onto the shallow flats, and along the southern beaches of the Cape. Like the bass, as the weather and water warms, the bluefish will spread east and up along the "backside." By June they will be in Cape Cod Bay for the summer. Throughout the summer, striped bass and blues can be found feeding along shore locations, particularly at dusk, during the night, and at first light. By the early part of August, the shallower water of Nantucket Sound has warmed to its summer peak and bonito will move in. Spanish mackerel, smaller in size than those in more southern waters, will also be in Nantucket Sound then. Around the first of September the false albacore arrive, providing additional sizzling action for anglers.

The albacore, Spanish mackerel, and bonito will remain the shortest amount of time and begin to disappear before the end of October. By then the bluefish are also on the move, leaving the colder waters of Cape Cod Bay. If weather conditions are good, they will linger around the south-facing beaches until late October. As they start their migration south, they stop and feed wherever they find food. This action can occur at any time of day since they take every chance available to feed, in preparation for their trip to the waters off North Carolina. The striped bass are also on the move, fueling up for their migration to warmer waters. Like the bluefish, they will not pass up

Joe Balboni carefully works a striped bass toward the shore of Mill Creek in Sandwich.

the opportunity for food at any time of day. By mid-November the majority of the bass have moved on.

In Cape Cod's shoreline waters, the primary food of striped bass, bluefish, bonito, and albacore is sand eels and silversides. Patterns like small Deceivers, Clouser Minnows, and sand eel patterns should be your first choice. Tan and white, chartreuse and white, plus olive and white are good color selections during daylight hours. After sunset and before sunrise, the flies should be darker in color, if not black. In fall schools of small menhaden, called peanut bunker, will be around. Therefore, make sure you have a variety of small bunker patterns in your fly box when fishing in fall.

Certain towns on Cape Cod provide access to their beaches for four-wheel-drive vehicles. This is an excellent way to fish some outstanding locations. Barnstable charges for a vehicle sticker to travel the long, sandy beach of Sandy Neck. This beach gives anglers access to fish Cape Cod Bay. For information about Sandy Neck, call 508-362-8306. The town of Orleans handles the fees and regulations for Nauset Beach. You can get information on fees and rules by calling 508-240-3700. To obtain the latest information about traveling the beaches within the Cape Cod National Seashore, plus access, fees, and regulations there, call 508-487-2100. Chapter 14 will tell you more about beach access, safety equipment, and driving the beach.

There are two good, very detailed books of maps for Cape Cod, Nantucket, and Martha's Vineyard. One is the *Cape Cod & Islands Atlas,* produced by the Butterworth Company; the other is the *Street Atlas Cape Cod, Including Martha's Vineyard & Nantucket,* printed by Arrow Map. Both can be purchased at most convenience stores or bookstores on the Cape or the Islands. These books, which show every street, town landing, and water access, are a valuable asset to the shorebound angler.

Cape Cod can seem like an intimidating place to fish, especially for the angler who hasn't fished there. With more than 300 miles of shoreline, there are numerous locations offering opportunities to catch fish. For the vacationing angler hoping to fly fish a time or two while on Cape Cod, the job of selecting a good spot may seem difficult. However, it doesn't take a secret location to find fish. Some of the most popular tourist destinations on Cape Cod are also excellent fishing spots, providing good fly fishing from spring to fall.

Given the amount of shoreline that Cape Cod has, an angler can feel unsure of where to fish, particularly if his time is limited. However, throughout the Cape there are numerous locations that afford easy access for the shorebound, wading fisherman. The book *Fishing New England, A Cape Cod Shore Guide,* by Gene Bourque, provides information on 41 locations, and I am sure Gene will agree that he has covered just the better-known spots.

The western end of Cape Cod, known as the Upper Cape, has many good locations for the fly angler. One of my favorite spots is in East Falmouth. Menauhant Beach, on Nantucket Sound, is an excellent location for striped bass throughout the season, with early spring and fall being the best times. The bass arrive here early in spring—primarily smaller fish that average about 18 to 20 inches. These early-May fish are hungry and are great sport on a 6-, 7-, or 8-weight outfit. As the season progresses, the fish get bigger.

Menauhant Beach has two parking lots, one on each side of the outlet of Bournes Pond. There are a number of short, stone jetties along the beach, and several of them will be covered at high tide. Fish love to hang around these structures, which should not be overlooked. The bass will also enter Bournes Pond to feed. This is a spot that can be very productive in the early morning and evening casting with silverside and sand eel patterns.

If you plan to fish Bournes Pond, make a visit at low tide to see where the holes are and where the shallow flats drop off sharply into the channel, especially near the bridge. On an outgoing tide the current can be strong; step off into the deep water and you'll be quickly swept under the bridge out into Nantucket Sound.

Menauhant Beach is located off MA 28, in East Falmouth. Going east on MA 28, take a right onto Central Avenue. Follow Central Avenue to the end and at the stop sign turn right onto Menauhant Road. In less than half a mile are the two town parking lots located on each side of the outlet of Bournes Pond. The town of Falmouth charges a daily fee of $10 to park there from Memorial Day to Labor Day. However, if you're fishing before 8 AM or after 6 PM, one of the parking lots is normally left open for anglers, and there is no fee to park then. If you want additional information about this location or any other Falmouth town beaches, call the Beach Committee at 508-548-8623.

On the north side of the Cape, in the town of Sandwich, are two locations that can be reached from the same parking area. Traveling west on MA 6A, at the second traffic light in Sandwich, just past the police and fire station, turn right onto Tupper Road. Not very far on the right is Town Neck Road. As you turn right, you will immediately go over the railroad tracks. In less than a mile you'll see the water; bear right here onto Freeman Avenue. Follow Freeman Avenue to its end and take a left onto Wood Avenue Extension. Just continue on this road a short distance to the Sandwich Town Beach. Parking there during the day, from Memorial Day to Labor Day, requires a $4 daily pass. Before 8 AM and after 6 PM, however, you should be able to park and fish without a pass.

From Town Beach, it's a short walk over the dunes to a beach, with jetties, that faces onto Cape Cod Bay. A short walk from the east end of the parking will take you to Mill Creek, which flows into Old Sandwich Harbor, along with Dock Creek and Old Harbor Creek. Old Sandwich Harbor empties into Cape Cod Bay at the end of Town Beach.

Town Beach has several large jetties and is a good summer and fall fishing spot. When the tide drops out of the Cape Cod Canal, whose eastern entrance is located just to the west of this beach, striped bass will spread out along the beach to feed. In fall bluefish will join the bass here to feed on sand eels, silversides, and menhaden, or peanut bunker. Dusk to early morning is the best time to fish this beach.

On the inside, Mill Creek to Old Sandwich Harbor is a great place to wade and catch some nice stripers. Fish can be taken here at any time of the day or night. Clouser Minnows, sand eel imitations, and sparse silversides patterns will take fish here. Depending on the depth of water and how fast it's moving, use an intermediate or slow-sinking line.

Let me give you a word of warning at this point: Several fishermen have drowned while wading and fishing different locations on the Cape. The opening at the end of Town Beach, where Old Sandwich Harbor drains into Cape Cod Bay, is one such dangerous location. There are several things you can do to avoid such a tragedy.

First, when at all possible, visit the area you intend to fish at low water to see where the holes and edges of channels are situated. This is especially important if you are going to fish that location at night. Know how far and where to wade. When you are fishing, wear an inflatable PFD, such as the kind that look like suspenders. Have a belt around your waist to keep your waders from filling with water. And finally, never fish such water alone.

If you travel farther east on MA 6, which is known as the Mid-Cape Highway, some 10 miles or so, you'll be in what's called the Mid-Cape area. There are a number of good fishing locations on both the north and south shores here. One such place on the south side is West Dennis Beach, which has good fishing from spring to fall. Look for striped bass to arrive first, followed by the bluefish about mid-May. This area's fishing will continue through the summer and into fall.

To reach West Dennis Beach, take exit 9 off the Mid-Cape Highway and proceed south on MA 134 to MA 28. Turn right there and drive less than 1½ miles east. At School Street in West Dennis, turn left and continue to the end. Turn left onto Lower County Road, and in just a very short distance you will come to Lighthouse Road on your right. West Dennis Beach is located at the end of Lighthouse Road, on the far side of a small rotary. Like most municipal facilities on Cape Cod, this one charges a parking fee between Memorial Day and Labor Day. As of this writing, it was $10 per day. The gate isn't staffed before 8 AM and after 6 PM, when most anglers would be fishing this beach. Note that no fishing is allowed in areas where people are swimming.

A long, sandy beach stretches from the entrance to the beach, west to where the Bass River empties into Nantucket Sound. Often, the fish will trap bait along this beach. Inside the jetty, along the Bass River, is an area that affords the wading fly angler a nice stretch of water to fish. When facing the river, wading to the right will take you to a side bay and marshes. Again, this is an estuary opening, so watch for the steep drop-off at the channel's edge.

A short distance to the east, and on the north side, facing Cape Cod Bay, is the town of Brewster. The water off the town of Brewster is an excellent wade-fishing location; it is known as the Brewster Flats. When the tide drops, there are literally miles and miles of cuts and channels to fish. Summer and early fall are good times to fish the Brewster Flats, especially if you have a dropping tide in the late evening or at first light. The abundance of sand eels here makes this a favorite striped bass feeding location.

If you're going to fish a late-evening tide into the dark, fish this area about two or three hours before low tide, and while it's still light, so you can see the deep channels and holes that hold fish. Additionally, do not be fooled by how quickly the tide comes in once it changes. A standard 9-foot tide can rapidly cover a sandbar, and the shallow channel you waded through could be over your head. Caution is the key here. Keep an eye on the clock and the tide.

Everyone who fishes the Brewster Flats should carry two very important items: a tide chart and a compass. The fog can move in quickly, and without a compass you can get disoriented. It's also useful for night fishing, helping you to retrace your steps to your car. A cautionary tale: A friend told me that one particularly dark night, he came upon an angler walking from his left, at right angles to his course. My friend asked where the other angler was headed, and he replied, "I am headed back to the parking lot." Luckily my friend and his compass were there to assist him.

There are a number of Brewster town beaches along the shore that will give you access to the Brewster Flats. All are within a very short driving distance of MA 6A. However, there is one location that gives you an added dimension to your fishing. It's found in the westernmost section of town that borders two creeks flowing into Cape Cod Bay. To reach the town of Brewster and this spot, take exit 10 off the Mid-Cape Highway and drive north on MA 124. Just before you reach MA 6A, turn left onto MA 137 and go a short distance to MA 6A, where you will turn left. In less than $1\frac{1}{2}$ miles, turn right onto Paine's Creek Road. A short drive will take you to a town parking area.

Paine's Creek is next to the parking area, and just beyond it is Quivett Creek. On the dropping tide, the mouths of both these creeks can be very productive. Fish a sand eel pattern here, casting just slightly upcurrent. Let the fly drift in the current and do not retrieve until it has made the swing back across the current. A striper will often take the fly as it starts that swing.

Brewster requires a parking permit for all its town beaches. The fee for nonresidents is $8 per day or $25 for a week. But before Memorial Day and after Labor Day, no fee is charged. Parking permits can be purchased at the visitors center, 2198 Main Street (MA 6A). While you're there, also get a copy of the *Visitors Guide to Brewster Beaches.* It contains a map for all the beach locations, a tide table, and additional information you will find helpful.

This eastern portion of the Cape Cod is known as the Lower Cape, and here at the "elbow" is the town of Chatham; it has another great site to fish, Harding's Beach. Facing the eastern end of Nantucket Sound, this beach is a good fly-fishing destination from spring into fall. This location, like many, is best fished in the early morning, at dusk, and after dark. From the parking lot, there is more than $1^1/_2$ miles of beach running east to where Stage Harbor empties into the sound.

The parking fee at this beach is $8 per day and can be paid at the lot. As with most Cape Cod beaches, no fee is charged in the off-season. To reach Harding's Beach when driving east on MA 28 into Chatham, look for MA 137 entering on the left. Less than 2 miles after passing MA 137 will be Barn Hill Road, on your right. Take Barn Hill a short distance and then bear right onto Harding's Beach Road. This will take you to the parking lot at Harding's Beach.

Beginning in spring and continuing through early fall, bluefish and striped bass can be found along this sandy shoreline chasing sand eels. Though the nearly 2-mile walk to the Stage Harbor Light and the opening to Stage Harbor may seem long, it can be well worth it. The flats, the small waterways between them, and the main channel should be fished on a dropping tide.

Not to be repetitive, but this is an estuary opening with a fast-moving current. Be careful and don't step where you can't see the bottom. It's better to be cautious than sorry; no fish is worth risking your life.

Though sand eels are the primary prey of the bass and blues into autumn, many fall seasons there have been schools of 2- to 4-inch peanut bunker cruising along Harding's Beach. When this happens, the bonito and albacore quickly discover these tasty morsels. This action can last for several days, with bonito and albacore slashing through the schools of bunker they have pinned against the beach—sometimes in just 3 feet of water.

If you want to fish the backside or Atlantic side of the Cape, a trip to Nauset Beach, in Orleans, should be on your list. This can be a heavy surf area, so plan accordingly; easterly winds and offshore storms can create a mean surf. However, big bluefish and bass feed in these waters from early summer until fall. During the summer, the prime time to fish here is early or late in the day and at night, but in fall the action of migrating bass and blues can happen at anytime. There is about $2^{1}/_{2}$ miles of good beach and surf, if you go north from the parking lot. The beach ends at the inlet for Nauset Harbor.

The beach to the south, from the parking lot, can be just as good. As with any location that you're going to fish for the first time, take a walk along the beach at low water to find the points, cuts, bars, and other structure that will attract fish. This whole beach has some outstanding striper fishing in fall, punctuated with occasional bluefish blitzes.

To reach Nauset Beach, take Main Street east from the center of Orleans; at the fork in the road, bear left onto Beach Road. The gate at the beach's parking lot is staffed 24 hours a day from Memorial Day weekend until Labor Day. When I last checked, the nonresident parking fee was $8.

No list of Cape Cod fishing destinations would be complete without Herring Cove Beach. Located in the Cape Cod National Seashore, Provincetown, this fly-fishing destination sits at the very tip of Cape Cod. It's where Cape Cod Bay meets the Atlantic Ocean. From June through October, this is an excellent place for the shorebound angler to fish for striped bass and large bluefish.

The parking lot at Herring Cove Beach is located at the end of MA 6. The Cape Cod National Seashore starts collecting daily parking fees there in late June, and does so until Labor Day. The parking lot is open from 6 AM until midnight, and no overnight parking is allowed. However, anglers can obtain a permit during the day at the visitors center, at no additional cost; the permit will allow them to park all night in the lot and fish. But be aware that regulations do not allow sleeping in your car.

Cape Cod has so many locations for the shore-bound fly angler to fish. There is, however, one drawback to fishing the Cape. It's a grand place to fish, but it's also a very popular tourist destination, so if you plan to stay there and fish for a time, make your reservations well in advance. Nevertheless, this is the kind of place where the whole family will enjoy themselves, and you will catch fish.

Nantucket

To the south and off the elbow of Cape Cod lies the Gray Lady—so named, I am told, for the fog that often envelops the island. Made famous by Herman Melville in his novel *Moby-Dick,* Nantucket was first settled by Native Americans. Nine Massachusetts Englishmen purchased it from them in 1659 for the amount of 30 pounds sterling and two beaver hats. Their aim

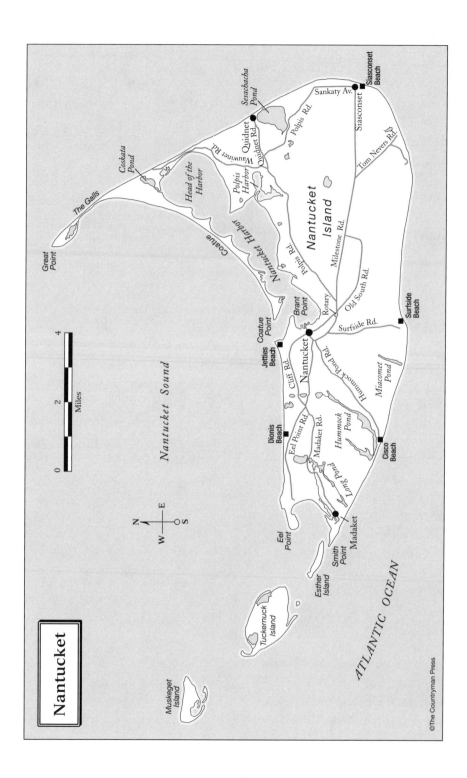

Nantucket

was to escape the intolerant Puritans and use the island for agricultural purposes. Among those men were Tristram Coffin and Thomas Macy—names that are woven into the history of the island.

Nantucket is most famous for its ties to the whaling industry from the early 1700s to the mid-1800s. At its prime more than 80 whaling ships listed Nantucket as their home port. These sailors were the first Americans to sail the Pacific. There is much on the island today to remind visitors of that time in our history. As an example, the cobblestones that are the surface of a number of Nantucket streets came from the holds of empty ships. They were used as ballast by the whaling ships when returning from delivering whale oil to Europe.

While researching the history of Nantucket, I discovered how the pineapple came to be the symbol of welcome and hospitality here. In whaling days, captains brought pineapples with them when they returned to Nantucket and displayed them as a signal that they were again home and all guests were welcomed.

Sitting at the edge of the Atlantic, Nantucket Island can be reached only by boat or airplane. Several airlines fly to Nantucket from Boston, New York, and Hyannis, on Cape Cod. It would be best to check with your travel agent as to airlines and flight schedules.

Currently there are a couple of ferries that run year-round, plus one seasonal service. The ferries that make the 30-mile run from Hyannis are Hy-Line Cruises and the Steamship Authority. Hy-Line Cruises provides only passenger service between Hyannis, on Cape Cod, and Nantucket. They also offer a high-speed ferry service, which makes the run in about one hour, but there is an additional cost for this quicker boat ride. For information on Hy-Line Cruises, schedules, and reservations, call 1-800-492-8082.

The Steamship Authority, which also operates out of Hyannis, has a passenger-only high-speed ferry service, as well. In addition, they have ferries that can transport vehicles to the island. However, the Steamship Authority requires that all reservations for this service be made well in advance. Vehicle reservations for the Nantucket ferry can be made by calling 508-477-8600. Walk-on passengers usually don't need a reservation. For information on schedules and rates, call the Steamship Authority at 508-548-5011.

There is also a seasonal passenger ferry service to Nantucket from Harwich Port on Cape Cod; it's run by Freedom Cruise. Call them at 508-432-8999 to find out more about schedules and cost, and to make reservations.

If you wish to stay on Nantucket, there are numerous hotels, inns, guest

The west jetty is located at the entrance to Nantucket Harbor. This location should be fished in the morning or evening when boat traffic is light.

houses, and bed & breakfasts on the island. Again, because this is an extremely popular tourist location, the earlier you book your reservations, the better your chances of getting the dates you wish. For information on island accommodations, contact the Nantucket Island Chamber of Commerce at 508-228-1700 or log on to their web site at www.nantucketchamber.org. Another good source of island information is the Nantucket Visitor Services and Information Bureau. You can contact them at 508-228-0925 or 508-228-7207.

When I was last on Nantucket, I spent some time with Captains Jeffrey and Lynn Heyer. This couple runs Cross Rip Outfitters, a well-stocked fly-tackle shop on the island. And as if that weren't enough to do, they both are guides on this island of about 50-plus square miles. On that last trip I gained additional information about fly fishing the nearly 80 miles of Nantucket shoreline.

Before telling you about some great fishing locations on Nantucket, let's take a look at the bait that will be around the island and the game fish that will be in hot pursuit. The first to arrive in spring are the herring, which normally appear in the waters around Nantucket from mid-April to the first of May. They will be moving into the estuaries and ponds of the island to spawn. A good fly choice would be a Lefty's Deceiver or similar pattern, all with a dark back and white sides.

The sand eels and silversides are not far behind the herring, showing up in mid-May. These baitfish will be around and on the menu until November. Look for bay anchovies along the shorelines during the early-fall months. Squid begin showing up at the end of May and remain until September. If you're fishing at night, try some squid patterns in Nantucket Harbor after the boat traffic has died down. This is a tip from Captain Jeff Heyer, so if you get a chance while there, do it.

Yes, there are some nice worm hatches on Nantucket. They occur in May, June, and July around the new and full moons. The hatch usually spans a time frame of two to three days prior to the new or full moon, until about a day thereafter. It's a short window, but it can offer productive fishing. Drifting your worm fly or "bunny" fly on the tide is the best approach.

The anticipated first striped bass will arrive in late April or early May. They are not only the first game fish to arrive but also the last to leave, usually sometime in November. Some of the biggest bluefish I have seen taken in New England have also come from the waters around Nantucket. They usually arrive in May and will depart on their return migration south in the latter part of October.

Near the end of July, fly rodders on Nantucket eagerly await the first bonito to make an appearance. These speedsters will be chasing bait along the beaches through October. The albacore arrive later, usually in mid-August, and provide sport for anglers until the end of September. Over recent years, Spanish mackerel have put in an appearance in September.

When packing for a trip to Nantucket, be advised that 8- and 10-weight rods will cover most of your fishing situations. Pack an extra reel or two in case one breaks down. For fly lines, take along intermediate, sinking, and floating or sinking-tip lines for use at night in the harbor and some of the other quiet-water situations you may encounter after dark.

When selecting flies for use on Nantucket, make sure you include a variety of patterns that are all white, chartreuse and white, and olive and white. These have been proven colors over the years. Also, don't overlook taking some flies that are brown and white. I have taken some of my nicest stripers on a small Lefty's Deceiver of that color combination.

If you, as a fly angler, do not like to fish the surf, the north shore of Nantucket has minimum wave action. However, it can get a bit rough there on strong, prolonged northerly winds. The major surf areas to fish are on the southern and eastern shorelines. And if you prefer to fish in a more leisurely manner, visit Nantucket during the summer. You can fish the flats and shallows in just a bathing suit. But no matter when you visit Nantucket, you'll find excellent fishing.

First of all, a number of the good fly-fishing spots on Nantucket require four-wheel-drive access. For these situations you can either bring your own vehicle or rent one on the island. Depending upon what beach area you want to access, you may need to purchase one or two beach access stickers; their price changes from year to year. You are also responsible for carrying the proper safety equipment for beach travel.

The town of Nantucket issues a sticker that covers all the beaches on the island that allow vehicle access, with the exception of Great Point. This sticker can be purchased at the Nantucket Police Station, located at 20 South Water Street. The vehicle permit for Great Point and its associated beaches can be purchased at the Great Point Gate House.

To drive to the Gate House for Great Point, travel out of town on Orange Street to the rotary, then onto Milestone Road; in a short distance turn left onto Polpis Road. Just past Polpis Harbor, which will be on your left, turn left onto Wauwinet Road. Follow this road to the Gate House. If you look at a map of Nantucket, you'll see that Great Point is reached only by traveling a good stretch of beach; this means that a four-wheel-drive vehicle is required. This section of Nantucket has much to offer the fly angler.

As you make your drive along the beach, toward Great Point, keep a watch on the water. This stretch of beach, which is approximately 5 miles to Great Point, has good fishing for stripers and blues. You'll often come across feeding fish close to shore, especially in fall.

Great Point has one of the larger rips on Nantucket that can be fished from shore. This is a prime location for both bass and bluefish; you'll find fish here at all times of the day, from sunset to sunrise being the best. But while you're there, don't ignore what lies behind Great Point and on the way to the mouth of Nantucket Harbor. This section of Nantucket Harbor is great fly-fishing water.

Traveling along the narrow spit of land that runs from Great Point in a southwesterly direction to the mouth of Nantucket Harbor is the area known as Coatue. The beauty of this long strip is that it offers first-class fishing on both sides. Look for striped bass, bluefish, Spanish mackerel, and albacore close to the outside shoreline, in what's usually a light surf.

Along the inside you should fish the bends and points, particularly early in the morning, evenings, and at night; also look for and fish the eelgrass beds along the way. This bit of Nantucket provides outstanding fishing from May through October. You can also experience worm hatches here in spring, but don't be afraid to try a worm pattern later in the season, on a quiet night's tide. Fish your fly on or very near the surface with an extremely slow movement.

On your way out to and back from Great Point, you'll pass Coskata Pond. This small salt pond is a good fly-fishing location in spring and early summer before its waters become too warm. A dropping tide in the early morning and late evening is the best, especially at the mouth of the pond. Coskata Pond can also be productive in late fall when its waters have cooled again.

If you were to continue on Polpis Road, you'll end up on Quidnet Road, which goes straight while Polpis Road turns south toward Siasconset. At the end of Quidnet Road and to your right is Sesachacha Pond. When they open this pond in spring to flush it out, there can be some very good early-season bass fishing. However, it only remains open for a couple of weeks.

On the southwest side of the island is Hummock Pond, which is also opened in spring, and sometimes in the fall, as well. Like Sesachacha Pond, it stays open for only a week or two, but if you are there when it happens, you will experience some very good striper fishing.

If you enjoy catching bluefish on a fly rod, concentrate on the south side of Nantucket. Bluefish cruise the surf all along this shoreline throughout the summer. When fishing the surf on the east and south sides, keep in mind that the fish can often be very close to shore, particularly the bass at night. They will travel the trough that has been cut by the waves, which is close to the beach and just below the low-water line.

On the southwest end of Nantucket Island sits Smith Point and more great water to fish, including a nice rip. Smith Point and adjoining Madaket Beach is a four-wheel-drive access location that is usually closed during the summer for the bird nesting season. The fishing here is good from Madaket Beach to Smith Point, with stripers, blues, bonito, and albacore providing the action. To reach Smith Point, simply take Madaket Road out of town to almost its end. Turn right onto Ames Avenue and, after crossing over the bridge, follow the road to the beach.

At the same end of the island, and north of Smith Point, is another excellent fishing location called Eel Point. This locale is very easy to get to; just follow Madaket Road from town and then go right on Eel Point Road. You will need a four-wheel-drive vehicle to get to the point, but once you're there, you'll be rewarded with some fine fishing. One great bit of structure there is

The lighthouse on Great Point stands a solitary watch over the waters of Nantucket Sound and the Atlantic Ocean.

a deep cut off the end of the point. Also take note of the flats area on the north side of Eel Point, running east. This is a very nice spot for the fly angler to wade and fish. Eel Point has striped bass and blues throughout the season, with the added attraction of bonito and albacore in late summer and fall.

In fall the whole north shore from Eel Point to the west jetty, at the entrance to Nantucket Harbor, offers outstanding fishing. An especially good area is Dionis Beach, which can be reached by several dirt roads off of Eel Point Road. I never knew which road was best until someone gave me a big assist; I was told to look for the rock with the number 40 on it. The rock marks a good access to the beach.

Farther east is the west jetty, which guards the entrance to Nantucket Harbor. It's accessible from the parking lot at the end of Bathing Beach Road. It's also very easy to reach; simply take Easton Street out of town and stay on it as it turns into Hulbert Avenue at Brant Point. Bathing Beach Road is a right turn off Hulbert.

There's normally a sandbar on the east side of the jetty that will give you access to the deeper water of the channel. This is a location that you want to fish in the early morning or evening when the boat traffic is at a minimum. Let me point out that this is one of those spots where care should be taken when wading, especially at night when you can't see where you are. Getting too close to the edge of a drop-off can cause it to give way, and you can be swept away by the current. You must also be cautious about not stepping off the edge into deeper water.

On your way to the west jetty, you passed by Brant Point Light. This is a very popular place for bait fishermen, but you can often find space to fish. The attraction here is the deep water close to shore.

There is one more good fly-fishing location on Nantucket that I want to tell you about: Polpis Harbor, which empties into Nantucket Harbor. You passed this location, which was on the left, as you traveled on Polpis Road toward Great Point. Take a left off Polpis Road onto Quaise Road, which will take you to a parking area. There are stairs here that will take you to the water. You want to move east and fish the mouth of Polpis Harbor; this spot is good in late spring and early summer for stripers. If you can time your visit there, fish the dropping tide in the early morning or late evening. The bass will be feeding on baitfish being carried out on the tide.

Nantucket is a grand place to fish and worth the effort to get there. If I were to pick a time to fish the Gray Lady, it would be fall. Of course, I think the fall in New England is a great time to be out fishing, regardless of where you are. Nantucket has good fishing throughout the season, but you can't beat the fall of the year for a shot at some outstanding fly fishing for trophy-sized fish.

Martha's Vineyard

Just 7 miles off the southern shores of Cape Cod sits the island of Martha's Vineyard. This island is larger than Nantucket and has a number of towns. Martha's Vineyard has a triangular shape, with the pinnacle pointed toward Cape Cod. The base, which faces seaward, is approximately 23 miles long, and the island is nearly 10 miles deep from the southern shoreline to its northern shores. Martha's Vineyard has a varied shoreline with numerous and outstanding fly-fishing locations for the shorebound angler.

First settled by Native Americans, Martha's Vineyard received its name in 1602 when the British explorer Bartholomew Gosnold discovered it. Seeing the wild grapes that grew there, he named the island for the grapes and after his young daughter Martha.

Today Martha's Vineyard is a very popular tourist destination. It's also a very popular fishing destination and has received much press in outdoor magazines. It has, in particular, become a favorite destination for fly fishermen. You will find local and visiting anglers fishing side by side on any given night when the word goes out that the stripers are in. It is indeed a fly-rod-friendly place.

One of the reasons that the island is so popular, aside from the good fishing, is that it's just a short and easy trip to the Vineyard. It takes 45 minutes to travel from Woods Hole, on Cape Cod, to either Oak Bluffs or Vineyard Haven via a Steamship Authority ferry. There are a number of other ferry services in-season from Hyannis and Falmouth, on the Cape, as well as New Bedford. Air service year-round is available from Boston, Hyannis, New Bedford, and Providence, Rhode Island.

As on Nantucket, car reservations to Martha's Vineyard need to be made well in advance. You can make reservations by calling the Steamship Authority at 508-477-8600; you can also request schedule and rate information at this same number. They have a web site that you can access for information at www.islandferry.com. If you intend to leave your car at one of the Steamship Authority parking lots, walk-on passengers usually don't have to worry about reservations.

For information on seasonal ferry services, accommodations on the island,

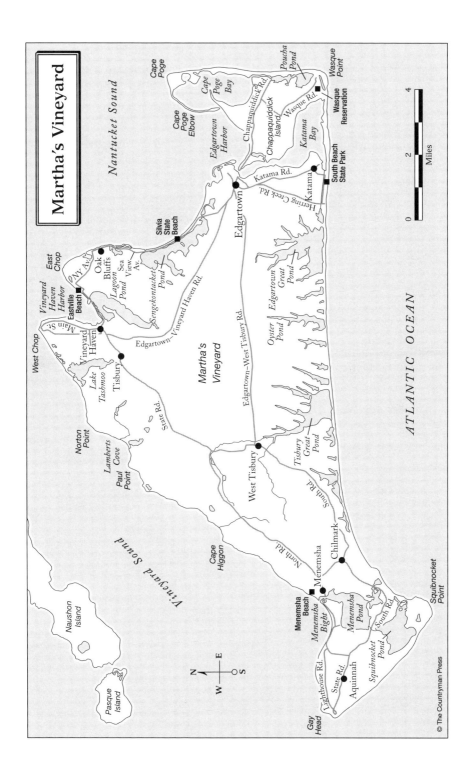

Martha's Vineyard

and ground transportation once you're there, contact the Martha's Vineyard Chamber of Commerce at 508-693-0085. They maintain a web site at www.mvy.com. They will be happy to send you a wealth of information on the island, how to get there, where to stay and dine, local events, and even fishing.

I would be remiss not to mention two great fishing events that occur annually on the island. The first is the Fly Rod Catch & Release Striped Bass Tournament held every spring on Martha's Vineyard. I have fished in this tournament and it is a great experience; it was here that I first met my good friend Chip Bergeron. This event lasts only one night, but a large number of people come to the island to be a part of this annual fly-fishing happening.

The second tournament is held in the fall and is the granddaddy of them all: the Martha's Vineyard Striped Bass & Bluefish Derby. The name may be misleading, since they do allow entries of other game fish that prowl the waters around the island. The derby runs from the middle of September through the middle of October, with daily, weekly, and overall awards. The category for fly-rod-caught fish has grown in participation over the years. Spending some time competing in the Martha's Vineyard Derby is a grand way to wrap up the fishing season.

When talking about the arrival of fish in spring and their departure in fall on the island, it easy to summarize by saying the fish arrive on Martha's Vineyard a bit earlier than Cape Cod and leave just a shade after the action dies to the north. Having said that, let's look at some of the bait and their predators.

The first significant bait to arrive in Vineyard waters is the herring in early May, followed by squid, which spread out through Nantucket Sound. You can expect the bass to be right behind the squid. Also showing up in May are the silversides; in June the sand eels take up residence. Both of these baitfish will be around until fall. Peanut bunker in the $2\frac{1}{2}$- to 3-inch range have been making an appearance recently in fall.

During one of my trips to Martha's Vineyard, Chip Bergeron gave me a great tip about how to better imitate the bait around. Chip varies the length of the flies he fishes as the season progresses. He starts in spring with shorter flies, gradually increasing their length as the season goes along to match the growth of the baitfish.

It's often said that simplicity works best when it comes to flies. Such is the case with the fly that Chip created and fishes, and which you'll see in this book's second color plate. Called the Fuzzy Bugger, it sure can catch fish. I

The Martha's Vineyard Surfcasters Association put these boxes at key locations to keep the beaches free of discarded fishing line.

have used this fly and can attest to its capabilities. Chip will fish different sizes of this fly, depending upon the time of the season.

The first bass to arrive off Martha's Vineyard are schoolies in early May, and sometimes even in late April; the bigger fish follow by a week or so. The stripers will be a prime target of island anglers until November, when the last of the migrating fish move through. Bluefish are around for almost as long. You can expect to start catching them from Vineyard shorelines about mid-May, and they will be around until late October.

In July anglers look for the bonito to show by the end of the month, and they will be chasing bait along various island shorelines until the end of October, if the weather remains warm. However, do expect to see the bonito action slow when the albacore show up. False albacore, depending upon water temperature, will appear by late August or early September. Their stay is short; they're usually gone by mid-October, when the bonito again get aggressive. If there are any Spanish mackerel around—which has been the case over the last several years—they will be mixed in with the bonito and false albacore from August until mid- or late September.

Here's a key piece of information to help you plan your fishing on Martha's Vineyard—especially if you need to move around the island to escape casting into a wind. The tides vary from one side of the island to the other. The tide rises from east to west and falls from east to west. It's best to get a tide schedule from a local tackle shop on the island when you arrive, then determine the times of the tides at the key spots you intend to fish.

Lake Tashmoo is special to me for two reasons. First, it's one of my favorite spots on the island, and is one of the closest places to fish once departing the ferry in Vineyard Haven. It is also special to me because on one of my first trips to Martha's Vineyard, and without a good map, I had a difficult time finding Tashmoo. But once I got there, the frustration was well worth it.

Like many things in life, now that I know how to get there, it's easy. Start at the Catholic church on Franklin Street in Vineyard Haven; it is easy to get there since everyone in Vineyard Haven knows where the church is. Continue out of town on Franklin Street and watch for Daggett Avenue, where you want to turn left. Near the end of Daggett Avenue, and on the right, is Herring Creek Road, which is a dirt road that can be a bit rough to travel.

While traveling on Herring Creek Road—which must be driven slowly—look for a sign for the Land Bank Area at Wilfrid Pond. You'll have to pay close attention because it's a small sign. You can park there and have access to some great shore fishing on Vineyard Sound. This is a good night-time location for striped bass.

Continuing to the end of Herring Creek Road will take you to Lake Tashmoo and a parking area just before the east jetty, which guards the entrance to Lake Tashmoo. The fishing from the jetty and saltwater pond is good throughout the season. The inside of Tashmoo is an excellent location to wade for bass at night, but do scout the area during the daylight, especially if you have never been there before; check out what sort of bottom structure you'll be fishing.

Lake Tashmoo hosts a worm hatch in spring during the full or new moon. The bass seem to know when this will happen. Stripers will also be feeding at night in the pond throughout the summer. Besides the good fishing on the inside, don't ignore the jetty. Stripers and blues are taken from there regularly. Starting about mid-July, the jetty becomes a prime place to fish for bonito, and the action will continue into October. Albacore hang around the entrance to Tashmoo beginning in September, as well. For some fast-action fishing for bonito and albacore, the two best months are September and October.

Another good fly-fishing location that's close to the ferry slip in Vineyard Haven, as well as the one in Oak Bluffs, is the Eastville Beach area from the drawbridge to the jetty, and inside the bridge at Lagoon Pond. When going from Vineyard Haven to Oak Bluffs on Beach Road, you pass over the drawbridge at Lagoon Pond. There is a good-sized parking lot just over the bridge, on the left, as you head toward Oak Bluffs. Park there to fish this location.

Lagoon Pond has some flats areas that will yield some nice bass on a nighttime tide. Both outside the drawbridge along the beach and inside in Lagoon Pond is good fly-fishing for striped bass and bluefish all season long. The beach that runs from the bridge to the jetty is a good area to fish in late summer and early fall for bonito and albacore. This location can save the day when the wind is a problem elsewhere on the island.

Continuing on Beach Road out of Oak Bluffs, and heading toward Edgartown, there is an area that is a bit similar to Lagoon Pond. At what the locals call the "Big Bridge" is easy access to a very popular fly-fishing area. Both along the beach and inside Sengekontacket Pond can be productive early in the season, around the end of April or early May, with some nice fishing for schoolie bass. Later in the season you can expect to find bluefish cruising along the beach in this area.

Two jetties on the Nantucket Sound side mark one of two openings from

Cape Poge at low tide reveals the structure that makes it such an exceptional fishing spot.

Sengekontacket Pond. This is a key spot to fish in late summer and fall for bonito and albacore. These speedsters will also be patrolling along the beach, chasing bait. Throughout the season the flats of Sengekontacket Pond, fished at night, will produce some very good striped bass.

From Edgartown, traveling south on Katama Road will lead you to South Beach, Katama County Beach, and, if you have four-wheel drive, Norton Point and Chappaquiddick Island. If you don't have a four-wheel-drive vehicle, you have two options. The first is soon after leaving Edgartown: Take the right fork off Katama Road, which is Herring Creek Road, and follow it to the parking lot at the west end of South Beach. To park at the east end of South Beach and access to Katama County Beach, stay on Katama Road, which is known locally as "the left fork." Katama Road will turn into South Beach Road just before the access to the east end of South Beach, Katama County Beach, and Norton Point.

If you plan to fish this area on foot, the parking at either end of South Beach will provide access to a good amount of beach to fly fish. This southern section of the island, whether on foot or four-wheel drive, provides the fly caster with some very good fishing. During the spring and fall this southern shoreline of Martha's Vineyard is one of the better places to tie into bluefish. If you want to fish for stripers here, then the best time is at night.

To travel along Katama County Beach and into Norton Point, you'll need a sticker for your four-wheel-drive vehicle; these can be purchased at the beach entrance. If you don't buy one there, they will catch up with you on the beach, and you will be asked to purchase one then. Remember that for beach travel here you'll need standard safety gear like a good tire pressure gauge, shovel, board, and towrope. An important piece of information to note is that from mid-May until August, this section of the beach is closed for nesting birds, as is the case with a number of Cape Cod and Islands beaches.

For information on Norton Point access and sticker costs, contact the Dukes County Commissioner's office. They are located on Main Street in Vineyard Haven, or you can call them at 508-627-5535.

You might expect the name Norton Point to indicate a spit of land surrounded by water. That was the case in the past, but currently Norton Point is a narrow piece of beach that connects to Chappaquiddick Island, which technically makes it a nonisland. Regardless, when driving east on Norton Point, it will lead you to Wasque Reservation and Wasque Point. Here you will need another sticker, the Trustees of Reservations sticker.

For information on the Trustees of Reservations sticker, which can be purchased at the Wasque Gate House, call 508-627-3255. If you don't buy one there but enter from Norton Point, the Trustees will find you on the beach and sell you a permit. Let me warn you that you should be prepared to pay a good price; in 2001 the fee for a nonresident sticker was $160. However, you will have access to the Wasque Reservation and Cape Poge.

Currently in spring and the fall, when you travel from Norton Point into Wasque Reservation, you are able to bypass using the "On Time" ferry that runs from Edgartown to Chappaquiddick Island. However, if you do not have a four-wheel-drive vehicle, you can take your car on the ferry and drive to the Fisherman's Parking lot at Wasque Point. This is one of the best and most popular spots to fish on "Chappy." However, fly-anglers should be warned that you may encounter a lot of surf casters using both bait and artificial lures; because it is such a productive fishing location, it can be crowded.

Departing the ferry, and once on Chappaquiddick, follow the paved road to the Trustees Reservation and from there on to the Fisherman's Parking lot. When you enter the property, make sure you follow the sign (it has an arrow pointing you in the right direction) since one road leads to the Beach Swimming lot and the other to fisherman's parking. Note that a third arrowed sign points to the beach access road.

Wasque Point is an outstanding location in spring for bass and blues. You will find striped bass in the rip by as early as the end of April, and the blue-fish usually show up by Mother's Day in May. Throughout the summer there will be blues there when the rip is "up" and running. During the summer months, a falling tide in the early hours of the morning, before sunrise and when the water is the coolest, is considered to be the best times to fish Wasque. This is a time when you have a good shot at finding bass moving closer to the shoreline to feed.

The fishing at Wasque gets really hot in fall, when the migration of stripers and blues begins. The "rip" is best fished on a falling tide, with a southwest wind. The tide will therefore be falling fast to the west, and the southwest wind will be pushing against it. At times this can create some very wild water, which the bass and blues just love. However, this is not the only time you'll likely find fish there since there are always exceptions; fish don't read books like this.

If Wasque Point is crowded, consider taking a short walk east from the rip to the next point. It can be very productive spot for a fly rodder when it's difficult working the main rip. This can be a particularly good autumn location for albacore, as well. There will be bonito, along with the albacore working this whole area around Wasque Point.

If you're using the ferry to get back and forth to Edgartown, remember that it doesn't run all night. Check the posted schedule, and make plans to either fish all night or leave before the last run of the night.

While on Chappaquiddick, there is another place that you can fish without a four-wheel-drive vehicle—East Beach. After you leave the On Time ferry, follow the signs for Cape Poge and East Beach. You can park at the Dike Bridge and then walk to East Beach. This east-facing shoreline is particularly good in September, with bonito and albacore along the beach. Don't be surprised if you run across a Spanish mackerel or two, as well. Bass and bluefish will also cruise and feed along this beach all season long. Both the rising and falling tide run fairly strong here, so it fishes fairly well at all stages of the tide.

If you're here at night, stop along the waterway that connects Poucha Pond and Cape Poge Bay, which is behind East Beach. Stand still, remain quiet, and listen for the bass feeding in the waterway. You'll often hear that familiar slap of a bass as it feeds. This can be an easy way to catch a striper or two. However, Chip Bergeron offers some friendly advice that I would strongly urge you to follow. When fishing this spot on a summer's night, do not forget the bug spray.

There is one last spot on Martha's Vineyard that you should visit, especially if you're vacationing with your family. Take a trip to the western side of the island and the public beach at Menemsha. Follow any of the signs on the island for the village of Menemsha, go through town, and continue to the public docks. Get there early, watch the sun as it sets over Vineyard Sound with your family, and then fish.

The beach on the north side of Menemsha Inlet has good parking and easy access to fishing. It's usually crowded until dusk with people watching the sunset. But the moment they leave is the time when you want to fish the beach from the inlet, north. This stretch of shoreline is a very good striped bass hangout and worth your time to fish thoroughly, particularly a bit north of the inlet, where there is some nice structure.

I have been fishing Martha's Vineyard since I first came to New England. My two favorite times to fish there are in spring and fall. Though the fishing is good during the summer months, this is also the peak of the tourist season and it can be a bit crowded. In fall the Vineyard can be crowded, as well, but with anglers enjoying the fishing. Regardless of when you go to Martha's Vineyard, you will have an enjoyable trip and fond fishing memories.

On the Way to the Cape

Those who travel to Cape Cod from the south will pass by two very good fly-fishing locations. Situated just 45 minutes from the Cape, the Westport River and Gooseberry Neck are worth a detour. They are close enough together that you can easily fish both locations on a single trip.

When heading east or west on I-195, and just east of Fall River, take the exit for MA 88 and Horseneck Beach. The Westport River is approximately 12 miles south on MA 88. As soon as you cross the bridge for the East Branch of the Westport River, turn right; on your right will be a large parking lot for the launch ramp. You can normally find room to park here.

The best fishing is on the opposite side of MA 88 from the parking lot. This is a beautiful estuary and marsh area. Large striped bass come into the Westport River to feed throughout the season; the fishing is especially good in May. There are shallows, channels, and deep cuts throughout this section of the river. If you can, scout this location during daylight hours if you plan to fish there at night. This will give you an idea of where to fish, plus identify where the deeper water and more dangerous wading areas are situated.

To get to Gooseberry Neck, simply continue on MA 88, which becomes

The East Branch of the Westport River is an estuary with marshes, deep channels, and shallow sections. It is an excellent striper location throughout the season.

John Reed Road and passes Horseneck Beach. Within 3 miles you will come to the end of the road and a stop sign at East Beach Road. Turn right and drive the short distance to Gooseberry Neck, which is part of the Horseneck Beach State Reservation; some people refer to this spot as Gooseberry Point. The road will take you along a sandy beach, over a rock causeway to the point and a dirt parking area.

The two best features of this location are the outstanding structure that will attract and hold fish, and the fact that you can always find a spot to get out of the wind. There is a sandy beach that leads to a rocky shoreline on the eastern side of the point. The rocky structure continues around the point to the western side. Depending upon wind direction and strength, you can have a good surf pushing onto the shoreline that will often blow bait in with it.

While there, and if wind and tide conditions are favorable, don't ignore the sandy flats on the east side of the causeway. Start from the parking lot and work that long stretch of water to the north. Gooseberry Point is a good fishing locale all season. Daytime fishing here is best in the spring and fall. Besides stripers, bluefish can be taken here, especially at dusk and dawn. Poppers or sliders on a floating line are your best choices for the blues.

CHAPTER 13

Rhode Island

It's a short drive down I-95 from Boston to Rhode Island. Though the smallest state in the Union, Rhode Island's shoreline is big in comparison to other states. With nearly 400 miles of coast, its license plate says it all; Rhode Island is truly the "Ocean State." For the fly angler, the opportunities in Rhode Island to pursue striped bass, bluefish, squeteague, bonito, and albacore are boundless.

Rhode Island was first settled in 1636, when Roger Williams, a clergyman banished from Massachusetts, established the settlement of Providence. Williams was the first of many to flee to what was to become Rhode Island to escape religious persecution, establishing the beginnings of such towns as Portsmouth, Newport, and Warwick. It was one of the original thirteen colonies that stood up against Great Britain. This is ironic since on four separate occasions between 1657 and 1678, Rhode Island had a governor named Benedict Arnold. He was the ancestor of the infamous Benedict Arnold who sold out his country to the British during its struggle for independence.

Before getting into specifics of the saltwater fly fishing in Rhode Island, I would like to recommend two great books about Rhode Island fly fishing. The first is *Striper Moon*, by J. Kenney Abrames. Kenney is not only a talented artist but also a writer, a fly tier, and an extremely experienced angler. His knowledge of fly fishing Rhode Island's salt water is known throughout New England, and the country. Read his book and you will get a first-class education in fly fishing Rhode Island.

With some 45 years of fly-fishing experience, Ray Bondorew shares his fishing expertise in the book *Stripers and Streamers,* a must read for any angler wishing to improve his fly-fishing knowledge. Ray is a fly tier, as well, who has created a number of flies that have been tested and proven in Rhode Island waters. Ray's flies are part of any serious striper fisherman's arsenal.

The game fish of Rhode Island are similar to those found around Cape Cod and the Islands. The one difference is that the season will start a bit sooner here and last longer into fall. As expected, the striped bass are the first to arrive in mid-April. The first arrivals are in the schoolie category, but the large fish are not far behind. The smaller, early fish initially move into estuaries and bays, where the water is warmer, to feed. Stripers are around throughout the season and depart Rhode Island waters in November. If the fall is mild, the striped bass fishing can continue into December.

The word of the first bluefish catches begins to circulate in early May. They will be around all summer, but those that are caught will often be smaller than the blues you'll find in May and again in fall. The schools of blues fueling up and migrating south will be along southern shorelines until October. If there is bait and the fall weather is mild, the bluefish can linger into November.

The squeteague or weakfish season begins in mid-May, and these fish can be caught throughout the season, into early fall. The peak time to catch the bigger squeteague is in May and June, and some of the best fishing at that time is in Narragansett Bay, on the west side above Jamestown. Though they are present all summer, it becomes more difficult to catch the larger-sized squeteague during the summer months. However, the smaller fish will still oblige anglers.

The bonito are a welcoming sight to fly rodders in late July. They will perk up the fishing during daylight hours, which has slowed due to the summer's heat. By August there are good numbers of them chasing bait along the shorelines. Look for the bonito fishing to wane by the end of October. Their partners in speed, the albacore, join the action in late August and will be around until mid-October, when the water begins to cool.

The bait situation in Rhode Island is typical of most New England areas, but with a couple of additional players. The adult herring begin to show at the mouths of estuaries in March, to spawn. In June this is the predominant bait in Narragansett Bay. Squid will be in the open waters of Rhode Island starting in April. They normally take up residence on the reefs from Watch Hill to Newport until fall. Silversides are common prey of game fish from late April into autumn. They move into the estuaries and salt ponds in late spring and early summer to spawn. When imitating this bait, start with smaller-sized flies and then increase the length as the season progresses. Another important baitfish is sand eels, which are resident all season in the sandy sections of the coastline, including the salt ponds. They are usually less than 2 inches in length in spring but will grow to more than 3 inches by fall.

Worm hatches are common in the Ocean State and a standard ritual of spring for fly rodders. Look for the hatches to occur primarily in the salt ponds, especially when you're fishing for the early-season schoolies. Another bait to imitate is grass shrimp, which are found in ponds, marshes, and estuaries from April through November.

I've witnessed an additional hatch in Rhode Island: the crab hatch. It happens in spring, but the time is unpredictable. The phenomenon will can cause the bass to go into a feeding frenzy, rolling on the surface and sipping in the tiny crabs like trout. It will drive an angler crazy because the bass will ignore most flies in favor of the transparent crabs, which are no bigger than the fingernail on your pinkie. One technique that has worked is fishing a large fly and using a slow, erratic retrieve that will cause the fly to twist or roll as if it were feeding on the crabs. The bass will often take this fly as an added course to their meal.

In August peanut bunker become abundant in the Upper Narragansett Bay, and the bluefish blitzes can be wild. As the summer progresses, the bunker will mature and move toward the open water. By September these fish will be about 4 inches long, and all of the game fish will key in on this bait. The menhaden will be joined by schools of mullet along the shoreline in fall. Though their abundance, or lack thereof, may vary from year to year, they're a major food source for all predators.

An important fall baitfish is the anchovy, which appears by late summer. Their large schools will attract any and all game fish. Albacore particularly enjoy herding them into a tight ball and then tearing through it. You'll have no problem determining when predators are feeding on these 4- to 5-inch colorful fish.

Rhode Island saltwater fly rodders have a style of fishing that has its roots in the traditional approach used in salmon and freshwater fly fishing. The techniques of drifting a fly, mending the line, and very little line stripping, along with a more subtle approach and presentation, are the legacy from the time when some pioneers began fly fishing for striped bass in the estuaries of Rhode Island.

When anyone speaks of these early days of saltwater fly-fishing in Rhode Island, Harold Gibbs is the first name mentioned. He is considered to be one of the first to saltwater fly fish for stripers. Gibbs helped fly rodders realize that the tactics used for Atlantic salmon were also effective for stripers. Many have heard the story, but I've been lucky enough to hear it from someone who was there and fished with Harold Gibbs.

I consider myself extremely fortunate to know Al Brewster. Al is a master fly tier and carves beautiful decoys. But more importantly, he always has time to teach people the joy of fly tying, especially children. He has given instruction and encouragement to my son David, who now loves tying flies as much as using them. Al is a treasure to the fly-fishing world.

Al Brewster was introduced to saltwater fly fishing by Pap Hinman, and through him Al came to meet Harold Gibbs. Harold and his brother Frank were avid salmon fishermen. During World War II, however, there wasn't much gas available for civilian use, let alone enough to go to New Brunswick, Canada, for salmon. So Harold, with his brother Frank, decided to find a fish just as worthy closer to home. He turned to the Palmer and Barrington Rivers near his home. The brothers set out to see if they could catch a striped bass on a fly. They knew that when bass were taken on a fly rod, it wasn't by casting a fly to them. Most were caught on bait, using a chum line or other methods of that type. They wanted to legitimately use a fly to catch a striper. About that time, Pap and Al started fishing with Frank and Harold; Al's first trip was about late April or early May. Al fished two or three nights a week and never caught a fish until October 15. Through their friendship, Harold Gibbs showed Al the flies he had created and how to tie them. Harold's flies are recognized as the earliest flies for stripers, and set the standard for others to follow.

Once when I was talking with Al, I couldn't resist asking him what his most memorable fish was. Considering all the places in the world that he has fished, I was expecting to hear of a near-record-sized fish taken at some distant or exotic destination. Instead, do you remember that first striped bass that he caught, after fishing all summer along the Rhode Island coast? That is Al's most memorable fish. It took nearly a season for Al to catch that bass on a fly rod. It weighed 8 pounds, but it was his first striped bass and he prizes that fish the most.

Al is especially proud of his friendship with Harold Gibbs, who also carved ducks and birds. Al, who is always ready to credit others, says, "You can't travel with a great man and not have it rub off." He laughingly con-

Captain Jim White with a 38-pound Narragansett Bay striper

tinues by saying that he "traveled with Gibbsie for so long, they used to think Harold was my father. He was a grand soul and carved great birds." He then showed me some of Harold Gibbs's decoys, which he proudly owns.

Al Brewster's fly, the Papie's Special, was originally tied at the urging of Pap Hinman. They were aware of Gibbs's fly but wanted to try something different. Pap told Al to move the blue to the top of the fly to imitate other baitfish that had dark backs. Harold Gibbs's fly was created to mimic the silversides that were prevalent in the estuaries he fished. When I asked Al about the red, white, and blue colors, he said that considering the times of World War II, it was a patriotic statement by both men.

This fishing heritage has left its mark on the Rhode Island fly anglers of today. You will find that they use floating lines quite a bit in situations you would expect, and in others you may not. As expected, floating lines are used when fishing estuaries; they do simplify the presentation to fish holding in the current, plus it's easier to mend a floating line during the drift. The pioneers of saltwater fly fishing in Rhode Island introduced this technique; they used the same approach that had been successful in their salmon fishing.

It didn't take long to realize that when fishing the whitewater around rocky structure, a floating line would prevent hang-ups on the rocks. It was also noted that the salmon-style approach of drifting the fly with very little stripping worked very well in these situations.

The flies of Harold Gibbs and Al Brewster appear in Lefty Kreh's book *Saltwater Fly Patterns*. These flies are of an early era but are still as effective as the time they were first fished; they appear on pages 139–142 of Lefty's book. And adjacent to them on pages 135–137 are the flies of Kenney Abrames and Ray Bondorew, who are carrying on the saltwater fly-fishing tradition of Rhode Island.

I am sure that any angler who has driven I-195 between Cape Cod and Providence, Rhode Island, has noticed the marshes and estuaries along the way, particularly just west of Fall River. There you will see the Lee and Cole Rivers, which empty into Mount Hope Bay. Farther east is the exit for Warren, Rhode Island; to the south from there is the Kickamuit River, which also feeds into Mount Hope Bay. Nearby, between Barrington and Warren, is the Warren River, which has the Palmer and Barrington Rivers as its tributaries.

If you look at a map of this area, you'll see this wonderful system of estuaries that feed Narragansett Bay and Mount Hope Bay. These rivers, where saltwater fly fishing began in Rhode Island, are excellent fly-fishing destinations. From the spring, when the first stripers arrive, through August, and into the fall when the bluefish feed on the abundance of bait there, these rivers are the epitome of estuary fly fishing.

Upper Narragansett Bay

Just south of where the Warren River empties into the Upper Narragansett Bay is one of the best fishing locales in Bristol. Colt State Park is a good fly-fishing spot throughout the season, and easy to reach. From I-195, take the RI 136 exit (exit 2) south to Warren. Turn left at RI 103 and travel less than a mile to RI 114, where you should turn left. As you approach Bristol, look for Asylum Road at a traffic light, and turn right. This will take you directly to the entrance to Colt State Park. Park in the lot that is closet to Mill Gut Pond.

This beautiful park, which is open from sunrise to sunset, has great fishing from spring into fall. Striped bass are around throughout the season, as are bluefish, which provide added sport for the fly rodder. In late spring you have a good shot at squeteague, especially in the morning and evening hours. A few of them are taken during the summer months, as well.

One of the better fishing locations is at the outflow of the salt pond and the boulder fields to the south. The left or south side of the opening of Mill Gut, as you look out toward the bay, will have a rip on a dropping tide. This is a good early-morning and evening spot when you have a dropping tide.

The view from the visitors center of Sachuest Point National Wildlife Refuge as you look down at Second Beach

Aquidneck Island

If you continue south on RI 114, it will take you over the Mount Hope Bridge and onto Aquidneck Island. Though the name may not be familiar, this is where the towns of Portsmouth, Middletown, and Newport are located. On the southeast tip of Aquidneck is Sachuest Point National Wildlife Refuge, and several fine fly-fishing sites situated within the refuge.

To reach Sachuest Point NWR from downtown Newport, go east on Memorial Boulevard (RI 138A). As you head toward Sachuest Point, you will come upon a long, sweeping beach on your right and close to the road. This is First Beach or Eastons Beach; though I have never fished this beach, I've been told that it can be a good early-season location. In summer this beach will be crowded during the day. If you do fish here early in the season, concentrate on the western end of the beach toward Cliff Walk.

In fall bluefish and stripers often drive bait into this area. If peanut bunker are around, check this beach on a regular basis. There have been seasons when the bait and the bass held along this beach for a good period of time. When this does happen, expect to have plenty of company considering its close proximity to downtown Newport.

Continuing east, there will be a traffic light where RI 138A swings north, as a left turn. You should continue straight on what is now Purgatory Road until you come to a fork. Bear right at the sign that directs you to Sachuest Beaches. This road—Sachuest Point Road—leads into Sachuest Point National Wildlife Refuge.

Sachuest Point NWR has a number of excellent locations to fly fish and has good action throughout the season. Parking here normally isn't a problem, and the fishing spots are easy to reach on foot. The first location I want to mention is Second Beach, which is located on your right and just before driving up the hill to the visitors center parking lot. This beach's varied structure of sand, boulders, and large rocks serves as a magnet for bait and, in turn, for striped bass and bluefish, plus bonito and albacore in late summer and early fall. The beach changes from west to east, beginning as sand, then turning to rocks and then to large boulders at the east end.

Southerly and southwesterly winds will push bait into this large cove. When this happens, expect the predators to show up. Early in the season, beginning in April, fish the west end of the beach when looking for your first striper of the season. You should also plan to fish this beach in the early morning and late evening during the summer months to avoid the crowds.

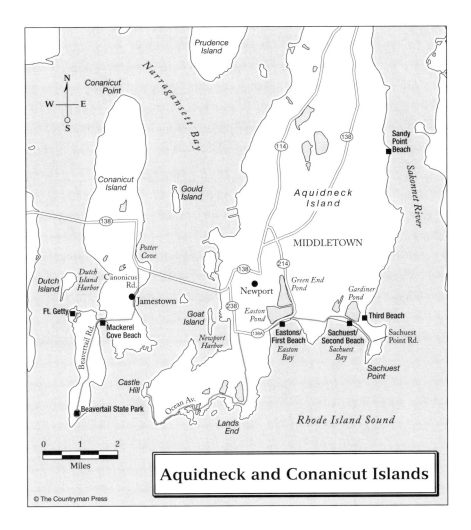

Aquidneck and Conanicut Islands

© The Countryman Press

From the visitors center parking lot, there are paths that will take you to Sachuest Point and the eastern shore of the refuge. I should note that fishing this rocky shoreline is not for the novice, even during daylight hours. The combination of surf and wet rocks isn't easy to handle, even for the most experienced. I recommend the use of an inflatable vest and steel-studded footwear in this situation.

The point's striper fishing, though good all season, is best in June. Throughout the season you'll also be able to catch bluefish here. You can fish the eastern side of the point using access spots from the path.

When standing in the parking lot at the visitors center, you can not only look down on Second Beach, but if you look more to your right you'll see

Third Beach, as well. You passed the road to Third Beach on the way to Second Beach. On your left is the Second Beach Campground, which has a number of trailers; turn left at the road by the campground. Follow this road a short distance to a fork, then bear right and continue to the parking lot for Third Beach.

Anglers will head for Third Beach when the wind is blowing too strong from the south, southwest, or west; however, it's a good location to fly fish regardless of the wind situation. This is a sandy beach, with some gravel, that has a northerly exposure and faces the open water of the Sakonnet River. Though it's considered a prime bluefish destination, anglers will head here in late summer and autumn for not only the bluefish but also the stripers chasing bait into this cove.

Sachuest Point National Wildlife Refuge is a first-class fly-fishing destination since there are multiple locations to fish. You can always get out of the wind at one location or another. The variety of structure in this small section of Aquidneck Island provides for good fishing from spring to fall. This is one of those places that you can spend the whole season learning and still not know all its secrets of where, when, and how to fish it—but it's worth the try.

Conanicut Island

Leaving Newport and Aquidneck Island via the Newport Bridge, you will drive onto Conanicut Island, which is often called Jamestown Island because it is where Jamestown is located. It's a long, narrow island running north–south, and the traveling angler passes through it on RI 138 in just a minute. However, local anglers know that this island has a number of good fly-fishing spots.

One of the first locations on the island that I would like to tell you about is Potter Cove; it's the closest location when coming onto the island from Newport. As soon as you cross the Newport Bridge and pay the toll, take an immediate right, which will take you back toward the bridge. As you are heading back to pass under the bridge, there is a break in median divider and a road to your left. Take that left, and a very short distance down this road is a gravel parking lot on your left. This parking lot overlooks Potter Cove.

Driving from the west on RI 138, you'll take the Jamestown Bridge onto the island. You should continue driving on RI 138 until you see the Newport Bridge and take the last exit before the tollgate for the bridge. The sign there indicates that you will be heading for Jamestown. The first left turn will take

Potter Cove, which is located next to the Newport Bridge, is a very good fly-fishing destination.

you under the bridge. The street immediately on the right after you go under the bridge is the one that takes you to the gravel parking lot for Potter Cove.

This is a fine location to fly fish for striped bass and blues, but don't be surprised to see bonito and albacore chasing bait here in late summer and early autumn. Potter Cove is primarily a spring and fall location best fished early and late in the day.

From the parking lot you can see the sweeping beach that runs to the left and borders the main part of Potter Cove. The beach has a flats area with a sand and gravel bottom. Though this a fairly firm bottom, you should take care because there are some holes here, as well as a few soft spots. To the right of the parking lot is the beginning of a rocky shoreline that leads east to Taylor Point. You will find bass hanging around this structure.

The next location on the island is south of Jamestown and called Mackerel Cove. To get there from Potter Cove, when you leave the parking area, turn right and then left at the end of the street; this will take you under the bridge. At the stop sign you should turn left. There is a sign here indicating that Historic Jamestown is to the left, in the direction you will be going. You are traveling on Conanicus Avenue, and continue on this road as it goes along the water on the east side of the island. At a stop sign, continue going straight and past the boat docks on left. After several streets that go off to your right and toward the center of Jamestown, keep an eye out for Hamilton Avenue, where you turn right. At the end of Hamilton is a stop sign at Southwest Avenue. Turn left onto Southwest Avenue and Mackerel Cove will be a very short distance ahead on your left.

To reach Mackerel Cove when coming east on RI 138 over the Jamestown Bridge, take the first exit after the bridge as you get onto the island. At the end of that road, which parallels RI 138, there is a stop sign. Turn right onto North Main Road, which will take you south into Jamestown. In Jamestown at the stop sign, Southwest Avenue will be a continuation of North Main Road, bearing slightly to right. Just proceed on Southwest Avenue until you see Mackerel Cove on the left.

There is parking lot for the town beach at Mackerel Cove, and you'll pay a fee to park there. The last time I was there it cost $10 to park from 9 AM to 5 PM, which is a bit steep. You're better off fishing either the morning or evening tide, when the fishing is better.

Mackerel Cove is a beautiful, large bowl of water whose opening is to the southeast, at the lower end of Narragansett Bay. The beach here is coarse sand, with rocky shorelines located at both ends. This is a gradually sloping, shallow beach with rocks just a bit from shore. Mackerel Cove has good structure, and you'll find striped bass and blues there throughout the season.

While you're at Mackerel Cove, don't pass up fishing the area on the opposite side of the road from the parking lot. On a high tide and at night, this area can provide very productive fishing for striped bass. Visit this marsh area at low tide and during daylight to see the structure you'll be fishing. The extra time spent to scout this location will pay off when fishing it at night.

Less than a quarter mile down the road from Mackerel Cove is the entrance to the Fort Getty Campground. Fort Getty Road is on the right, and it's just a short drive to the main campground. As you reach the park, take notice of the beautiful marsh area on your right; this is the Fox Hill Salt Marsh. On the left is a small parking lot with access to Narragansett Bay. There are different spots throughout the campground to park and fish.

At end of the road is Fox Hill, and a launch ramp for boats. Just prior to that is a small parking lot on the right, away from where the cars and boat trailers would park. Between this point and Dutch Island is a channel with deep water and good tide movement.

This is an ideal destination to take the family for the day to picnic and fish. It's also a good campground in the heart of New England fishing; it's open for camping from May to October. If you plan to camp here, you'll need to book your reservation well in advance with the Jamestown's Parks and Recreation Department; call 401-423-7200 and ask to be connected to that department. A fee is charged to camp at Fort Getty, as well for daily use of the picnic area, or simply to fish. I've been told that if you intend to fish at night, you should check with attendant and let him know of your intentions.

The waters at the northern end of Fort Getty from the channel into Dutch Island Harbor and the marsh area provide good fishing for stripers, blues, and squeteague. Look for blues to be working the Narragansett Bay shoreline; bonito and albacore will often cruise along this rocky shore.

On the southernmost tip of Conanicut Island is Beavertail State Park, and a spectacular shoreline to fish. To reach Beavertail Point, turn right when leaving Fort Getty Campground; the road is called Beavertail Road from this intersection, south. In less than 3 miles, you will reach the entrance to Beavertail State Park. Once inside the park, you should proceed to the lighthouse. There are parking lots just prior to and after the lighthouse, on the east and west side of the point.

This whole area is a rocky shoreline that can be difficult to fish, even on the best of days, but it's a good white-water spot. The point under the lighthouse faces out into the Atlantic Ocean and has some strong currents sweeping around the rocks. With the right wind and tide, this can be wild water. Korkers or similar footwear outfitted with studs are needed to negotiate the sloped, slippery rocks. The water is very deep here, even close to the rocks. It's also worth wearing an inflatable vest when you fish Beavertail.

You may find that the eastern side of the point is a bit easier to fish. They do allow fishing after dark, but I would exercise great caution, especially if you've never fished here at night before. Become familiar with the terrain during daylight hours before attempting a night trip. Even daytime hours will produce fish, and this location has good fishing all season long. Striped bass, bluefish, bonito, and albacore are the main targets of those fishing from the rocks of Beavertail Point. Over the years some very large stripers have been landed here in late spring and fall. But I'll say it again: It's is not worth risking your life for any fish. Enjoy your angling here; it is a spectacular setting to fish. Just maintain caution at all times.

Western Narragansett Bay

On the western side of Upper Narragansett Bay are two locations that are favorites of fly fishermen. One is Goddard Memorial State Park and the other

Foggy days like this one can be as productive as fishing during the early-morning or late-evening hours.

is Sandy Point; they are within a few miles of each other. Let's take look at Sandy Point first, which is located in a small town with the very strange name of Potowomut.

Driving south from Providence on I-95, watch for large overhead signs for RI 4 south. You should bear to the left on RI 4, but keep in the right-hand lane of that road. This is important, because you'll take the first exit off RI 4, for RI 401 and East Greenwich. At the top of the exit ramp turn right onto RI 401 (Division Street). At the split in the road, bear right and stay on RI 401. The third traffic light on this road is Main Street (US 1); you should turn right at this traffic light. There are two service stations at this intersection. As you proceed south on US 1, at the first traffic light, which is at the bottom of a hill, turn left. This is Old Forge Road, and there is a sign for Goddard Memorial State Park. Stay on the main road as it curves to the left and becomes Ives Road. Continue past Goddard Memorial State Park and the golf course. In approximately 3 miles you'll come to a small parking lot that holds about 10 cars. This is what anglers call Sandy Point, though it's actually just south of Sandy Point.

Traveling north on I-95 from Connecticut, take exit 8 for RI 2 south. In a short distance you'll come to the traffic light for RI 401. Turn left there and follow RI 401 into East Greenwich. From Jamestown, go west on RI 138, over the Jamestown Bridge and then north on US 1 to East Greenwich. On the way, be sure to go straight at the intersection where RI 4 bears off to the left. In East Greenwich, at the foot of the hill, turn right at the traffic light onto Old Forge Road, and follow the directions previously given.

Sandy Point is an outstanding sunrise-to-sunset location for the shore-bound fly angler. You can wade out a good distance and approach the mouth of the Green River, to your right. Sandy Point is to the left. It's a good idea to view this area at low water to determine where any holes, drop-offs, and other structure are located.

Sandy Point is a very good early-spring spot for small bass. In late spring and early summer there can be some fine squeteague fishing here, and around into Greenwich Cove. In May there has also been a nice run of bluefish in recent years; the smaller blues return in August to chase peanut bunker, and will continue to do so into the fall.

On the way to Sandy Point, you passed the main entrance to Goddard Memorial State Park on your left. It's only about half a mile from the main gate to parking for the beach. The park is open from sunrise to sunset.

This beach is a prime location for you to have a shot at some good-sized squeteague in spring. Remember to use a slower retrieve and keep your fly on or near the bottom. These fish are moving in and out of Greenwich Cove, feeding on the baitfish there. The last few years, in the spring, there have been some big bluefish moving into Greenwich Cove, as well. As the tide floods, they will feed almost to the back end of the cove, and then move out as the tide drops. As with Sandy Point, the stripers are here in spring and fall. The blues will be back in August chasing bait, and will remain until fall. The beach can be crowded as the weather warms, especially on weekends, so your fishing will be confined to the ends of the beach. The best direction to fish is to the right of the beach, toward Sally Rock Point.

South County Beaches

The southern shore of Rhode Island, which faces Block Island Sound, has some of the better fishing spots in the state. Many of these locations are classic fishing destinations made famous by generations of surf casters. It's a shoreline where the angler can fish breachways, salt ponds, and sandy or rocky beaches all within a short driving distance. Many times these varying forms of structure can be fished on foot without even moving your vehicle.

When driving south on US 1 from East Greenwich, two of the many great places along Rhode Island's southern shore to fish are East Matunuck State Beach and Matunuck Beach. The former is reached by taking Succotash Road south from US 1 in South Kingston. It is less than a 2-mile drive to one of the more frequented fishing locations in South County. During the summer season you'll have to pay to park in the beach lot, and it's often crowded. Since I recommend that you fish this location in spring and fall, this should not be a factor.

East Matunuck State Beach in Jerusalem is a location that has, over the years, produced large stripers and bluefish for those anglers willing to learn how to fish its shoreline. From the West Wall that guards the entrance to Point Judith Pond, and running west toward Matunuck Beach, with the right wind, this beach is a spectacular striped bass and bluefish destination.

Fish the east end of the beach near the West Wall in early spring for the first stripers of the season. Since the water off this beach is deep, it's a good location for fly rodders. Concentrate on sunset, night, and dawn hours when you fish here; these are usually the better times for the bigger fish. Still, in fall you'll enjoy the typical autumn action of migrating bass and blues during the day.

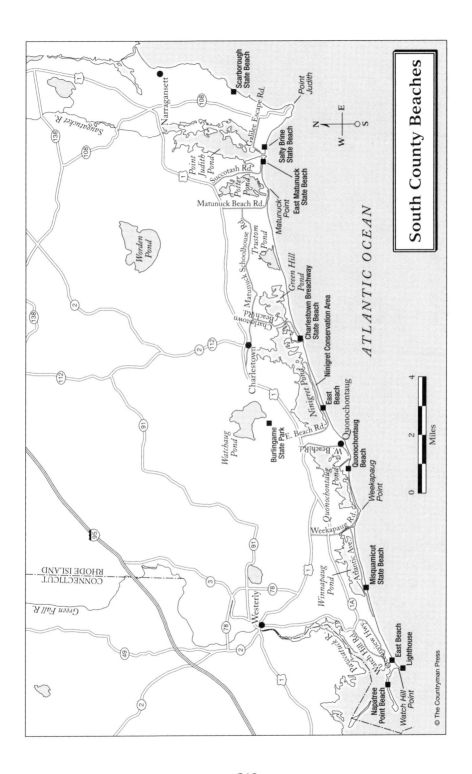

South County Beaches

ATLANTIC OCEAN

© The Countryman Press

219

The Rhode Island coastline has a variety of structure, often within a short section of shoreline, like this area of Napatree Point.

One caution applies to most of the South County beaches: When there is a strong southwesterly wind, it will drive in the baitfish, followed by the stripers and blues—but too much of a good thing may not be favorable for the fly caster. The stronger winds, which surf casters can tolerate, will make for difficult if not impossible conditions for the fly fisherman. If you plan to fish these beaches, keep an eye on the wind forecast and have alternative plans to fish an area where you won't have the wind in your face.

If you continue south on US 1 to the next exit and take Matunuck Beach Road south for about 2 miles, you will come to the Department of Environmental Management fisherman's access parking lot for Matunuck Beach. Like East Matunuck Sate Beach, which is just to the east, this is one of the locations where the first schoolies of the season are caught.

When you reach the beach after leaving the parking lot, look to your left and you will see an area known as Deep Hole. The name describes exactly what it is—a section of deep water that's accessible at the lower stages of the tide. Deep Hole is not hard to find since its edges are marked by the breaking waves. It's very rocky here, with medium to large rocks, and care should be taken when moving out to and around this area. It goes without saying that metal-studded footwear is a must in this situation.

You should fish Deep Hole at the lower stages of the tide so as to reach the drop-off and the deeper water. This is not always an easy place for fly rodders to fish. The rougher the weather, the better the fishing gets, but there comes a point when the fly angler is at a definite disadvantage. Your ability to reach the productive water will be diminished by the increasing wind and surf.

To the west of Matunuck Beach are the three breachways of Charlestown, Quonochontaug, and Weekapaug, and situated between and beyond are Misquamicut, Watch Hill, and Napatree Point—names that for years have made surf casters' hearts beat a little faster. These locations around Charlestown and Westerly, Rhode Island, are now providing the same excitement for fly anglers.

The Charlestown Breachway is one of the more popular fishing destinations for Rhode Island anglers. This may be because it's the first one you reach going south from Providence and because of its proximity to the popular campgrounds at Burlingame State Park. Regardless of the reason, this breachway can get very crowded at times. To reach the parking lot for this location from US 1, go south on Narrow Lane for a very short distance before turning left onto Matunuck Schoolhouse Road. Almost immediately on your right is Charlestown Beach Road. Follow this road about 2 miles to the parking lot for the beach and breachway.

Charlestown Breachway guards the opening to Ninigret Pond; I point this out because in spring there will be a worm hatch in the pond. This is when the fly rodders have a ball with the striped bass that move into Ninigret Pond to feed on these delicacies. If the hatch, which is based on the moon phases, comes early in spring, the bass that will be feeding in the pond will be predominantly schoolies. But if the hatch occurs late enough that the larger bass have shown up, then the fishing will be extra special.

On the western side of the Charlestown Breachway is the Ninigret Conservation Area and East Beach, which is one of the beaches along the southern shoreline of Rhode Island that allow access to four-wheel-drive vehicles. To reach East Beach, simply take East Beach Road from US 1; in a mile you'll reach your destination. Remember to obtain your permit to ride the beach at Burlingame State Park. This is an outstanding fall fishing location for the four-wheeler. The bass and bluefish will be all along this sandy beach during this part of the season. Also spend the time to fish at night, especially in fall. Big stripers like to cruise the surf here after dark.

If you're on foot, you should also fish to the west, from the parking lot at East Beach. The shoreline becomes rocky, but the fishing can be very good. Several people who fish this area on a regular basis have told me that the section in front of the Blue Shutters Beach parking lot is a prime spot, and I always heed good advice.

Not that far to the west of East Beach is the Quonochontaug Breachway and Quonochontaug Pond. Quonny, as it is known locally, is another easy-to-reach Rhode Island destination. Traveling west on US 1 past Burlingame State Park, look for West Beach Road and take that road south toward the water. At West End Road, go left to the parking lot at the back end of the breachway, where it enters Quonochontaug Pond. There is also a state boat ramp located there.

The fishing season here begins about mid- to late April with schoolie-sized striped bass in the backwaters of Quonochontaug Pond. The bass are feeding on small herring, grass shrimp, and other baitfish. The pond also hosts a worm hatch later in spring. Spring and fall are the better times for fishing Quonny Pond, but fish are taken in the early morning, late evening, and at night during the summer. During the early fall both small bass and snapper blues visit Quonny Pond to feed. Hickory shad are also there in spring and fall, giving the fly rodder an added bonus. This is a great wading spot that is easily accessible.

Access to these flats and the pond is from the east side, at the parking lot. When working Quonochontaug Pond, fish both the flats and the drop-offs, at the edges of the flats. When the bass are feeding there, they will move from the deeper water to the flats and back as the tide and water temperature change.

This is an excellent spot for the beginning fly angler. You can practice your casting and retrieves without the surf or the swift currents associated with the breachway. An 8-weight rod with an intermediate line is a good choice in spring. For flies at that time of the year I suggest Clouser Minnows, small Deceivers of about 2 to 3 inches, or similar patterns. Fly colors of olive, all white, chartreuse, and chartreuse and white are among the local favorites.

The beach to east of the breachway can be very good, but access during the summer is difficult since the property along the beach is private. This beach is also excellent in fall—and by then most of the cottage owners have left. To reach the beach from the parking lot, walk back on the road about half a mile to a dirt road that leads to the beach. You can also make the long walk from East Beach, and have good fishing along the way. This area has a lot of rocky structure to fish; the bass just love this environment

The primary targets of fly anglers fishing the South County beaches during July and August are bass and blues. That is the case until the bonito

The breachways along the southern coast of Rhode Island are popular fly-fishing destinations because they do produce fish.

show up and add another player to the game. Until then, those fishing on foot should concentrate on the morning and evening plus the hours of darkness for best results. Though you'll have good fishing throughout the season, this section of Rhode Island is at its best during the fall.

Bonito will appear in Block Island Sound in August and should remain until late September, and sometimes even into October. The false albacore or "Fat Alberts," which are the most exciting and sought-after fish of the early-fall action, arrive after the bonito and leave a bit sooner. For the land-based fly fisherman, one of the best spots to fish for false albacore is from the rocks of the Weekapaug Breachway. The incoming tide is the favored time for these fish to appear. This is an easy breachway to fish; there's public parking on both sides of the Atlantic Avenue Bridge.

To get to the Weekapaug Breachway when you are traveling west on US 1, look for RI 1A, which bears off the left as you enter the town of Westerly. Follow RI 1A a short distance to Weekapaug Road, and turn left. In about a mile you will come to Atlantic Avenue, which goes left and over the upper end of the breachway, which is the outlet for Winnapaug Pond. The parking lots for Weekapaug Breachway are on each side of the bridge on your left, and are clearly marked.

Traveling east from Westerly on US 1, look for Langworthy Road on your right at Dunn's Corner, and head south on Langworthy. When you reach RI 1A, make a right turn followed quickly by a left turn onto Weekapaug Road.

When you are fishing for striped bass at Weekapaug Breachway, concentrate on the outgoing tide, and fish at the ends. The hours after dark are the prime times, and the key locations on the breachway can get crowded then. Also note that waves sometimes wash right over the ends of this breachway during strong southerly winds and when sea conditions are heavy.

During the fall when bluefish and bass are on the move, the high-percentage locations are again at the ends of the breachway, on an outgoing tide. This is when the baitfish move out of the ponds and meet with this migration. Bluefish have been known to hang around the breachways as late as Thanksgiving, if bait like blueback herring are around.

In late August to early September this section of Rhode Island sees the arrival of densely packed schools of bay anchovies in Block Island Sound. This rust- or root-beer-colored baitfish is from 1 to 3 inches in length, so flies of that size and color work well. There are a number of fly patterns that imitate the anchovies, including smaller Deceiver patterns, and epoxy and silicone flies. Striped bass seem to have special liking for this baitfish, as witnessed by anyone who has come across a school of bay anchovies being driven skyward by the bass.

If you have the opportunity to fish a school of bay anchovies under attack, take special note. Often the false albacore and striped bass will be feeding on the same pod of bay anchovies. When this happens, the albacore will be near the surface while the bass will often be underneath the bait. If you're after bass, you'll need a sinking line to get down to them. But be alert, since an albie will go after a fly as it is sinking.

Close to Weekapaug Breachway is a section of shoreline that has produced some large striped bass and blues over the years. The problem is that Weekapaug Point is not an easy place to fish, and the area has difficult footing. It is a beach of rocks and large boulders. You need to pay special attention to your back cast here since the barnacle-covered boulders can do a number on flies and line.

To reach this section of beach from the breachway, take Atlantic Avenue east to Wawoloam Drive and turn right. Look for parking places along the street or park in the third lot of the Fire District Beach Parking Area. You can walk from there over to the beach. When you get to the beach, fish to the west toward the rocks and the bowl just before Weekapaug Point.

If you travel west on Atlantic Avenue from the Weekapaug Breachway, you'll pass along Misquamicut Beach. This is a choice spring and fall location for fly fishing. One place that many locals frequent is the Andrea Hotel and Resort, which is on the beach in Westerly. It's a good after-dark location in summer and fall, and you can use the lot adjacent to the hotel when it's closed. The key here is that the lights from the hotel attract bait, and this in turn draws in the bass.

If you own a four-wheel-drive vehicle, you can access most of Misquamicut Beach in fall. If you are walking the beach and fishing in spring or fall, you can park your car in the lots of closed businesses. During the summer, however, this is not permitted.

Another beach that allows four-wheel access is East Beach, in Watch Hill. The entrance to the beach is at the west end of Atlantic Avenue. Look for the blue-roofed house that sits next the access point for the beach.

Watch Hill has two fly-fishing spots that are very good. The first is at the Watch Hill Light; fish both at the point in front of the light and around to the west side, inside the small bowl. During the spring and fall you may be able to park up the road from the light, at the Inn at Watch Hill's parking lot. However, during the summer tourist season, this may be difficult to do. You should be able to use the municipal parking lot if you're fishing at night, but during business hours it's reserved for people accessing the businesses in the area. Also be careful when parking on the street, since many are spots marked for resident use only. Obviously, in spring and fall the parking situation is a bit easier.

If you were to ask an old surf rat to describe the perfect beach to fish, I'd be willing to bet that the description would closely match Napatree Point, in Watch Hill. Though it's a good location for the fly angler throughout the season, I believe it's one of the best fall fishing locations in southern Rhode Island. This point has a variety of structures that really attract fish. There are two small jetties on Napatree Point, while the outer end has excellent rock structure. Near the point is a nice mussel bed that is a productive spot to fish. Along the north side is a small bay, with some shallow flats near the end and a $1\frac{1}{2}$-mile sandy beach on the south side. Almost every fall you'll hear of several bass over 40 pounds being caught here, plus an occasional striper exceeding 50 pounds.

Watch Hill is located in the southwest corner of the state. Traveling west on US 1, bear left onto RI 1A and follow the signs for Watch Hill. A left onto either Ocean View Highway or Watch Hill Road will take you to Watch Hill. If you are on I-95, take exit 1 at the Rhode Island border with Connecticut. Follow RI 3 south into Westerly and the downtown area. You should then continue on RI 1A south for less than 4 miles to Watch Hill Road. Turn right, proceed south for less than 2 miles, and turn right onto Bay Street, where Watch Hill Road becomes Ninigret Avenue. The best parking for Napatree Point is the municipal parking.

Striped bass are caught at Napatree Point as early as late April, and until June on north side facing Little Narragansett Bay, which is at the mouth of Pawcatuck River. The bass return in fall to this side when the shallow water begins to cool. Besides bass, Napatree has bluefish around throughout the season, with the bigger blues in fall. In late summer and early fall, albacore and bonito often chase bait along the north shore of Napatree Point.

When I was last here, John Prigmore, who knows this area well, told me of an interesting location at Napatree Point that has an odd name. The "Kitchen" is located on the north side of Napatree and is a good all-season fishing spot. The area got its name from the appliances and other debris strewn over the bottom as the result of a 1938 hurricane that destroyed homes located on Napatree Point.

If structure is the one of the keys to finding fish, you'll have a hard time deciding where to fish first along the shores of South County. Within just a small number of miles there are estuaries, sandy beaches, rocky shorelines, and breachways to fish. From East Matunuck Beach to Watch Hill you'll find fish waiting to make an easy meal of your fly. Not only is there great fishing, but the scenery will add that much more to your experience. In fall southwest winds will drive bait right up against the beaches. Just keep a lookout for the birds; they will signal feeding fish and great fishing action.

Striped bass and bluefish remain along this shoreline until November. While most bluefish action is during the day, most experienced anglers agree that the bigger striped bass are usually caught between sundown and sunrise. But whenever you fish this area, enjoy the beauty and grand fishing.

Block Island

Block Island stands at the entrance to Long Island Sound with its eastern shore facing the Atlantic Ocean; to the southwest is the tip of Long Island, and 14 miles to the north, Point Judith, Rhode Island. Native Americans

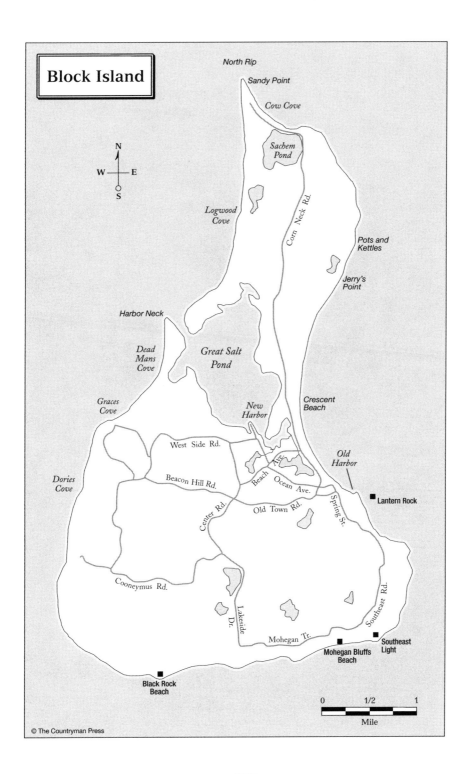

Block Island

North Rip

Sandy Point

Cow Cove

Sachem
Pond

Logwood
Cove

Corn Neck Rd.

Pots and
Kettles

Jerry's
Point

Harbor Neck

Dead
Mans
Cove

Great Salt
Pond

Crescent
Beach

Graces
Cove

New
Harbor

West Side Rd.

Old
Harbor

Dories
Cove

Beacon Hill Rd.

Beach Ave.

Ocean Ave.

Lantern Rock

Center Rd.

Old Town Rd.

Spring St.

Cooneymus Rd.

Lakeside Dr.

Southeast Rd.

Mohegan Tr.

Mohegan Bluffs
Beach

Southeast
Light

Black Rock
Beach

N
W E
S

0   1/2   1
Mile

© The Countryman Press

North Light is located on Sandy Point, which is an outstanding striper destination. However, the rip there can be very dangerous with the right wind and conditions.

known as the Manisses, who were part of the Narragansett tribe, were the first to live on Block Island. In 1660 there were approximately 1,000 of them on the island. Adrian Block, a Dutch explorer, was the first white man to set foot on the island; then in 1661 European settlers from the Massachusetts Bay Colony came here to farm and fish.

Known as the Bermuda of the North, Block Island is a popular resort famous for its Victorian architecture and saltwater fishing. It may be small in size, but it is a place where a fly rodder can experience a wide variety of fishing conditions. Striped bass, bluefish, bonito, and false albacore are in the waters surrounding Block Island from May through November, and provide fine fishing.

Though Block Island is just over 8 miles long and 3 miles wide, the fishing opportunities are boundless. And when the wind is blowing, you can always find a sheltered location to fish, regardless of the direction. Additionally, if you like sandy beaches, or sandy beaches with intermittent rocks, or rocky shorelines, or rocky shorelines with boulders, you'll find them on this beautiful island. And unlike many other locales in the Northeast, access is not a problem.

An 1840s regulation assures anyone fishing the shores of Block Island that they need not worry about restricted access. That regulation prohibits the closing of any access to the water for the purposes of fishing or the gathering of seaweed. Believe me, you can put in a great deal of time before you fish all the shoreline of Block Island.

There is year-round car and passenger ferry service between Point Judith, Rhode Island, and Block Island. To reach the ferry terminal on the mainland from US 1 in Narragansett, take the exit for RI 108; there will be signs for Point Judith. Keep an eye out for the BLOCK ISLAND BOAT sign, which is about 3 miles down RI 108. At that point you will turn right and then left to get to the ferry.

From June until September a car and passenger ferry service operates from New London, Connecticut. During the summer, there is also passenger service from Providence and Newport, Rhode Island, plus Montauk, New York. Scheduled air service to Block Island from Westerly, Rhode Island, is also available.

To help with the planning of your visit to Block Island, here are some telephone numbers. The Interstate Navigation Company, which runs the ferry service to the island, can be reached at 1-860-442-7891 or 401-783-4613. Calling 1-800-243-8623 will connect you with Action Air, a charter service, while New England Airlines can be reached at 1-800-243-2460 for information about their flight schedule from Westerly to Block Island. Lastly, the Block Island Chamber of Commerce has a web site at www.blockisland-info.com; or you can call them at 1-800-838-2474.

As the water temperatures around Block Island reach the 50-degree mark, which will be sometime in May, look for the striped bass to make their appearance. They will be the prime target of fly anglers until late November. Arriving soon after the bass, bluefish move into the Block Island waters on their migration north. As with the striped bass, their numbers and appetite greatly increase in fall before they begin their journey south in early November. Bonito usually make their appearance by mid- to late July, with false albacore joining them in August. The albies will depart around mid-October, while the bonito will hang around until about the end of the month.

The island is easy to traverse, though there are a small number of roads. Following Corn Neck Road north from the ferry, you will reach Cow Cove, North Light, and the access to Sandy Point. This is where the first settlers landed because there were no natural harbors on the island. The story goes that the cows were dropped off the ship at this location so they could get to shore, hence the name.

This is the island's northern tip and where you'll find the Block Island North Reef and rip; also called the North Rip, it runs from Sandy Pont in a northeasterly direction and consistently holds stripers throughout the season. You can reach the point with a four-wheel-drive vehicle but the sand is often deep and soft, so take care and be sure your tires are properly deflated. Sandy Point has great bass fishing—but let me sound another note of caution. At certain times the waters and rip of Sandy Point can become one mean piece of water to fish. Anglers should take extra care when fishing here.

Leaving Sandy Point and heading south on Corn Neck Road, there is easier fly fishing along the eastern side of the island. Anglers should fish the stretch of beach from the Pots and Kettles to Jerrys Point, and even down to Crescent Beach. Striped bass often cruise along this shoreline, just beyond the last wave. Stripers, particularly during the summer, can be a sucker for a crab fly drifted like nymph fishing on the outside edge of the last wave.

While you're on the east side of the island, do spend some time working the shoreline from the jetty at Old Harbor, south to Lantern Rock, and beyond to Old Harbor Point, hitting each jetty along the way. This is an excellent dusk, dark, and early-morning section to fly fish. Sand eel patterns are good choices here, plus Tabory's white-and-black Snake Flies. Chartreuse-

These steps near Southeast Light will take you down the steep cliffs of Mohegan Bluffs to Block Island's southern shoreline.

and-white Deceivers, as well as chartreuse-and-black Clouser Minnows, are also good bets. Guide Johnny Glenn's silicone fly, Charlie's Angel, is another very popular Block Island fly.

On the south side of the island the terrain changes and there is where you'll find high cliffs and narrow, rocky shorelines. At certain sections these cliffs are 250 feet high, so you can descend to the water only at certain points. One good location that has a stairway from a parking lot to the water is just past Southeast Light. This area is known as the Mohegan Bluffs and is a fine bass fishing location.

To the west is a well-known striper spot that has produced some large stripers over the years, particularly in fall. It is Black Rock Point, and the shoreline just to the west of it. However, it is the most difficult of the Block Island locales to reach. When you leave town for the Southeast Lighthouse, you are on Spring Street; this becomes Southeast Road, and then Mohegan Trail. When it turns north or to the right, it becomes Lakeside Drive. If you go left there on the dirt road and then take the first dirt road to the right, it will take you to Black Rock Road, which is a left turn onto another dirt road. This road leads to the water.

There is another way to Black Rock Point by continuing north on Lakeside Drive past Fresh Pond, which is a good-sized pond. Turn left after Fresh Pond onto Cooneymus Road. Black Rock Road is a left off that road. Let me warn you that these dirt roads are narrow and rough in spots. The bushes growing alongside the roads will scratch your vehicle. And when you get to Black Rock Point, the trail down to the water looks like it was made by a mountain goat. However, for those who do fish this location in the fall, the fishing can be outstanding.

The western side of the island has some great locations for fly anglers, as long as the wind is not too strong. If you are on Cooneymus Road, it will turn north and become West Side Road. This road will give you access to several good spots as you make your way north toward the Great Salt Pond.

When there are light westerly winds, be sure to head to this side of Block Island. The breezes will push bait against the shoreline, setting up a buffet for bluefish and striped bass. Fish your way along the western side, checking the beaches at Southwest Point, farther north at Dories Cove and Graces Cove, Charleston Beach, and around the entrance to the Great Salt Pond at Dead Mans Cove. You'll find fish feeding at any or all of these spots.

Besides the stripers and blues that feed along the western shoreline, in late July the game gets an added dimension. Like annual summer tourists, bonito followed by false albacore move into Block Island's waters to add to the fishing action. About the end of July, the first bonito will begin chasing the local baitfish. The false albacore make their appearance in August and are the first of the two speedsters to depart as early-fall temperatures begin to cool the water. By mid-October the bonito will move out for warmer southern waters. To get the attention of the albacore and bonito, use sand eel patterns, sparse Clouser Minnows, and small minnow patterns.

The consistently good spots to look for bonito and albacore action are in and around the entrance to Great Salt Pond, by the Coast Guard Station, at Beanes Point, and along the shores of the pond. To reach this section of the island, take Coast Guard Road, which branches off West Side Road as it runs along the southern shoreline of the Great Salt Pond. Though not receiving as much press as other spots in the Northeast, a strong argument can be made for this being one of the best bonito and false albacore fisheries in the region.

For some of the best fly fishing along uncrowded shorelines, you should head to Block Island. With its Victorian architecture and rolling farmland, the island is also a great destination for a family vacation. There is access to a variety of fishing conditions, and they are all very good. In fall the weather is still mild and the fishing reaches its peak. Block Island's beauty and fly fishing will provide you with a trip you'll long remember.

Chapter 14

Driving the Beach

The biggest problem that all shorebound anglers face is access. As more and more people are seeking to live along our coastlines, places that we once fished are lost. Development is the biggest culprit when it comes to the loss of shoreline fishing access. Some existing fishing locations can only support a small number of anglers; added fishing pressure will only result in their loss as neighbors and towns react to the increased activity. On the positive side there are, through efforts on the federal, state, and local levels, some sections of the coastline that have been preserved. Many of these coastal areas include beaches that provide the fly fisherman with added angling opportunities, particularly if they allow vehicle access.

One way that you can make full use of the fishing possibilities of such beaches and expand your angling options is with the use of a four-wheel-drive vehicle. You can cover a greater area than on foot, and in less time. However, this does require the large investment of a vehicle with four-wheel drive that can run the sand. But even if you own a four-wheel drive, you can't just roll out onto the beach without preparation and an understanding of what sort of conditions you will encounter.

Driving the beach is not one of those things that can be learned from a book. I can give you suggestions and pointers, but you must learn firsthand. Initially you should have someone with experience ease you into it. Use your own vehicle, because each four-wheel drive will handle a bit differently. Your

The driver of the vehicle on the left thought that he could drive through this section of beach that was covered with about three inches of water. He did not know that the sand underneath was like quicksand.

buddy can teach you about proper tire pressure, steering, and how to avoid getting stuck under different situations.

I currently own a four-wheel-drive Suburban that I use to fish East Coast beaches. I bought my first Suburban 18 years ago, before it was fashionable to have an SUV. Back then people on the beach would stop and stare; they were use to smaller vehicles like jeeps and pickups. In fact, the first four-wheeler I owned was a Jeep. I bought it in the early 1960s when I first came to New England. Fishing the beaches of New England with a beach buggy was a dream I had pursued since high school.

When I'm not fishing, I love to slowly roll along the beach while watching the water and waves. Though this activity may seem like a waste of time, think again. Besides being very relaxing, I can't tell you how many times I have come upon fish that were making just a few, faint signs of feeding on the surface. These were often so subtle that even the seagulls hadn't detected the activity. I can also easily follow the fish as they feed along the shoreline. If you've ever tried to keep up with a school of bluefish, you'll appreciate how fast they can move. Being able to drive to a point ahead of them means that you can get in more than one cast, rather than just one desperate cast at the tail end of the school.

A four-wheel-drive vehicle also gives you an excellent means to scout a beach at low water. I often do this if I plan to fish the area at night. Driving the beach during the day and low water helps to establish a better picture in my mind of what structure I will be fishing that night. It also aids with putting together a plan of where and when to fish.

There are numerous advantages of being able to fish a beach with a four-wheel-drive SUV or pickup truck. For someone like me who likes to carry more gear than I probably need, my Suburban is ideal. I should note that I purchased the larger four-wheel drive because I take extended fishing trips that usually include several people, their gear, and my dog. The larger vehicle is ideal for me because it is a good highway vehicle for long trips yet handles very well on the beach.

Though I do get kidded at times for the amount of gear I carry, there have been times when it has paid off. I have even been able to bail out buddies who needed to replace gear or use something they weren't carrying. One great addition to my Suburban for fly fishing is a set of straps called the Vehicle Rod Carrier. These two straps, which are strung across the inside of the vehicle, allow me to carry up to seven rods fully rigged and ready to go. You obviously need a vehicle that's long enough to accommodate the rods, but these straps can also be used to carry rods above the bed of a pickup truck.

I do have one word of advice about these rod straps. They work great but the rods will sway back and forth when driving over any irregular surface, so do put on reel covers; I prefer the foam type because they do a good job of protecting the reels in all conditions. Without some kind of covers, your reels will bang together, causing damage.

In addition to the safety gear listed in this chapter, I strongly suggest that you invest in an air compressor of the type that plugs into your vehicle's cigarette lighter. These compressors are normally less than $80 and take up very little room. They can be very handy if you get stuck and have to drop the pressure in your tires to get your four-wheeler free. Though it may take some time, a small compressor can inflate your tires back to the pressure they were.

I believe that a slower pace while driving the beach works best for most situations. Also, at night, turn your lights off when passing someone who is fishing. If you have difficulty seeing, you can use your parking lights to illuminate the trail you're driving. Be aware that the quickest way to become the least popular person on the beach is have your headlights light up a fishing area or swing over water that is being fished by anglers. A sudden, bright light like that will spook the fish.

There will be times when even with your headlights on you won't have good visibility. Fog on the beach can be the thickest you'll ever experience. You can become disoriented very quickly, even if you're familiar with the beach. There have been cases of experienced people driving into the water when there was heavy fog, especially at night.

In his book *Twenty Years on the Cape*, Frank Daignault tells his readers of making a very minor error of just 10 degrees, going off course, and ending up in the water on a foggy night. He nearly lost his life, as well as that of his wife. And let me tell you, as a friend of Frank, he knew that beach as well as anyone who fished it.

If you can find a copy of Frank's book, get it and read it. You'll not only be reading the exploits of one of the best anglers I know, you'll read about how the fishing was in the 1960s. You may hear people like myself complain that though the current striped bass fishing is good, it's nowhere close to what it was like in the 1960s. If you weren't fortunate enough to fish during that great striper era, not only does Frank tell you about that time, but his pictures of striped bass caught then will put things into perspective.

A word of caution about where you park your four-wheeler on the beach. I have witnessed several instances of vehicles sliding into the Atlantic because they were parked too close to a bank or cut. As the tide comes in and the sand absorbs the water, the sand becomes less firm and weakens. Eventually it gives way, sending the vehicle into the water. Even if you can salvage your vehicle, once it has been immersed in salt water, it isn't worth much.

A washout is where the area of the beach between the high-water mark and dune line has been cut out and the water reaches the dunes at high tide. Driving through one of these washouts is an extremely dangerous situation, even at low tide when the water has receded. The sand in the washout is soft, and the washout itself usually has a steep incline from the dunes to the water. I recommend that you not cross a washout, even at low water. The rear end of your vehicle will usually start to slide toward the water, and if you aren't careful, the rear tires will begin to dig into the sand; you'll end up stuck. If you cannot get your four-wheeler out and onto the level beach in time, the incoming tide will claim it.

I write of this situation from experience. Several years ago while fishing the beach at the Cape Cod National Seashore, I encountered one nasty washout that was between me and a section of the beach I usually fished. Though I didn't lose my four-wheel drive, I did have a moment of panic as the Suburban's rear end started to slide. I knew that I shouldn't have tried to cross it even though I could see the tracks of someone who had driven across it a bit earlier. I was lucky because I didn't panic and step on the gas, which would have buried the rear end to the axle. I slowly and carefully worked my way out of the washout; I knew that I had a couple of hours before the surf got to me.

One last thing you should remember about driving the beach, and that is not all sand is the same. Certain types of sand are softer than others, and driving through these can be more difficult. I believe that the beaches in the Cape Cod National Seashore's northern portion are the hardest to drive. The sand conditions there require a lower tire pressure. I start my tire pressure at 14 pounds; if I do get stuck, I can then drop that pressure to as low as 10 pounds. This is in comparison to when I drive the beaches on the Outer Banks of North Carolina, where my tire pressure is usually 18 pounds. That is because the sand on the Outer Banks is finer and compacts better than that in the Cape Cod National Seashore.

As a general rule, the finer the sand, the easier it is to drive. Also, watch for changes in the color of sand. For example, many washouts have sand that has an orange or reddish tint. This is a good indicator that this sand is coarser and will be much harder to drive through. Even on the flat section between the high-water line and the dunes, you'll find areas of more coarse sand; you can tell them by that change in the color.

After it has rained, driving the beach is almost like being on a dirt road. It is a lot easier. But if there has been a sustained period of time with no rain, the driving will be more difficult and usually requires lower tire pressure. Very dry sand conditions are difficult to drive and will often necessitate going to tire pressures lower than that of other times.

To save both time and aggravation when applying for a permit to drive the beach, there are a few things that you need to know in advance. Be sure to find out about what safety equipment and tire size is required for your vehicle when it is inspected, which is often done prior to issuing a beach permit. Ask what the permit cost will be; most locations will not take a check, and many are strictly cash transactions. Inquire about any beach closures. Sections of many of these beaches are closed at some time during the summer to protect nesting birds. You don't want to pay for a vehicle permit to fish a particular section of a beach and then find out it's closed for the next month or more.

There has been a recent increase in the number of vehicles on the beaches. Many of these drivers aren't fishermen; the increased sales of SUVs

A four-wheel-drive vehicle can greatly expand your fishing opportunities.

have probably contributed greatly to this situation. Therefore, like it or not, as mobile anglers we have to work harder to keep beach accesses open. Keep the beaches clean, obey all the regulations, and support organizations that are working to maintain access for fishermen on these beaches.

Massachusetts and Rhode Island have the greatest number of beaches with four-wheel-drive access. Besides those noted in previous chapters, there are additional beaches within Massachusetts that you can travel and fish. Actually, they are all located on Cape Cod. The first, Sandy Neck, which is about 5 miles long, is located just off MA 6A on the town line between Sandwich and Barnstable. For information on permit costs and regulations for Sandy Neck, call 508-362-8306. The town of Barnstable issues permits at the beach gatehouse.

Nauset Beach is under the control of the town of Orleans; they set the fees and regulations for beach access. This is another location where the permit cost is rather expensive for a nonresident. As of this printing, that cost was $160. However, on the plus side, Nauset Beach offers outstanding fishing, on both the ocean and the bay side. You can get the latest information on fees and regulations by calling 508-240-3700.

To obtain information about traveling and fishing the beaches within the Cape Cod National Seashore, including access, fees, and regulations, call 508-487-2100. This area also offers some excellent fishing opportunities for the mobile fly rodder. However, note that the park service has placed a limit on the number of beach permits issued each year. In 2001 that limit was reached in July; in 2002 it was hit by the end of May. More and more non-fishing vehicles are using these beaches.

If you are serious about using a vehicle to fish the beaches and want to preserve that access, I suggest that in Massachusetts you contact and join the Massachusetts Beach Buggy Association. Started in 1950, the MBBA is a family-oriented organization dedicated to beach conservation and working to keep the beaches open for the use of the public, including anglers. I have been a member for nearly 40 years and I can tell you that if it weren't for the MBBA, there would be few, if any beaches available to the four-wheel-drive angler today.

Each year the MBBA conducts various projects aimed at preventing beach erosion, plus yearly spring cleanups of the beaches their members use. They will stop and help anyone on the beach who is in trouble, whether he's a member or not. For more information about the organization, who they are, beach travel and access, and how to join, go online to their web site at www.mbba.net.

In Rhode Island four-wheel-drive vehicle access to the beaches requires a Rhode Island Coastal Resource Management Council (CRMC) beach permit. This permit can be purchased from the Burlingame Campground and State Park, located off US 1 in Charlestown. You must have the vehicle to be permitted with you at the time you purchase that permit, plus proof of insurance, the vehicle's registration, and your driver's license. You are also required to have certain safety equipment for inspection. To get additional information on the permit and current costs, call the ranger station at the Burlingame Campground and State Park; the telephone number there is 401-322-8910. The telephone number for the Rhode Island's Coastal Resources Management Council in Providence, Rhode Island, is 401-222-3577.

The CRMC has a list of safety equipment required for granting a permit. I believe it's a good idea to have this gear regardless of where you're driving the beach. An investment in the proper safety equipment is far less expensive than the cost to be towed off the beach or, even worse, the loss of your four-wheel-drive vehicle.

- **Shovel** Use either a heavy-duty shovel or military entrenching tool. The military style folds up and occupies little space.

- **Tow rope or chain** Either must be 15 feet or more in length, with a load strength of 1,800 pounds. If you use a chain, it should have links that are of minimum size of $5/16$ inch.

- **Jack and support stand** I prefer a hydraulic jack since it takes up little room and is easy to use. The support stand should be a board or piece of plywood that is a minimum size of 18 inches by 18 inches, and $5/8$ inch thick.

- **Tires** Street-legal tires with four-ply treads and two-ply sidewalls work well on the beach. Snow or mud tires are not recommended since they perform poorly on the beach.

- **Tire gauge** A low-pressure tire gauge with a range of 0 to 20 pounds pressure is a must. The gauge should allow you to easily read the pressure to the nearest pound.

- **First-aid kit** A well-stocked unit with antiseptic, band-aids, gauze pads, tape, aspirin, and, if you can find one, a kit to remove hooks from people. Check the first-aid kit every year and replace used items.

- **Fire extinguisher** It should be either a Coast Guard– or Interstate Commerce Commission–approved model.

- **Road flares** I keep mine in a closed plastic container. Replace old flares that appear to be beyond their time.

- **Flashlight** I prefer to carry a couple of them. One of mine casts a wide beam of light, enough to illuminate the work area while I'm changing a tire.

- **Spare tire** Check it at least yearly to see that the pressure is okay and that it's ready for use.

Appendix:
State Agencies

Each state sets the regulations for both the recreational and commercial fishing of saltwater fish in its waters. They are, however, operating within the parameters set by the Atlantic States Marine Fisheries Commission. The ASMFC, which is comprised of 15 Atlantic coast states from Maine to Florida, was formed in 1942 to provide a cooperative interstate fisheries management effort, especially for such migratory species as striped bass, bluefish, and weakfish.

Using the guidelines established by Atlantic States Marine Fisheries Commission each state manages and sets its own regulations, along with size and bag limits for species under the ASMFC jurisdiction; these will usually vary from state to state for particular species. When fishing a state for the first time, you should check with a local tackle shop regarding current regulations. For additional information as to species-specific management and regulatory action, you can contact that state's agency directly.

Maine Department of Marine Resources
21 State House Station
Augusta, ME 04333-0021
207-624-6550

New Hampshire Fish & Game Department
2 Hazen Drive
Concord, NH 03301
603-271-3421

Massachusetts Division of Marine Fisheries
100 Cambridge Street
Boston, MA 02202
617-727-3193

Rhode Island Division of Fish and Wildlife
Oliver Stedman Center
4808 Tower Hill Road
Wakefield, RI 02879-2207
401-789-3094

Bibliography

I've read many books that have helped to make me a better angler. Many of these books were invaluable references and guides as I put this book together.

Blues, John Hersey. New York: Vintage Books.

The Fisherman's Ocean, David A. Ross, Ph.D. Pennsylvania: Stackpole Books.

Fishes of the Gulf of Maine, Henry B. Bigelow and William C. Schroeder. Washington, D.C.: U.S. Government Printing Office.

Fishing for Weakfish and Sea Trout, William A. Muller. New Jersey: The Fisherman Library.

Fishing New England, A Cape Cod Shore Guide, Gene Bourque. Massachusetts: On The Water.

Fishing New England, A Rhode Island Shore Guide, Gene Bourque. Massachusetts: On The Water.

Fly Fisherman's Guide to Atlantic Baitfish & Other Food Sources, Alan Caolo. Oregon: Frank Amato.

The Fly Fisherman's Guide to Boston Harbor, Jack Gartside. Massachusetts: Jack Gartside.

A Fly-Fisher's Guide to Saltwater Naturals and Their Imitation, George V. Roberts Jr. Maine: Ragged Mountain Press.

Fly Fishing in Salt Water, Lefty Kreh. New York: Lyons & Burford.

Fly Rodding the Coast, Ed Mitchell. Pennsylvania: Stackpole Books.

Greased Line Fishing for Salmon and Steelhead, Jock Scott. Oregon: Frank Amato.

Inshore Fly Fishing, Lou Tabory. New York: Lyons & Burford.

L.L. Bean Fly Fishing for Striped Bass Handbook, Brad Burns. New York: The Lyons Press.

Lou Tabory's Guide to Saltwater Baits & Their Imitations, Lou Tabory. New York: Lyons & Burford.

The Orvis Guide to Saltwater Fly Fishing, Nick Curcione. New York: Lyons & Burford.

Practical Fishing Knots II, Mark Sosin and Lefty Kreh. New York: Lyons & Burford.

Prey, Carl Richards. New York: Lyons & Burford.

Profiles in Saltwater Angling, George Reiger. New Jersey: Prentice Hall.

Saltwater Fly Patterns, Lefty Kreh. New York: Lyons & Burford.

Sport Fish of the Atlantic, Vic Dunaway. Florida: Florida Sportsman.

The Striped Bass Chronicles, George Reiger. New York: Lyons & Burford.

Striper, John Cole. Massachusetts: Atlantic Monthly Press.

Striper Hot Spots, Frank Daignault. Connecticut: The Globe Pequot Press.

Striper Moon, J. Kenney Abrames. Oregon: Frank Amato.

Striper Surf, Frank Daignault. Connecticut: The Globe Pequot Press.

Stripers and Streamers, Ray Bondorew. Oregon: Frank Amato.

Through the Fish's Eye, Mark Sosin and John Clark. New York: Outdoor Life.

The Trophy Striper, Frank Daignault. New Jersey: Burford Books.

Twenty Years on the Cape, Frank Daignault. Connecticut: MT Publications.

Maps

The following maps were used as reference to verify directions and street names. I have found them invaluable when fishing a new location for the first time.

Arrow Map, Inc.
50 Scotland Boulevard
Bridgewater, MA 02324
508-279-1177
Street Atlas Cape Cod, Including Martha's Vineyard & Nantucket

DeLorme
P.O. Box 298
Yarmouth, ME 04096
207-846-7000
www.delorme.com
Maine Atlas & Gazetteer
Massachusetts Atlas & Gazetteer
New Hampshire Atlas & Gazetteer
Connecticut Rhode Island Atlas & Gazetteer

The Butterworth Company
1022 Main Street
West Barnstable, MA 02668
508-375-9998

Cape Cod & Islands Atlas and Guide Book
Martha's Vineyard Map with Guide Information
Nantucket Map with Guide Information

I have also found that either www.mapquest.com or www.yahoo.com can provide good maps of an area.

Index

Page numbers in italics indicate photographs or illustrations.

F

Falmouth (MA), 178–179
Fat Alberts. *See* Bonito and false albacore
Fat back, 61–62
Ferry Beach (ME), striped bass, 156–157
First (Eastons) Beach (RI), striped bass and bluefish, 210
Fish. *See also* Baitfish, worms, and crustaceans; specific fish
  importance of understanding the habits of, 40, 60–61
  learning more about the behavior of, 70, 76
  as opportunistic feeders, 40
  sense of hearing, 71–74
  sense of sight, 74–76
  sense of smell, 70
Fisherman's Ocean, The (Ross), 36, 70, 76
Fishes of the Gulf of Maine (Bigelow), 44, 45, 46, 49, 52
Fishing logs, 99–100, *101*
Fishing New England (Bourque), 178
Five Sisters (MA), striped bass, 115
Flagg, Lou, 145–146
Flats
  anticipating tidal changes, 27
  best flies for, 27
  fishing the channels and deep pockets, 27
  identifying good areas, 27
  sight casting on, 27
  using a compass on, 28
Flies
  basic colors, 88
  for Block Island, 230, 232
  for Cape Cod (MA), 177
  for flats, 27
  keeping contact with, 20
  for the Kennebec River (ME) area, 153
  limiting fly movement, 20–21
  for Martha's Vineyard (MA), 194, 196
  matching the local bait, 88
  for Nantucket (MA), 187
  for New Hampshire, 171–172
  for Portland (ME) south, 163
  for rocky beaches, 23
  standard patterns, 87
  for weakfish, 55
Flounder, 139, 161
Fly Fisherman's Guide to Atlantic Baitfish & Other Food Sources, A (Caolo), 60
Fly Fisherman's Guide to Boston Harbor (Gartside), 109, 112, 118
Fly Fishing in Salt Water (Kreh), 78, 93
Fly Line Winder, 102
Fly Rod Catch & Release Striped Bass Tournament, 194
Fly Rodding the Coast (Mitchell), 14, 23, 38
Fly-Fisher's Guide to Saltwater Naturals and Their Imitation, A (Roberts), 60
Fort Getty Campground (RI), striped bass, bluefish, and weakfish, 215
Freshwater herring, 63

G

Gartside, Jack, 109–111, 112, *113,* 115, *116,* 117–119, 123
Gear. *See* Tackle and gear
Gibbs, Frank, 206
Gibbs, Harold, 206, 208
Gilbert, Percy, 123, 134
Glut herring, 63–64
Goddard Memorial State Park (RI), striped bass, bluefish, and weakfish, 218
Goose Rocks Beach (ME), striped bass and bluefish, 158
Gooseberry Neck (MA), striped bass and bluefish, 202
Grass shrimp, 68
Gravel beaches. *See* Sand, gravel, and cobblestone beaches
Gray trout. *See* Weakfish
Greased Line Fishing for Salmon [and Steelhead] (Scott), 21
Great Molasses Flood, 106–107
Great Point (MA), striped bass and bluefish, 188
Green crab, 68–69
Green smelt, 62
Grill, Chris, 151, 152
Groins. *See* Jetties

Books from The Countryman Press
and Backcountry Guides

We offer many more books on hiking, bicycling, canoeing and kayaking, travel, nature, and country living. Our books are available at bookstores and outdoor stores everywhere. For more information or a free catalog, please call 1-800-245-4151, or write to us at The Countryman Press, P.O. Box 748, Woodstock, Vermont 05091. You can find us on the Internet at www.countrymanpress.com